PROMOTING SOCIAL COHESION

Implications for policy and evaluation

Edited by Peter Ratcliffe and Ines Newman

First published in Great Britain in 2011 by

The Policy Press
University of Bristol
Fourth Floor
Beacon House
Queen's Road
Bristol BS8 1QU
UK

t: +44 (0)117 331 4054
f: +44 (0)117 331 4093
tpp-info@bristol.ac.uk
www.policypress.co.uk

North American office:
The Policy Press
c/o International Specialized Books Services
920 NE 58th Avenue, Suite 300
Portland, OR 97213-3786, USA
t: +1 503 287 3093
f: +1 503 280 8832
info@isbs.com

© The Policy Press 2011

British Library Cataloguing in Publication Data
A catalogue record for this book is available from the British Library.

Library of Congress Cataloging-in-Publication Data
A catalog record for this book has been requested.

ISBN 978 1 84742 694 9 paperback
ISBN 978 1 84742 695 6 hardcover

Cover design by Qube Design Associates, Bristol.
Front cover: image kindly supplied by www.istock.com
Printed and bound in Great Britain by TJ International, Padstow.
The Policy Press uses environmentally responsible print partners.

Contents

—

iv

List of figures and tables

Figures

Tables

Notes on the contributors

Clare Batty has over 20 years' experience as a public sector policy maker and manager, specialising in social policy and partnerships at the centre of local government. Her work has included five years with the Local Government Centre, Warwick Business School, University of Warwick, where she co-manages the Local Authorities and Social Exclusion Network and led an European Union-funded transnational project on social inclusion, the results of which were presented at the Fourth European Roundtable on Poverty and Social Exclusion in 2005. Most recently, Clare has been working with the Beth Johnson Foundation in support of its local authority intergenerational programme.

Juan Camilo Cock is based at Praxis Community Projects and PACE, Goldsmiths, University of London. He recently finished a PhD in human geography at Queen Mary, University of London, in which he carried out research on the social spaces created by Colombian migrants living in London. He has collaborated with, and worked for, several migrant community organisations in London, including the Indoamerican Refugee and Migrant Organisation, Praxis Community Projects and the Migrants' Rights Network where he currently leads on their work in London. As part of a collaborative project between Praxis and the Professional and Community Education Department at Goldsmiths, Juan carried out a literature review on evaluating the impact of voluntary and community organisations on community cohesion. His academic interests are in the collective identities of recent migrants, the urban geography of migrants in cities of reception and integration policies towards migrants.

Rose Doran is community cohesion advisor at Local Government Improvement and Development. She is based in the Equalities and Cohesion team and leads on a range of work to facilitate learning, dialogue and the sharing of good practice across the local government sector, and linking national policy to local delivery. Prior to the general election, Rose managed Local Government Improvement and Development's programme of work on Prevent – the previous government's national strategy to prevent people from becoming or supporting violent extremists. She is currently working closely with colleagues in the Local Government Association, local authorities and national government to contribute and respond to equality and community cohesion policy emerging under the new coalition government.

Prior to joining the IDeA in 2007, Rose worked in the Policy and Partnerships team at the London Borough of Tower Hamlets.

John Eversley is an expert in the field of public policy and management. His experience spans the voluntary sector and director-level posts in the National Health Service (NHS), local government and as a university researcher and teacher.

He is currently a part-time senior lecturer in the Department of Public Health, Primary Care and Food Policy at City University, a part-time senior lecturer in voluntary and community organisations in the Department of Applied Social Sciences at London Metropolitan University and managing director of a Community Interest Company research company – ppre CIC.

John has carried out research and published on a wide range of subjects, including equalities, measuring quality and social history. Details of his work can be found at http://ppre.org.uk/

Crispian Fuller is a lecturer in public policy at Aston University. His research interests centre on the spatial political economy of urban governance, neoliberalism, urban regeneration and economic development. This research has been published in journals such as *Antipode*, *International Journal of Urban and Regional Research* and *Environment and Planning A*. He is presently undertaking research on the spatial restructuring of the nation state, and the crisis of neoliberal urban governance.

Roger Grimshaw is research director at the independent Centre for Crime and Justice Studies. His recent studies have ranged over the evidence base for criminal justice policy, including 'gun and knife' crime, criminal justice expenditure, interventions and services for people in the criminal justice system and for their families, as well as the particular needs of migrants. Previously he was responsible for research on services for children and young people, at a national voluntary organisation. He has published work on truancy, parenting programmes, and the care and education of 'at-risk' children.

Alan Hatton-Yeo has over 30 years of working in the voluntary sector with roles that have included principal of a residential college and principal education advisor of the then Spastics Society. For the last 12 years he has been chief executive of the Beth Johnson Foundation and he has a national and international reputation for his work in the fields of intergenerational practice and active ageing. He has written extensively and is an honorary research fellow at Keele University.

Vaughan Jones is the founding chief executive of Praxis. He holds a Masters degree in pastoral theology from Heythrop College, University of London. He is both a qualified teacher and minister of the United Reformed Church. He writes on migration for the Ekklesia website (www.ekklesia.co.uk) and has managed Praxis research projects in the area of communication support for migrants, frameworks for refugee and migrant community development, approaches to housing and homelessness, and the impact of demographic change on local communities. He has a strong interest in popular education methodologies, migration policies, community development, human rights and inter-faith relationships.

Michael Keating is currently on secondment to Local Government Improvement and Development as the national advisor for equalities and cohesion. Michael leads on Local Government Improvement and Development's contribution on strategic issues affecting equalities and community cohesion within local government. He is also leading on the development and implementation of the Equality Framework for Local Government and other public sector frameworks.

Michael's substantive role is the service head, Scrutiny and Equalities, at the London Borough of Tower Hamlets where he has worked since 2003. During that time Michael has had responsibility for reshaping the council's Overview and Scrutiny service, developing a corporate performance management team and also managing the third sector and equalities teams. In 2007, he created the Scrutiny and Equalities service. By marrying the key policy and delivery agendas of community leadership and partnership, the service works to ensure that scrutiny + equalities = community cohesion. Between 1994 and 2002, Michael was an elected member and has also previously worked in higher education and the NHS.

Les Mayhew is a professor in the Faculty of Actuarial Sciences and Insurance at Cass Business School, City University London. He is a former senior civil servant with nearly 20 years' experience in the Department of Health, the Department of Social Security, HM Treasury and the Office for National Statistics where he was also a director. Currently he is director of Mayhew Harper Associates, which specialises in the use of administrative data to address wide areas of social policy including health, crime, deprivation, service development and evaluation at local and other levels and was a founder of *nkm*. He is an honorary fellow of the Institute of Actuaries and a fellow of the Faculty of Public Health. Details of Les's work on *nkm* can be found at http://nkm.org.uk

Marjorie Mayo is professor in community development at Goldsmiths, University of London. She has worked in the community sector and local government, and has experience of working internationally. She has published widely on community development, including *Imagining tomorrow: Adult education for transformation*, (National Institute for Adult Continuing Education, 1997), *Cultures, communities, identities: Cultural strategies for participation and empowerment* (Palgrave, 2000), *Global citizens* (Zed, 2005), with Paul Hoggett and Chris Miller and *The dilemmas of development work* (The Policy Press, 2008).

Ines Newman is a town planner who has specialised in economic development, community advocacy and community development. She is currently a principal research fellow in the Local Government Centre at Warwick Business School. She is director of the Warwick University Local Authorities Research Consortium and led a Consortium economic development research stream. She managed a research project for the Audit Commission scoping a national study on community cohesion and has contributed to the national evaluation of Local Strategic Partnerships (LSPs)/Local Area Agreements (LAAs), particularly on Multi Area Agreements and the equalities dimension of LSPs/LAAs. She was the strategic advisor for the IDeA on economic development from October 2007 to March 2009 and has contributed many articles and reviews in the journal *Local Economy*. Ines was previously (1999-2007) head of policy at the Local Government Information Centre (LGiU). At LGiU, she managed a range of research projects focusing particularly on neighbourhood renewal and social inclusion, the frontline councillor role and parish and town councils.

Audrey Osler is visiting professor at Birkbeck, University of London and at the University of Leeds, where she was founding director of the Centre for Citizenship and Human Rights Education. She also holds an honorary position at the University of Warwick where she is a member of the Centre for Rights, Equality and Diversity (CRED). She is interested in sociocultural aspects of education and has published widely on exclusion and inclusion, education for democratic citizenship, child rights and racial justice. Her two most recent books

–

are *Students' perspectives on schooling* (Open University Press, 2010), which explores how young people might contribute to educational policy development, and *Teachers and human rights education* (Trentham, 2010, with H. Starkey), which examines the potential of human rights to enable justice in and through education in a range of international settings.

Peter Ratcliffe is professor of sociology at the University of Warwick and director of the Centre for Rights, Equality and Diversity. He is also director of the UK National Focal Point for the RAXEN network managed by the European Union Agency for Fundamental Rights (FRA). In 2006, he was elected president of the International Sociological Association's research committee on racism, nationalism and ethnic relations.

Peter's major publications include *Racism and reaction: A profile of Handsworth* (1981), *'Race', ethnicity and nation* (ed, 1994), *Social geography and ethnicity in Britain: Geographical spread, spatial concentration and internal migration* (ed, 1996), *'Race' and housing in Bradford* (1996), *Breaking down the barriers: Improving Asian access to social rented housing* (2001), *The use of public sector procurement to enhance 'racial' equality in employment* and *Working for an inclusive Britain* (2003, with Michael Orton). More recently, he has authored *'Race', ethnicity and difference: Imagining the inclusive society* (2004). His major report for the UK government on the 'managing diversity' and the 'community cohesion' agenda was published in July 2006.

Ludi Simpson is professor of population studies at the University of Manchester, and was a demographic and census analyst in local authorities for 20 years. He works with population, census and survey statistics, aiming to extend their use by communities and governments. He has worked closely with local authorities and government departments, and statistics associations in Britain and abroad. His publications include *Statistics in society* (1999, edited with Danny Dorling) and *'Sleepwalking to segregation'? Challenging myths about race and migration* (2009, with Nissa Finney). He is currently vice-president of the British Society for Population Studies and co-organiser of the Radical Statistics Group.

Kate Smart is director of policy, communications and advocacy at the Welsh Refugee Council and has previously worked for the British Refugee Council, Oxfam, the Kosovo Humanitarian Evacuation Programme and the European Council on Refugees and Exiles. She is the author of a number of publications on refugees and asylum, including research reports on how the media reports asylum.

Helen Sullivan is professor of government and society at the University of Birmingham. Her research and writing explore the changing nature of local governance. She has a longstanding interest in the evaluation of complex policy initiatives and has been involved in a wide range of government-funded studies, including the national evaluations of: Health Action Zones, Local Area Agreements, Local Strategic Partnerships and the take-up and use of the Power of Wellbeing. She has published widely on different aspects of evaluation in academic and practitioner media. Her publications on theory-based evaluation include *Building capacity for health equity* (Routledge, 2005, with M. Barnes, L. Bauld, M. Benzeval, K. Judge and M. McKenzie).

Acknowledgements

First, the editors would like to acknowledge the valuable contribution played by the Audit Commission who commissioned the University of Warwick in the first quarter of 2008 to carry out an extensive programme of research into the extant literature on the policies, practices and evaluation of various aspects of local and national 'community cohesion' policy. It was this research that provided the initial stimulus for the current volume.

Second, we owe a huge debt of gratitude to all of our contributors. Without exception, they responded in a timely fashion to all the deadlines we set (however tight), in so doing ensuring that the project remained on schedule throughout its life. Given the extremely busy, and highly pressured, working lives that are currently the norm, this was no mean feat. To also do so while retaining a positive demeanour was particularly impressive.

Third, we would like to thank our external referee who helped to shape the book and then went beyond the call of duty and commented in detail on each chapter. We have no doubt that he has helped us to raise the quality of this volume.

Last, but by no means least, we are delighted to be able to express our enormous gratitude to our colleagues at The Policy Press. Although it is invariably somewhat invidious to single out individuals for praise, we would especially like to thank Emily Watt and Leila Ebrahimi. Without their generous support and enviable efficiency, the volume would not have been such a delight to undertake. We can only hope that the final product justifies their confidence and faith in our work.

Acknowledgements

Promoting social cohesion

Peter Ratcliffe and Ines Newman

National social policy agendas tend to be dominated by a relatively small number of key concepts. In Britain,[1] one such concept, 'community cohesion', has assumed a pre-eminent role over the past decade. It has been the subject of a host of government enquiries, policy papers and even a national Commission – the Commission on Integration and Cohesion (CIC). There is also a policy institute, the Institute of Community Cohesion, committed to propagating its use as a guiding theme for national policy and practice.

In addition, it has spawned a voluminous academic literature, much of it, to one degree or another, critical of its central tenets. What is currently lacking, however, is a serious engagement with the evaluation agenda: in other words, the question of how one might assess the fruits of 'community cohesion' policy in its various guises. As Khan (2007, p 40) argues, 'providing linkages between policies and concepts is a difficult enterprise but one that is necessary for justifying and ultimately evaluating the implementation of government measures'. The existing academic literature engages with the concept and outlines alternative ways of interpreting the key policy challenges facing Britain, but fails to elucidate appropriate policies in any detail and, even more noticeably, fails to provide any guidance on evaluation strategies.

This book aims to address this lacuna. In doing so, it builds on the excellent work of, for example, Wetherell et al (2007), Flint and Robinson (2008) and Finney and Simpson (2009). It evaluates the theoretical and substantive arguments for moving from a focus on 'community cohesion' to the rather broader notion of *social* cohesion and then looks at the implications for policy and evaluation. In other words, it addresses not only how one might evaluate existing cohesion policies, but also how one might do this given a restructured and reformulated cohesion policy context.

As a consequence of this shift in emphasis, our approach places a much greater emphasis on material inequalities. This in turn has significant implications for the evaluation of policy and practice around 'community cohesion'. The book provides a thorough critique of current measures based on national indicators, clarifies the aims and objectives of what we see as the 'social cohesion' paradigm and provides alternative frameworks for policy development and evaluation.

While there is a fairly substantial body of work on the general policy terrain, a literature and data review for the Audit Commission undertaken by the editors of the current volume revealed that there is currently very little literature (academic or otherwise) on the evaluation of community cohesion interventions. Given the increasing importance placed by government on this policy area in the recent past and the shift towards Comprehensive Area Assessment (before it was abolished by the incoming coalition government in May 2010), this vacuum is surprising. The New Labour government under Gordon Brown placed a great deal of emphasis on the importance of effective evaluation and of policy being based on 'what works'. Yet there is very limited guidance as to how to actually evaluate work on community cohesion.[2]

Because of its prominent position in current policy discourse, community cohesion is widely debated in both policy and academic circles, as noted above. This book aims both to reflect these different strands of thought and provide a synthesis that unites the theoretical and historical realm with that of contemporary policy and practice. To achieve this, the analysis is organised in four parts: Part One outlines the context and substance of community cohesion policy and practice and looks at appropriate theories of evaluation; Part Two assesses the broad methodological problems underlying evaluation strategies; Part Three examines key policy strands; and Part Four ties the arguments together and assesses a possible future trajectory of policy and evaluation in this area. What follows, in this introductory chapter, aims to survey the core elements of each of these parts.

Theoretical perspectives

Although one might not gather this from a reading of much of the literature, the ontological status of the concept 'community cohesion' is deeply problematic. True, as already pointed out above, it has been questioned as a general model for policy and practice but this, we feel, does not go far enough. Chapter One in Part One of this volume should be read as an attempt to rectify this problem.

'Cohesion', in the sense of a stable society, is clearly a *sine qua non* for most contemporary societies.[3] As to whether the particular route to such an end is desirable, however, depends on the balance of consent and coercion. Put very simply, a police state may generate a stable polity and cohesive society *de facto* but would be unacceptable in a modern democracy. This is not an either/or situation, however. Some would argue, for example, that increasing levels of surveillance and the targeting of particular sections of a population for close monitoring (and even demonisation) go beyond the realms of acceptability and may even undermine the very aims of such a policy approach, that is, that of generating a stable cohesive society.

The notion of 'community' has, of course, exercised the minds of social scientists for many decades.[4] In the recent past, and certainly within cohesion policy, however, it has tended to be heavily ethnicised.[5] Yet, in the context of 'community cohesion' policy at least, its status and meaning are highly questionable. As Ratcliffe argues in Chapter One of this volume, 'community' is commonly operationalised in official publications in terms of those from 'different backgrounds' or even conflated with the idea of 'neighbourhood' (which may, or may not, contain those from different 'backgrounds'/ethnicities/faiths/ social-class groups). These are not mere pedantic quibbles: they are extremely important issues that go to the heart of policy, practice and the evaluation process.

Policies and their aims and objectives need to be clear and unambiguous. In this case, however, there is not only a great deal of confusion surrounding the use of the term 'community', there is also a failure to see cohesion as referring as much to intra- as to inter-group relations. We argue that sustainable 'community cohesion', as it is normally viewed, cannot be achieved without addressing the *prior* challenges posed by material inequalities rooted in, and reproduced by, endemic racism and widespread and enduring deprivation.[6] We argue further that the government focus on cohesion has, thus far, downplayed equalities and a rights-based approach to public services and life chances.

We advocate an understanding of 'community' that highlights its heterogeneous nature; hence the importance of the focus on the broader notion of *social* cohesion. Success in terms of social cohesion (as a policy end) would be evidenced by sustainable harmonious relationships stemming from a substantive reduction in material inequalities among those of different age/generation, gender and socioeconomic backgrounds (irrespective of ethnicity/faith/migrant status and so on). Hence, 'success' is judged by sustainable, that is, lasting, stability based on the firm foundation of *achieved* equality targets.[7]

All of this poses major questions for evaluation: how do we evaluate a concept as complex and multifaceted as 'social cohesion'? This clearly has to begin with conceptual clarity and definition. Having tackled these issues, in Chapter Two Sullivan reviews ongoing debates about the merits of different approaches to evaluation and highlights the potential contribution of recent developments in 'theory-based evaluation'. Drawing on 'theories of change' – a much-favoured example of theory-based evaluation – the chapter explores both how these challenges may be met and the implications for evaluators.

The major theoretical challenge raised by this process relates to the thorny question of causality. Specifically, how do we know that the policy interventions being proposed are making a contribution to the objectives being sought? This invokes a common sociological dilemma: in a scenario involving multiple actors with differing structural positionings, how do we evaluate those changes that have resulted as a direct or indirect consequence of policy intervention?

Evaluation and data: methodological issues

The key conclusions of Part One of the book are threefold. First, theoretical clarity and conceptual clarification are paramount: we need to understand (a) the core issues that are to be the subject of policy intervention, and (b) how, in terms of a 'theory of change' approach, these interventions can be expected to produce the desired results. Second, we need the put in place an evaluation process that assesses these results. Third, we need data of the appropriate nature and quality to facilitate the desired evaluation exercise.

Part Two of the volume focuses on the second and third of these points. In other words, it addresses the core methodological issues involved in policy evaluation. The starting point has to be current understandings of 'community cohesion' and so in Chapter Three, Fuller complements the analysis in Chapter One by looking in detail at the way in which the concept has been developed and measured in official circles. Central to this are the 'community cohesion indicators' developed by the Home Office et al (2003).

The key point here is that these indicators are flawed in a number of ways, and derive largely from the perspectives, values and beliefs of policy makers and politicians. Fuller's analysis demonstrates that many of the existing indicators are based on the 'snapshot' perceptual and attitudinal responses of participants, within a framework where there is a reliance conceptually on ambiguous terms such as 'background' and 'belonging'. To make matters worse, issues of faith, gender, age and socioeconomic class are effectively subsumed within simple descriptors. Such data present very real drawbacks in the context of developing an effective performance management regime. If effective evaluation is to be undertaken, one arguably needs specially tailored measures that take account of the complexity of place and the 'stretched' social networks of actors.

Much cohesion policy has relied on developing positive relations between those of 'different backgrounds', as we have seen. Attitudes are therefore central to the evaluation process. But, given the superficial 'snapshot' nature of existing data, and the fact it is focused on negative elements of ethnic relations (tension and community disturbance), rather than the role of more positive elements, there is a pressing need for a more sophisticated methodology.

In Chapter Six, Grimshaw and Smart examine the tension between popular perceptions of relations between groups (however defined) and external, material (objective, empirical) evidence on the state of such relations and show how strategies for increasing cohesion must take into account the ways in which communication flows influence perceptions and attitudes. They reflect on how a mixed-methods approach to evaluation might address some of the difficulties in measuring the impact of cohesion initiatives.

Fuller, Simpson, and Doran and Keating, in their respective chapters (Chapters Three, Four and Seven) highlight the importance of data on, and qualitative understanding/knowledge of, place and neighbourhood. To understand the nature of cohesion or disharmony, the neighbourhood clearly plays a crucial role as a site where citizens experience everyday lived experience through a multitude of networks. In keeping with the central theme of the book, however, all of these authors argue that material inequalities underscore, mediate and condition these social relationships. Doran and Keating's chapter (Chapter Seven) is crucial here in focusing on the potential impact of the new Equality Act at a local level. In particular, it looks at the work of the IDeA (now called Local Government Improvement and Development) in developing a framework for evaluating equalities, arguing that promoting community cohesion and race equality (and indeed wider equalities) can be brought together through the concept of social cohesion and information auditing across an 'equality measurement framework' such as that proposed in the Equalities Review (DCLG, 2007).

One of the issues at the heart of national debates on 'community cohesion' is ethnic segregation. Simpson, in Chapter Four, takes up the central theme of his recent book with Nissa Finney, *'Sleepwalking to segregation'?* (Finney and Simpson, 2009). The argument in effect is that much of the public and policy discourse over the recent past has been based on a misnomer. The dominance accorded to segregation levels and friendship patterns is misplaced, he argues, and the commonly voiced suggestion that particular communities 'self-segregate' is simply erroneous, or at the very least a crude caricature of household decision-making processes. But indicators of population change are nonetheless seen as essential contextual information for social programmes.

This provokes an obvious question – how do we measure population change? Eversley and Mayhew concur with him in Chapter Five in pointing to major problems here. Data from the decennial Census of Population is of limited use for three principal reasons. First, by definition, the data become increasingly unhelpful over the 10-year period of its life. Second, the latter problem becomes even more serious in the context of rapid population churn of the sort experienced in Britain over the past decade. Third, in so far as ethnic heritage and faith group feature in the population change analysis, additional problems emerge. Not only have migration flows increased in volume and intensity, they have also become much more diverse; and diverse in ways that do not gel with the ethnic categorisations deployed in the national Census.

Because of this, both chapters look to alternative sources of data. Simpson reviews existing advice on local demographic monitoring and provides practical guidance on the necessary contextual information for the evaluation of local initiatives. The chapter also defines more precisely the measures that could be used for an assessment of demographic change, school choice and other components of social cohesion. It illustrates how the development of a sound methodology can lead to the evaluation of policy and practice at the local level.

Eversley and Mayhew explore the possibility that normal routine administrative data, available at local authority level, can be used in creative ways to provide vital data to aid the evaluation process. To illustrate this, they discuss a system called Neighbourhood Knowledge Management.[8] Administrative data, in conjunction with survey data, can be used to explore attitudes, behaviour and status (subject to the practical and ethical issues involved in using such data).

We can sum up the principal conclusions of Parts One and Two of the book as follows:

- A reconceptualisation of national policy debates is required so that these focus on social, rather than community, cohesion.
- This revised agenda needs to be accompanied by detailed evaluation strategies grounded in a clearly formulated 'theory of change' framework.
- For the latter process to be effective, a great deal of further work is needed on developing an understanding of how to use data

sources that meet the complex challenges posed by rapid population movements and structural inequality.

In Part Three we move on to consider the core issues emerging from a detailed consideration of a wide range of policy arenas.

Implications for policy of the need for enhanced social cohesiveness

From all of the foregoing it is clear that social cohesion demands various things from a policy agenda that is demonstrably fit for purpose. Inevitably, we have had to be somewhat selective in terms of policy areas covered in this book. However, we feel that those we have targeted span the central debates emerging from the literature and much of the discussion on measuring value for money and addressing risk assessment. The selected areas also demonstrate at times key tensions in government policy, with major policy streams conflicting with efforts to promote cohesion and equality.

The key policy areas impacting on social cohesiveness are seen as education, the labour market and housing.[9] All of these are central to the material conditions experienced by all communities. But we must remember that 'communities' refer to highly differentiated, and often internally conflictual, entities. Any consideration of policy must therefore address two issues in particular: tensions between generations (across all communities, majority or minority) and relations between settled and 'new' migrant groups. Summarising the core themes here, starting with the three policy arenas, should help the reader to identify what we see as the most pressing issues for future policy, practice and evaluation.

As noted above, in Chapter Four Simpson demonstrates the need for a much more nuanced approach to understanding the relationship between the shifting demographic composition of neighbourhoods and social cohesiveness. In particular, he disputes the centrality accorded to (ethnic) segregation in current policy debates. In Chapter Eight, Ratcliffe situates these propositions in the context of housing and the built environment, arguing that policies geared to reducing segregation levels, even if considered desirable, are destined to be ineffective and possibly even counterproductive (in the sense of increasing local tensions). This is because the core problems are historical and structural in nature: the specific form of 'segregation' that is viewed as problematic has stemmed from a combination of poverty, the structure of local housing markets, discriminatory market operations and wider racism and racist harassment, all of this compounded more recently by rapid population churn.

All of these problems have become more acute given the descent into financial crisis. In this context, there are serious dilemmas facing the interrelated spheres of education and work. As Osler argues in Chapter Nine, English schools are required to have policies that promote 'community cohesion'. In practice, however, these appear to be honoured too often in the breach. Moreover, in the areas most affected by significant flux in school roles, day-to-day pressures are dominated by the need to cope with linguistic diversity given a lack of resources. This is deeply problematic for job prospects in the context of an increasingly demanding credentialism and the need to provide all children of whatever background with key transferable skills.

Central to our conception of social cohesion is the issue of economic 'inclusion'. Indeed, labour market position more generally is vital to our analysis. Given this fact, it is particularly important to acknowledge the growing evidence that, as in previous economic downturns, the effects of the 2008/09 recession are highly uneven in terms of their impact on different sectors of the British population. The (already) most vulnerable tend to become the victims, and this encompasses large swathes of the country where the lack of 'cohesion' was already most visible. Spatially, these tend to be the areas with large concentrations of migrants (whether settled or 'new') and/or poor white communities. These issues are at the heart of Newman's chapter (Chapter Ten), as are current and possible future ways in which policy intervention can be evaluated.

As noted above, intra-communal as well as inter-communal tensions demand attention. Furthermore, 'inter-communal' implies not simply relations between various 'settled' minority communities or those between minority and majority communities but also relations between settled groups and newly arrived migrant groups from the European Union and beyond. The issue of intra-communal tensions is addressed by Hatton-Yeo and Batty in Chapter Twelve, who take a detailed look at multigenerational policy strategies and their evaluation. They focus, in particular, on a recent cross-government-funded 'Generations Together' programme designed to help close widening generation gaps through volunteering and other intergenerational approaches. Critically, material inequality is once again seen to be at the fulcrum of social instability and 'social exclusion'.

Our shared future (CIC, 2007), along with subsequent government pronouncements, preserves the term 'integration' for relations between new migrants and the 'host society', and 'cohesion' for broader relations between communities. Our Chapter One, however, makes the case for a wider definition of integration, which, rather than being a matter for new migrants alone (or indeed [necessarily] for migrants/ minorities at all), should be seen as a more generic, inclusive concept. *Social* integration, then, refers to a much broader set of issues relevant to relations between all population segments. Chapter Eleven, by Mayo, Jones and Camilo Cock, addresses these issues through the lens of research with a non-governmental organisation that aims to help new migrants to settle, to foster reconciliation and to promote human rights and social justice. The chapter pays particular attention to the mechanisms by which both new migrants and existing communities are involved in the evaluation process.

Part Four of the present volume aims to pull together the various strands of research and evaluation on cohesion policy and practice and to look to possible future state policy in the light of the formation of a Conservative–Liberal Democrat coalition government following the May 2010 General Election. Our research demonstrates considerable confusion about the focus of existing policy, conflicts within government agendas, a lack of evaluation, an agenda dominated by 'race' and faith issues (often within the context of 'internal security'), and policy and practice in which those who are the intended targets/ beneficiaries of the policy often have a limited role in defining the objectives of the policy or how it should be delivered. Despite these problems, we show that some important work is being developed that tries to bring together equalities and cohesion policies and address some of the exclusionary processes, for example those rooted in racism or gang culture, in deprived neighbourhoods and schools.

We conclude that any evaluation should address the wider issue of social cohesion rather than focusing solely on the narrower, and more problematic, term 'community cohesion'. The ultimate aim would be to move towards a society driven by consensual, rather than externally enforced, stability/cohesion. Social cohesion would not be confined to global comparisons between groups defined in terms of ethnicity and/ or faith. It would involve looking at social divisions encompassing class, gender, age, sexual orientation, disability and other dimensions of social difference and diversity. The ultimate goal of policy and practice around social cohesion is a substantial narrowing of differentials between those from diverse social backgrounds *within* ethnic and faith groups, *and* a more egalitarian social structure more generally (thus invoking the socioeconomic duty enshrined within the new Equality Act). This implies that evaluations will need to integrate equality and cohesion measures and look at outcomes for different groups, not just their perceptions of inter-group relationships and interactions (harmonious or otherwise).

Our final chapter draws out some important practical implications for national and local policy evaluators in a rapidly shifting national context. We also present a brief preliminary assessment of the general policy terrain likely to be occupied by the new coalition government. Evidence from the Spending Review presented on 20 October 2010 suggests that welfare claimants are to be increasingly targeted on the pretext that (an assumed) welfare dependency is at the root of 'broken Britain'. As to the suggestion in the previous paragraph that action towards a generally more equal society is needed, the omens are not good. The clear intention is that the 'big society' will replace 'big government', meaning that poor, disadvantaged communities will effectively be forced to rely largely on their own efforts backed up by the voluntary sector, rather than looking to the state (central or local) for support. The Spending Review confirmed this by outlining a severe programme of cuts to the latter sectors over the next four years. What this means for social cohesion in the longer term remains to be seen.

Notes

[1] The policy paradigm assessed in this volume strictly relates to England and Wales only, although somewhat similar approaches are in force in Scotland (and indeed in Northern Ireland).

[2] In undertaking this work, we liaised closely with the Improvement and Development Agency (IDeA), now called Local Government Improvement and Development.

[3] Strictly speaking, we should characterise cohesion as an *aspiration*. It would be difficult to conceive of a society devoid of internal conflicts and tensions: cohesion should therefore be viewed as a relative, rather than absolute, state.

[4] See, for example, the extremely thoughtful analysis of the ontological status of the concept in Parekh (2000).

[5] It also increasingly became infused with faith issues.

[6] As is acknowledged throughout the current volume, addressing inequalities will not in itself eliminate inter-/intra-communal, inter-faith tensions. These invoke a very different policy programme.

[7] As implied by the previous note, addressing material inequalities is part of a much broader cohesion policy agenda.

[8] This uses anonymised datasets from local authorities (including local education authorities), the National Health Service, the criminal justice system and so on.

[9] Although there is no chapter focusing specifically on crime and the policing of communities, issues arguably of central concern in the context of cohesion, the core issues are addressed across a number of both theoretical and substantive chapters in this volume.

References

CIC (Commission on Integration and Cohesion) (2007) *Our shared future*, London: CIC.

DCLG (Department for Communities and Local Government) (2007) *Fairness and freedom: The final report of the equalities review*, London: DCLG, pp 40-58.

Finney, N. and Simpson, L. (2009) *'Sleepwalking to segregation'? Challenging myths about race and migration*, Bristol: The Policy Press.

Flint, J. and Robinson, D. (2008) *Community cohesion in crisis? New dimensions of diversity and difference*, Bristol: The Policy Press.

Home Office, Local Government Association, Commission for Racial Equality, Office of the Deputy Prime Minister and Neighbourhood Renewal Unit (2003) *Building a picture of community cohesion*, London: Home Office.

Khan, O. (2007) 'Policy, identity and community cohesion: how race equality fits', in M. Wetherell, M. Lafleche and R. Berkeley (eds) *Identity, ethnic diversity and community cohesion*, London: Sage Publications.

Parekh, B. (Commission on the Future of Multi-Ethnic Britain) (2000) *The future of multi-ethnic Britain: The Parekh Report*, London: Profile Books.

Wetherell, M., Lafleche, M. and Berkeley, R. (eds) (2007) *Identity, ethnic diversity and community cohesion*, London: Sage Publications.

Part One
Theoretical perspectives

ONE

From community to social cohesion: interrogating a policy paradigm

Peter Ratcliffe

Background

In the wake of rapid, increasing and increasingly complex, international migratory flows, most European Union (EU) host countries are facing serious challenges to their internal social stability. Policies, variously labelled 'integration', 'cohesion' or 'community cohesion', are commonly seen as the way forward, but there is much confusion as to what these mean and how they should be translated into policy and practice. The focus of this chapter, and indeed the book, is on Britain but this wider context is vital for the core arguments.

The emergence in Britain of what one might call the 'cohesion paradigm' is relatively recent yet the events that proved the catalyst (for its emergence) were not, in essence, a new kind of phenomenon. The arrival of Huguenots after 1685 and the Jewish migrants in the 19th century, for example, prompted widespread unrest and consternation among the political classes and citizenry. More recently, Britain witnessed many instances of urban unrest in the past four decades (Rowe, 1998) with immigration (and 'race') at the fulcrum. It is instructive to ask, then, why this new policy tack was taken. Among the plethora of reasons that could be mooted, two stand out: (a) historical amnesia and (b) the pervasiveness of neoliberalism as a guiding philosophy.

This chapter first of all traces, in what is inevitably a rather abbreviated and oversimplified form, the historical and ideological backdrop to the emergence of cohesion policies. It then interrogates the concept of 'community cohesion' and outlines the development of the associated policies and practices. The narrative then shifts to the relationship between the latter phenomena and the rapidly evolving equalities agenda. This reveals a series of tensions that undermine the utility of the existing cohesion paradigm. The conclusion is that the focus on 'community cohesion' is misplaced, and that policies should be driven by the much more fundamental notion of 'social cohesion'; the reasoning being that the tensions in Britain's towns and cities have roots much deeper and more extensive than divisions based on 'race', ethnicity and faith.

The genesis of a policy paradigm

Following the Second World War, Britain was in desperate need of workers for its factories, offices and public services. However, instead of turning to the New Commonwealth (as is often wrongly surmised), the country looked in the first instance to Europe for this replacement labour supply. Under the European Volunteer Workers (EVW) initiative, those with appropriate skills were recruited (principally) from Eastern and Southern Europe (Solomos, 2003). Crucially, at that time such European workers were far more likely to be 'white'. It emerged that 'race' was, even at this stage, a key defining logic behind national policy. It was this, rather than culture or language, that was seen as likely to generate tensions and slow the pace of migrant 'integration' (Carter et al, 1987).

As early as 1948, however, there had been a trickle of economic migrants principally, although not exclusively, from the Anglophone Caribbean. The rate of flow gathered pace during the 1950s. As with poor migrants in other parts of the world, they largely settled in impoverished inner urban areas of major cities, not least London (Patterson, 1965), Birmingham (Rex and Moore, 1967) and Nottingham (Lawrence, 1974). Here they suffered discrimination, racist abuse, harassment and violence on a daily basis. Not surprisingly, it was in these cities, in 1958, where the first major urban disturbances took place. Reflecting on the events in Notting Hill (London) and Nottingham (Phillips and Phillips, 1998; Rowe, 1998), many policy makers saw this as a vindication of their earlier stance, namely that the presence of 'black' workers was the source of conflict. In other words, they (and not, for example, racism among white communities) were to blame. Arguably, it was a similar story in the case of subsequent outbreaks of violence in St Pauls (Bristol), Toxteth (Liverpool) and Brixton and Southall (London) in 1980/81 (Wallace and Joshua, 1983; Solomos, 2003; Ratcliffe, 2004); Handsworth (Birmingham) and Tottenham (London) in the mid-1980s (Gifford, 1986; West Midlands County Council, 1986); and Bradford in 1995 (Bradford Commission, 1996; Ratcliffe, 1996).

The wide swathe of academic literature, on the other hand, has tended to draw attention to the key role played in these urban disturbances by ethnic concentrations and segregation combined with poverty, deprivation and the corrosive power of racism, epitomised by organisations such as the British National Party (BNP). Significantly, they have also focused on the role of the police and, in particular, on heavy-handed police tactics and the institutionalised racism within individual police forces that has led to the harassment of innocent residents via the indiscriminate use of such practices as 'stop and search' (Macpherson, 1999; Kalra, 2003).

Government thinking in the 1950s and early 1960s was driven by a stated commitment to 'integration'. The problem, however, was that this was seen as the one-sided process illustrated by the popular adage 'when in Rome....'. Essentially, the onus was on migrants to fit in. Only when it became clear that this policy was not working did it provoke a radical rethink. This came with a Labour government in the mid-1960s. Roy Jenkins, as Home Secretary, saw the way forward as working towards a society where cultural diversity could flourish in an atmosphere of mutual tolerance. Thus began a sustained period of policy and practice driven by the idea of 'multiculturalism'.

From 1965, a series of (unfortunately named) Race Relations Acts were enacted (although not without considerable resistance from the Conservatives in opposition). Although not radical pieces of legislation in themselves, the first two Acts (passed in 1965 and 1968 respectively) did fulfil the extremely important purpose of establishing the principle of equity (Lester, 1998). The next significant legislative change was a strengthening of the Race Relations Act 1968. The Race Relations Act 1976 both widened the definition of discrimination (to include 'indirect' as well as 'direct' variants) and made the execution of cases easier by including new powers of subpoena in relation to documents and witnesses (Ratcliffe, 2004). It also brought into being the Commission for Racial Equality (CRE). The existing Race Relations Board was closed and its statutory duties transferred to the CRE. Whereas the former was restricted to the pursuit of cases involving individual complainants, the latter had new powers to launch investigations (where *prima facie* evidence of discrimination had come to light) into organisations or even whole industries/professions.

Merely having the legislation in place did not, of course, solve the problems of minorities or the areas in which they lived. For one thing, the next government (and Prime Minister Margaret Thatcher in particular) disapproved of both the legislation and the CRE. It realised, however, that it could not shut the CRE down summarily so it did the next best thing (from its perspective) – systematically starving the CRE of the funds it needed to do its job effectively (Sanders, 1998). Neoliberalism had no place for a body that sought to threaten what were assumed to be the inalienable, sovereign rights of the private sector.

Preparing the ideological basis for the shift to 'community cohesion'

With the election of the first New Labour government led by Tony Blair in May 1997, some assumed that there would be a radical re-evaluation and overhaul of the ways in which previous Conservative administrations had dealt with issues such as racism and 'racial' discrimination. In reality, what we initially witnessed was merely a continuation of the CRE cuts regime and an indifference towards any suggestion that the Race Relations Act 1976 should be strengthened further. One event, ironically from four years prior to its election, changed the picture: the murder of a black teenager, Stephen Lawrence, in Eltham, South London.

The national campaign for an independent inquiry, launched and fronted by his parents Neville and Doreen, garnered massive popular support and generated a widespread feeling of disgust directed at both the white youths who had perpetrated the crime and the Metropolitan Police. What followed was effectively a show trial revealing systematic incompetence on the part of the officers investigating the case and institutional racism infecting the organisation's body politic (Macpherson, 1999).

The Race Relations Act 1976 had been drafted in such a way that certain people and organisations were specifically exempted from its provisions: the police and immigration service were two such bodies. Given the outcomes of the Macpherson Inquiry, there was clearly a compelling argument for amending the legislation. The Race Relations (Amendment) Act 2000 not only imposed certain key statutory responsibilities on the police, it also contained a much broader definition of a 'public authority': the latter meaning that any private organisation undertaking work for a public body would (by virtue of the relationship) also assume the mantle of a public authority.

Public authorities covered by the new Amendment Act were required to draw up Race Equality Schemes by May 2001. There was also a mechanism for ensuring that policies already operated, or drawn up and proposed, by an authority were evaluated for 'impact'. These Race Equality Impact Assessments were intended to ensure that equality considerations were mainstreamed in all areas of policy and practice. Had they been effective they would have been a powerful tool. The problem was that, despite the fact that they were a statutory requirement, public authorities were for a number of reasons reluctant to adopt them (Ratcliffe, 2004). This underlines the obvious point that *having the right legislation in force is not enough*: the enforcement of the associated statutory regime has to be effective. We shall return to this issue later, but before doing so it is important to appreciate that this was part of a much larger New Labour agenda.

With the election of the first New Labour administration in May 1997, it rapidly became clear that there had been a radical repositioning of the Labour Party in ideological terms. It emerged that the neoliberal policies adopted by successive Conservative governments over the previous 18 years were in many cases being given little more than a glitzy makeover, with a series of reassuring labels and sound bites. Primary among the latter was 'social exclusion', a concept lifted directly from EU policy discourse. At one level, this was a catch-all for a cluster of highly disparate concerns that were (implicitly) deemed a little too 'Old Labour' (for the 'brave New Labour world'): poverty, racism, violence against women, homophobia, morbidity/ill-health/obesity, antisocial behaviour, substance abuse and so on. More significantly for the current chapter, however, it marked the most obvious evidence to date of a *culturalist approach to policy*. Those who were 'socially excluded' were viewed as a community apart: in other words, 'they' were not like 'us'. They were beyond the mainstream, and they were (frequently) 'hard to reach'. This effectively meant that it was *they* who were to blame for not being assisted by the (assumed) benevolent state: their 'opting' for a place beyond mainstream culture demonstrating a lack of personal, or collective, responsibility (Gough et al, 2006). It therefore mirrors the classic theorisations of the sub-proletariat or underclass (Morris, 1994).

To the government, the solution to these problems was a policy agenda it labelled 'social inclusion'. Levitas (1996, 1999) quite rightly characterised this as a classic exemplar of Durkheimian methodology. Policies were to be designed to cure an ailing body politic. The government's Social Exclusion Unit duly established a plethora of Policy Action Teams to cover the key areas of policy, and consulted widely across the country. There were undoubted successes, for example 'Sure Start', public money being invested in the early education of deprived children and the idea of joined-up policy working at a local authority level.

What especially interests us about this agenda, however, was its heavy focus on 'community' and neighbourhood as the route to sustainable social change. This is best viewed through the lens of the New Deal for

Communities (NDC) programme. Thirty-nine of the most deprived neighbourhoods in the country were to be given a major injection of public finance as part of a radical experiment seeking to involve local communities in key decisions about how local investment should be deployed. Although in one sense the initiative could be viewed as merely the most recent in a long series of urban regeneration/ renewal programmes over the last three decades, it was distinctive in its stated intention of minimising the role of the local authority in decision making. It also aimed to generate real sustainable change on the ground, something mostly lacking in the case of previous central government interventions. There is little evidence to suggest that the previous urban regeneration programmes had reduced inequalities between neighbourhoods or their residents.

Rather than relying on centralised decision making, local neighbourhood NDC offices were set up, the hope being that these would provide the context for a more effective dialogue between the local state and residents, including those disparagingly labelled 'hard to reach'. The exercise was viewed by central government as an attempt to increase the stock of social capital in the area, encourage local people to work together and thereby avoid the usual problems associated with top-down policy making (for example, disempowerment and the lack of feeling of ownership on the part of residents).

The theoretical underpinning for this approach came from the United States (US), where there was renewed interest in the concept of social capital. Although Robert Putnam had been working on this idea for a number of years (for example, Putnam, 1993), one particular book, *Bowling alone* (2000), seems to have captured the most attention from policy makers and academics on this side of the Atlantic. The problem of modern society, and especially poor urban communities, was seen to stem from atomisation. People were viewed as having become isolated from the sources of help and support, and most especially from those services that would *help them to help themselves.* The solution, therefore, lay in reconnecting such people to their local 'community', first by encouraging voluntary associations between residents and then using this as a bridge to the wider voluntary sector and education and training facilities. Reconnecting with community was crucial in that the development of relationships, the theory suggests, would generate 'bonding capital', vital for knowledge sharing. Being linked to the third sector and local state services would then enhance the level of 'bridging capital' by helping people to avail themselves of opportunities beyond the confines of the locality. The argument, in short, is that 'social capital that is built through encouraging voluntary associations is the cure for social inequality and lack of cohesive social trust' (Cheong et al, 2007, p 29).

While it is difficult to deny the appeal of this approach, critics were quick to point out that the evidence on which Putnam's book was based came from urban areas of the US and might therefore not be transferable to the UK (Kalra and Kapoor, 2009). The two welfare systems are totally at variance and there are critical differences in the way in which citizens of the United Kingdom (UK) traditionally relate to the local state. In addition, much of urban America is rigidly segregated on class and ethnic lines. (This, somewhat ironically, may well assist in the generation of bonding capital in local neighbourhoods [albeit probably at the expense of bridging capital].)

Critics have argued that residents 'are often more concerned about access to jobs, decent housing and public services rather than engaging in the shared, time-consuming project of community building' (Cheong et al, 2007, p 41). This argument runs directly counter to the communitarian agenda promoted by New Labour as the solution to inner-city decline. The key point in relation to the NDC initiative is that poor, relatively under-educated, NDC residents could never be expected to make a meaningful contribution to decision making where the professionals had control of the contours of the agenda, the technical language, the performance management framework and know-how and the hegemonic discourse surrounding change processes (that is, what is possible and over what timescale).

The basic problems exhibited *in extremis* in these 39 areas were also widely in evidence throughout urban, and indeed rural, Britain. Although no one had yet deployed the term 'broken Britain', it was clear that there was interest in government circles in finding a way to re-socialise those who had become left behind by the economic advances of many fellow citizens. As the wording here suggests, however, the solutions were sought through a change in culture, via communitarianism, a revitalised civic culture and the promotion of the idea of an inclusive (rather than exclusive) citizenship. This was viewed as the most effective route to a 'cohesive' society, thereby implicitly downplaying the importance of material inequality.

In a seminal paper, Kearns and Forrest (2000) spelt out an agenda for progress towards a *socially* cohesive society. This, while recognising the importance of fostering strong relationships between citizens, placed a major emphasis on economic inequality. This, they argued, had to be at the core of any overarching policy strategy. Flint and Robinson (2008, p 4) argue that the government subsequently took some core elements of this argument but replaced the term '*social* cohesion' with '*community* cohesion', the key point being that the focus on economic inequality was lost.

The emergence of 'community cohesion' as a policy strategy

In recent times, at least since the end of the Second World War, immigration has remained a highly contentious issue in Britain, with both major political parties constantly vying with each other to see who could appear tougher on immigration policy. Throughout the early years of the first Blair government, there were rising levels of what can best be described as paranoia surrounding the alleged dangers that inflows of refugees and asylum seekers posed (McGhee, 2005; Kundnani, 2007; Fekete, 2009). The concern was whether the refugees/asylum seekers might not only be a burden on the state purse but might also be dangerous – and here the 'victim as potential aggressor' took a particularly racialised/ethnicised form. What follows needs to be seen with this as a backdrop.

In the summer of 2001, there were serious disturbances in a number of towns and cities in Northern England (Clarke, 2001; Ritchie, 2001; Kalra, 2003). The Home Office committee formed in their wake, chaired by Ted Cantle (a highly experienced local government figure), sought to address the causes and consequences of these events and suggest appropriate policy responses. The subsequent report (Home Office, 2001a) and that of Home Office minister, John Denham (Home Office, 2001b), laid the blame on societal instability caused by the fact that groups of residents, defined by ethnic origin, were following 'parallel lives'. In other words, residents from the respective groups lived in separate localities, went to different schools, worked in different organisations and did not socialise or ever pray together. In a word, 'segregation', in all its guises, was the prime culprit for the disturbances. Ironically, then, it now seemed that high levels of bonding capital, which had once been lauded as an extremely positive feature of South Asian community life in the UK, were now a 'bad thing' (Cheong et al, 2007, p 25).

Although acknowledging that poverty, inequality and a longstanding animosity between communities (*grounded in racism*[1]) were also relevant factors, the Cantle Report, as it became known, gave these rather less prominence. It contained some 67 recommendations and was seen by its principal author as providing the basis for 'a new framework for race and diversity', to quote the subtitle of Cantle's subsequent book (Cantle, 2005). The report is also credited with coining the concept of 'community cohesion'. One could regard this as the point at which the prospects for a central policy focus on *social* cohesion receded (Flint and Robinson, 2008). The potential tension between policies on 'cohesion' and inequality (in its broadest sense, encompassing the end product of multiple 'exclusionary' forces) is central to our later analysis. We will be arguing that policy formulation and 'community cohesion practice' have largely failed to grasp the 'bigger picture'.

In 2002, this new agenda sparked a flurry of activity across central and local government, the CRE and faith groups. The result of consultations spanning the Local Government Association, the Office of the Deputy Prime Minister, the Home Office, the CRE and the Inter Faith Network was the publication of *Guidance on community cohesion* (LGA et al, 2002). This included the first formal definition of the concept in question. A *cohesive community*, they argued, is one where:

- there is a common vision and a sense of belonging for all communities;
- the diversity of people's different backgrounds and circumstances are appreciated and valued;
- those from different backgrounds have similar life opportunities; and
- strong and positive relationships are being developed between people from different backgrounds in the workplace, in schools and within neighbourhoods. (LGA et al, 2002, p 6)

The guidance document also provided a good deal of practical advice on how to approach this challenging agenda: challenging not least because the historically entrenched racism and prejudice that lie behind most outbreaks of disorder are not readily counteracted by local authority policies and practices in the here and now.

In 2003, the Home Office established the Community Cohesion Unit and set about the task of devising the means by which the level of cohesion in a particular locality could be measured. Its conclusions were contained in *Building a picture of community cohesion* (Home Office et al, 2003). Each of the elements identified in the above definition were to be measured by a small number of indicators (2003, p 5). Crispian Fuller in Chapter Three of this volume asks what these questions tell us about the level and nature of the underlying tensions that create problematic relations between the constituent 'groups' within a local authority area. He concludes: 'not as much as the government might hope'. Even discounting serious questions about the methodology itself (vague and ambiguous question wording, sampling design, and even the choice of the particular mode of interview adopted), a snapshot of people's answers to such general/broad questions at a particular time and place can generate a high degree of data unreliability. More importantly, what people *say* about an event clearly does not constitute direct evidence about the event itself.

Where direct evidence is invoked, for example the number of 'racial incidents' recorded by the police, this provides only a very partial picture as comparatively few instances are actually *reported* and not all of these are *recorded*. Furthermore, there is the question of what, say, an increase in incident numbers might mean. It may simply be the case that confidence in the police has improved to the point where people are more willing to report such events. The same argument, of course, holds in the reverse case (a drop in the figures). This means that the analysis of such data needs to be undertaken carefully, taking relevant contextual evidence into account.

This being said, the Home Office indicators did at least include a focus on the material factors that affect life chances and, as we argue later, there has been some extremely useful proactive policy development, for example in the crucial area of education. Also important is the inclusion of deprivation indices, which provide a vital indication of overall levels of inequality (although they do not permit geographically fine-grained analysis that would enable us, for example, to assess evidence on ethnic differentials at a localised level). Their presence in the list of indicators does, however, at least suggest that regeneration was to remain a significant element of future policy thinking.

Promoting 'community cohesion'

While it is clearly instructive, and potentially illuminating, to build a 'picture' of community cohesion and assess how this changes over time, the key question for this book is how positive change can be ensured (and the results evaluated). As noted earlier, it is clear that the government, for its part, intended to place great store on the idea of 'social capital', which explains why the Cabinet Office commissioned a major review of the evidence around this time (Aldridge et al, 2003).

Our earlier assessment of the social capital approach, however, casts considerable doubt on its efficacy. It appeared to us that there were a number of key areas that needed to be subjected to sustained policy focus: policing, (tackling) racism and discrimination (both individually and collectively based and including, crucially, *state policies and practices*, housing and regeneration, education and (increasing) access to the labour market. The chapters in Part Three of this volume explore some of these areas.[2] We look now, however, at the issue on which the UK government has placed much emphasis in terms of cohesion policy – *intercultural understanding*.

The 'Pathfinder programme' (Home Office and Vantagepoint, 2003), which focused on increasing the level and quality of cross-cultural interaction, resulted in government funding for 14 local authorities and a similar number of authorities adopted such policies and practices despite the absence of such external financial support. Smaller local initiatives such as the Swapping Cultures project (Hall, 2006; DCLG, 2007) also demonstrated what could be done to increase understanding between young people from different ethnic, cultural and faith backgrounds. While perfectly acceptable as a way of attempting to increase knowledge of 'the other', it rather assumes (a) that historically entrenched/endemic racism, ignorance and prejudice can be educated away and (b) that material inequalities between groups can be ignored, or downplayed, in this process.

Potentially more effective is a strategy adopted by Britain's more forward-thinking local authorities. This is the practice known as '*myth-busting*' (DCLG, 2006a). The idea is to counter mischievous untruths circulating within a locality; untruths, in particular, that are driven by an explicit or implicit racist agenda. The authority acts in conjunction with local media outlets to project a rather different message. Liaison between these agencies is promoted via the Local Strategic Partnership, involving representatives of the local authority, public service providers, 'the third sector', politicians, local media and the police. (The role of the media is discussed in more detail in Chapter Six of this volume.)

The major Achilles heel, however, lies in the degree of trust in the local authority. In other words, where there is a breakdown in the relationship between local government and citizen, 'myth-busting' is likely to be ineffective (and may even lead to more people believing the 'non-establishment' version of a story). Importantly, the local authority also needs to be sensitive to the everyday lived experiences of local people. Immigration tends to impact disproportionately on already poor, deprived communities and, as a direct consequence, some local inter-communal tensions are to be expected.

Attempts have been made to counter this breakdown of trust by invoking the '*civic values*' *agenda* based on a more inclusive notion of citizenship. A recent study, for example, welcomed many of the initiatives undertaken locally to improve the lives of residents, encourage inter-cultural dialogue and build a consensus over civic values, for example the concept of an 'Oldhamer' as an attempt to encourage residents of Oldham (in North West England) to identify with the town and not to a narrower, and more exclusionary, ethnicised form of self-identity

(DCLG, 2006a[3]). Ultimately, this, along the lines of the 'myth-busting' strategy, is about *civic leadership*, about countering negative forces by projecting a rather different message about the role of the citizen and their relationship to a social milieu and to fellow citizens.

The message of the study was essentially that there has to be a firm, unambiguous and unwavering political commitment from the top to promote sustainable change. The findings concurred with the thrust of a document published the previous year. Targeted specifically at chief executives and council leaders, this advocated a *corporate approach* to community cohesion (LGA, 2005). As to day-to-day practice, this was addressed in a 'toolkit' (Community Cohesion Unit, 2005).

Importantly, however, the DCLG study also explored the limits to the spheres of influence open to local forms of governance. It acknowledged, for example, that the economic fortunes of an area (a key factor in relation to levels of deprivation) are to a large extent determined by regional, national and global factors. As Kearns and Parkinson (2001, p 2103) had argued five years earlier:

> [G]overnments and policy-makers are neither able to control global capitalism and its effects, nor at the other end of the scale to direct or manage the fortunes of individual neighbourhoods within their jurisdictions. Neighbourhood change is proving unpredictable and resulting in ever-wider gaps in fortune and prosperity between places within single regions and countries.

And this is the crux of the matter. Echoing an earlier point, however much one promotes positive ideas and encourages a greater understanding between people, material circumstances still hold sway. The focus therefore has to be on what can be achieved within these larger constraints.

Cohesion, integration and the equalities agenda

By mid-decade, the government was formally (that is, in theory) committed to a policy of tackling inequality *and* promoting cohesion. This led to the publication of *Improving opportunity, strengthening society* (DCLG, 2005), a wide-ranging document supplementing the focus on promoting cohesion with an appraisal of levels of inequality in various institutional areas, most notably education, employment, housing and health. Here it drew attention to particular areas of concern.

The equalities agenda has been moving inexorably towards a generic model. In theory, this has the potential to facilitate the promotion of a more nuanced, multidimensional (rather than additive) approach to questions of equity. In other words, it should be able to address the challenges stemming from intersectionality. Accordingly, a major government review was launched alongside a review of the current legislative context applicable to the separate equalities arenas. The Discrimination Law Review and the Equalities Review (Cabinet Office, 2007) acted as the backdrop to the establishment, on 1 November 2007, of the Equality and Human Rights Commission (EHRC), which replaced the three former Commissions: the CRE, the Equal Opportunities Commission and the Disability Rights Commission.

At the same time, increasing concerns about social instability were sparked by two factors: evidence that immigration flows were becoming increasingly diverse (and unpredictable) in the wake of the expansion of the EU from 2004, and apparently increasing rates of radicalisation among young Muslims, exemplified by the London bombings of July 2005 (seen within a wider European context in EUMC, 2005). The national agenda and government thinking, as a consequence, began to focus on both cohesion and the need to 'integrate' migrants. The Commission on Integration and Cohesion (CIC), chaired by Darra Singh, chief executive of Ealing Borough Council, attempted to fuse these two streams of ideas, although there is a strong case for suggesting that the 'real' (that is, underlying but unspoken) agenda was to explore ways of addressing 'the Muslim question'.

The interim report of the CIC appeared in February 2007 (CIC, 2007a). This highlighted the need for widespread improvements to the availability of good-quality training in English for migrants and, while acknowledging that much good work was being done locally, the need for more initiatives to bring communities together. There were clear echoes of the integration agenda of the 1960s here, especially in the centrality accorded to the ability to communicate in English. But, although given much less prominence in public debate following its publication, it did state very clearly that 'bringing communities together' could not be achieved without addressing the *prior* question of levels of inequality and deprivation. It could be argued that the thrust of this latter point was rather lost in the final report (CIC, 2007b).

In the latter, the CIC presented its vision for the 'open communities' of 2020 and proposed 'four key principles … underpin[ning] a new understanding of integration and cohesion': 'shared futures', 'a new model of rights and responsibilities', 'a new emphasis on mutual respect and civility' and 'visible social justice' (2007b, p 1). It also provided a comprehensive definition of an integrated and cohesive community. This, the CIC suggested, is one where:

- There is a clearly defined and widely shared sense of the contribution of different individuals and different communities to a future vision for a neighbourhood, city, region or country
- There is a strong sense of an individual's rights and responsibilities when living in a particular place – people know what everyone expects of them, and what they can expect in return
- Those from different backgrounds have similar life opportunities, access to services and treatment
- There is a strong sense of trust in institutions locally to act fairly in arbitrating between different interests and for their role and justifications to be subject to public scrutiny
- There is a strong recognition of the contribution of both those who have newly arrived and those who already have deep attachment to a particular place, with a focus on what they have in common
- There are strong and positive relationships between people from different backgrounds in the workplace, in schools and other institutions within neighbourhoods. (CIC, 2007b, p 10)

The third bullet point is particularly relevant to our core argument in that it relates to social inequality. However, mirroring a broader ideological shift in New Labour thinking, the focus is quite explicitly on 'life opportunities' rather than outcomes.

There is also an attempt by the authors of the report to define, and distinguish between the concepts of 'cohesion' and 'integration'. In their view, '[c]ohesion is principally the process that must happen in all communities to ensure different groups of people get on well together; while integration is principally the process that ensures new residents and existing residents adapt to one another' (2007b, p 9).

They say that the processes go side by side as the local population evolves and communities move forward to their (projected) 'shared future'. One can see a certain logic in this, that is, distinguishing between the ongoing relations between groups and the issues concerning the settlement of newly arriving migrants, but the wording is ambiguous and the definition of 'integration' questionable. As to the former, there is the not unfamiliar issue relating to use of the term 'community' (see Commission on the Future of Multi-Ethnic Britain, 2000). The CIC really means by this 'local population' but there is also an issue to do with the lack of *internal* cohesiveness of some putative groups. As to the notion of 'integration', the obvious question is: why is 'integration' purely concerned with newly arriving groups? Is this not in truth a much broader issue, affecting sections of all population groups, irrespective of ethnicity?

It is important to recognise, however, that this interpretation of integration as a process concerned with 'new' migrants is in accordance with normal usage within wider European debates. In these countries, as noted earlier, the term 'cohesion' has little resonance in policy discourse as yet. It is clear that the rapid population flux in member states as a direct result of EU expansion has stimulated these debates further: 'further' in the sense that there were already vigorous debates about policies across Europe towards refugees and asylum seekers. The *Third annual report on migration and integration* (Council of the European Communities, 2007) sees the fundamental aim as promoting unity in diversity. It regrets the fact that 'structural initiatives targeting the host population to reinforce its ability to adjust to diversity are still underrepresented in national strategies' and suggests that 'fostering integration as a genuinely two-way process is a major challenge that requires further efforts'.[4] *Integration is therefore viewed as a two-way process involving an acceptance of diversity on the part of existing residents of the receiving country.* Britain's approach has, however, been markedly at variance with this. In a highly illuminating publication from the Department for Communities and Local Government (DCLG, 2008a), 'integration' policy appeared essentially to be about informing migrants how 'we' behave and what is therefore expected of 'them': notably absent is any tangible sense of these European ideals of integration as a two-way process.

The role of the new edition of the European Commission's *Handbook on integration* (Council of the European Union, 2007) was to set out the respective roles of the existing residents and newly arriving migrants. Member states are advised to set out clearly the rights and responsibilities of migrants; the latter in turn being expected to adjust their mindsets to conform to these injunctions. The ultimate aim is to improve participation in the economic, social and political life of a country, this being regarded as vital to the 'integration' process *although not totally synonymous with it (thereby leaving discursive space for the essence, if not the explicit terminology, of 'cohesion').* There is no clear attempt across Europe to assess wider integration policies by deploying the idea of 'value for money'. It would, after all, be extremely difficult to find a rational means of doing so, especially as many European countries do not collect data on 'ethnic group/origin' (and have no plans to do so).

As to how 'acceptance of diversity' is to be achieved, the *Handbook on European integration* argues that the media should play a critical role both by presenting an accurate picture of migrant populations and by countering misleading stereotypes. This resonates well with the current 'myth-busting' strategies of some local authorities in the UK, which, as we saw earlier, are seen as a central plank of existing community cohesion strategies (DCLG, 2006a). It also fulfils one of the other core aims of the wider policy strategy, namely that which appeals for a greater level of understanding and tolerance on the part of majority society. It should be stressed, once again, that the pressures on local resources generated by immigration fall unevenly on the population, being essentially heavily concentrated in what are already relatively impoverished neighbourhoods. Thus, tensions arise despite the presence of multi-ethnic friendships, tolerance and respect within working-class communities.[5] Put simply, and as quite rightly argued by Ed Miliband when announcing his candidacy for leader of the Labour Party in 2010, migration is a class issue.

In February 2008, the UK government published its formal response to the CIC's definitions of integration and cohesion and to its recommendations on the way forward (DCLG, 2008b). First, it somewhat simplified the CIC's definition:

> 'Community Cohesion is what must happen in all communities to enable different groups of people to get on well together. A key contributor to cohesion is integration which is what must happen to enable new residents to adjust to one another.
>
> Our vision of an integrated and cohesive community is based on **three foundations**:
> • People from different backgrounds having similar life opportunities
> • People knowing their rights and responsibilities
> • People trusting one another and trusting local institutions to act fairly
>
> And **three key ways of living together**:
> • A shared future vision and sense of belonging
> • A focus on what new and existing communities have in common, alongside a recognition of the value of diversity

- Strong and positive relationships between people from different backgrounds. (DCLG, 2008b, p 10, emphasis in original)

This new definition/approach is worthy of some comment at this stage. The first, rather obvious, point is that although it appears neater and more straightforward, it illustrates very clearly our earlier point about ambiguities surrounding the term 'community'. Here it is used in two completely different senses, first to refer to 'population' and second to 'groups', or should that read 'people from different backgrounds'? The key point here is that the drivers of a lack of 'cohesion' may or may not be related to ethnicity, culture or faith. This appears to put the case for a wider, more inclusive, notion of '*social* cohesion' (DCLG, 2006a). Furthermore, we arguably need to move to a much more nuanced 'de-racialised' or 'de-ethnicised' interpretation of both 'integration' and 'cohesion'.

The vision of a future where 'similar life opportunities' are the norm is part of a much more extensive policy agenda. In previous definitions of cohesion, such as that produced by the CIC, it was simply one of a list of elements, and even then a good way down the list. The problem for policy makers faced with this agenda is that they need some pointers towards a rational strategy. We would wish to argue that:

- What is needed is a clear unambiguous statement that addressing the issue of inequality/unequal life chances is a *necessary but not sufficient condition* for the achievement of *social cohesion* as a sustainable condition.
- Social cohesion is a more fundamental concept than *community* cohesion. It effectively acknowledges the presence of intra- as well as inter-'community' divisions. Social cohesion refers to a situation where these internal divisions (based, for example, on age/generation, gender and socioeconomic background) have been addressed. Here, 'success' would be judged by sustainable, lasting stability based on the firm foundation of *achieved* equality targets.

This implies that any attempts to achieve good relations between people from different backgrounds in the absence of a serious push on equality are destined to fail. But equally, the achievement of a more equal society does not inevitably ensure harmonious relations between these groups.[6] That is why both are needed, but *within a clearly prioritised policy strategy*. The definition in the government response document (DCLG, 2008b) is more convincing than the earlier versions in that, by referring to 'foundations' and giving pride of place to 'life chances', it does at least hint at an official preference for prioritisation. This 'prioritisation' needs, however, to be backed up by a clear, unambiguous policy strategy and the firm political will to drive it through to a successful conclusion.

Three updated versions of *Improving opportunity, strengthening society* (DCLG, 2005) have been published over the last five years (DCLG, 2006b, 2007, 2009). Once again, as well as pointing to positive advances, these draw attention to ongoing substantive material inequalities. This concern with structural disadvantage suffered by the more impoverished members of some groups was also underlined in a series of significant publications in the final year of the CRE as an independent body. The first, entitled *30: At the turning of the tide* (CRE, 2006), reflects on its achievements since establishment in 1976 by collating a series of personal accounts from people from a wide range of backgrounds.[7] A rather more systematic account, essentially taking the form of a balance sheet, was published a little more recently (CRE, 2007). This spelt out what had been achieved but also warned that there was much more to do (in the period following the handing over of the baton to the EHRC). The other equalities bodies would undoubtedly concur with this assessment of the tasks ahead.

Concluding thoughts: the challenges ahead

> Britain's Labour administration has clearly indicated the policy weight behind the community cohesion agenda. It remains to be seen to which extent this will be matched by as clear an agenda in the area of equalities with the launch of the unified Equality and Human Rights Commission. (Karla and Kapoor, 2009 p 1411)

In many ways, this is the crux of the matter. The Equality Act 2010 is of course only the start of a challenging policy process. As already noted, it is one thing to have legislation in place that spells out the statutory responsibilities of the various public bodies: quite another to ensure the deployment/activation of these responsibilities in such a way that meaningful, sustainable change is generated. The lessons, drawn from more than three decades of 'race relations' legislation, are instructive here. Attempts to curb overt discriminatory behaviour often simply had the effect of driving such practices underground. Years of cajoling the private sector to adopt fair practices have produced mixed results as the CRE (2007) admits. In addition, successive CRE chairs had bemoaned the fact that the political will (at the highest level) to help them push through real change was simply not there.

Throughout the 1980s and 1990s, tight fiscal controls meant that they were effectively fighting racism and discrimination with one arm behind their backs. The Conservative administrations during this period had little time for what they saw as a socialist agenda driven by 'political correctness'. The pervasive neoliberal mantra was that the private sector, comprising essentially sovereign entities, had certain inalienable rights, which included being permitted to run their businesses as they saw fit without interference from government-funded quangos such as the CRE (Orton and Ratcliffe, 2008). As noted earlier, the position did not change materially with the election of New Labour in 1997.

Even among local authorities that displayed a high degree of commitment to the spirit as well as the letter of the law, progress was slow. This is because Race Equality Impact Assessments – potentially the key motor for change – are an intrinsically complex idea. It is not easy, for example, to assess the likely impact of a proposed new policy on a multi-ethnic citizenry: not least because most policies have a variety of unintended consequences. In the context of tight fiscal control, there is always the temptation to focus on delivery of frontline services rather than engage in exercises that inevitably slow down that process. Mainstreaming, the only long-term, sustainable solution, tends to take time in any large organisation. Public authorities need logistical and technical support backed up by an effective inspection regime if progress is to be made. More relevant, given the current trajectory of the equalities regime heralded by the Equality Act, this applies even more so in the context of the much broader, and even more complex, Equality Impact Assessment.

The sheer complexities involved in promoting real social change by such administrative tools combined with the apparent keenness of government to pursue the 'community cohesion' agenda raised an uncomfortable question (somewhat obliquely raised in the Cheong et al quote at the head of this section). Has the latter effectively *supplanted* the equalities agenda as the core policy terrain followed by public bodies such as local authorities, schools, colleges, hospitals and housing associations? If so, the prognosis for a stable, sustainable social formation and polity is deeply compromised. At the risk of overstating the case, it is infinitely easier to bring people together for social events than it is to solve the material differences that divide those same people.

The EHRC, as its name implies, also has a core remit to pursue the attainment of basic human rights for all citizens (and would-be citizens). This invokes a much broader and more fundamental agenda incorporating 'equality' as a basic right (Phillips, 1999). This is an 'equality' that goes far beyond the idea of equalising the income or wealth *distributions* defined by ethnicity, gender, age, sexual orientation and so on. It is about pursuing a fairer, more equitable society that rejects the pathologisation of fellow citizens as 'hard to reach' or 'socially excluded'. In short, it involves taking very seriously the first strand of the New Labour government's own stated agenda for an 'inclusive and cohesive society', namely that 'people from different backgrounds' really do have 'similar life opportunities'.

It seems extremely unlikely, however, that the new coalition government headed by David Cameron will pursue the 'socioeconomic duty' as a policy option. This notwithstanding, we need to consider the implications of the broader agenda for evaluation strategies. In terms of pursuing social cohesion, much would depend on whether, and if so how vigorously, the Equality Act 2010 is deployed by government. This, after all, contains the basis of a framework for policy and practice. In terms of evaluation, much would rely on a wider application of Equality Impact Assessments or their successors. In order to do this effectively, however, two things are urgently needed. First, more work is required on the methodology of Equality Impact Assessments across differing substantive contexts. Second, much better and more up-to-date data on population size and flux are needed (see Chapters Four and Five by Simpson, and Eversley and Mayhew, respectively).

'Community cohesion': a research footnote

By way of a footnote to these discussions, in the same month that the Department for Communities and Local Government published the CIC report (2007b), it also released an important analysis of the predictors of community cohesion from a research team at the University of Oxford containing one of the UK's top quantitative social scientists, Anthony Heath (Laurence and Heath, 2008). This featured the multilevel modelling of data from the 2005 Citizenship Survey. Of particular interest are two findings: first, that 'it is ... deprivation that undermines cohesion, not diversity' (2007, p 47) and second, that 'individual level disadvantage (ie low socio-economic status) is ... a negative predictor of cohesion' (2007, p 47). In other words, it is deprivation, low socioeconomic status and poverty that are the principal correlates of 'cohesion', and not ethnicity. This explains the rather obvious empirical point that ethnically diverse middle-class neighbourhoods do not feature in debates about cohesion. As we have noted at various points in this chapter, it is the more deprived areas, both urban and rural, that bear the brunt of new immigration flows in the sense of increased pressures on local infrastructure such as housing, education, and health and welfare services.

As to 'integration', the CIC had attempted to distance itself from earlier interpretations of the concept,[8] in particular its association with the idea of 'assimilation'. This is understandable given that 1960s assimilationism (and the implication within 1960s political discourse of *acculturation* as a positively valued end) was the prime cause of the failure of related social policy during that decade. Indeed, it led directly to the adoption of 'multiculturalism' as a core paradigm (Solomos, 2003; Ratcliffe, 2004). It appears that in social policy circles, as with the fashion industry, those at the helm find it difficult to resist the temptation to recycle earlier approaches (even when, as in this case, they have been thoroughly discredited). Indeed, given a general acceptance in the contemporary world of the 'politics of identity', the chances of success are even more remote.

Notes

[1] The crucial point is that animosity is seen in the cohesion literature as largely to do with culture and ethnicity (and not with racism). The implications for policy and practice are wide-ranging.

[2] There is insufficient space to cover many other important issues here, notably policing, health and social welfare.

[3] This major study examined the policy response of four local authorities in East Lancashire to the urban disturbances in 2001. Running in parallel with this, the Community Cohesion Panel published its final report in 2004 (Home Office, 2004) essentially to review progress since the Cantle Report (Home Office, 2001a).

[4] See the press release at http://europa.eu/rapid/pressReleasesAction.do?reference=MEMO/07/351&format=HTML&aged=0&language=EN&guiLanguage=en

[5] For further reading on tolerance and respect within working-class communities, see Collins (2004).

[6] *Our shared future* (CIC, 2007b) does refer, if only fleetingly, to a lack of 'cohesion' in more affluent areas.

[7] The catalyst was a major national conference convened by the CRE and held in London during November 2006.

[8] The Department for Communities and Local Government (DCLG, 2008a) suggests, however, that it has not distanced itself very far.

References

Aldridge, S., Halpern, D. and Fitzpatrick, S. (2003) *Social capital: A discussion paper*, London: Performance and Innovation Unit, Cabinet Office.

Bradford Commission (1996) *The Bradford Commission report*, London: The Stationery Office.

Cabinet Office (2007) *Fairness and freedom: The final report of the equalities review*, London: Cabinet Office.

Cantle, T. (2005) *Community cohesion: A new framework for race and diversity*, Basingstoke: Palgrave Macmillan.

Carter, B., Harris, C. and Joshi, S. (1987) 'The 1951-55 Conservative government and the racialisation of black immigration', *Immigrants and Minorities*, vol 6, no 3, pp 335-47.

Cheong, P.H., Edwards, R., Goulbourne, H. and Solomos, J. (2007) 'Immigration, social cohesion and social capital: a review', *Critical Social Policy*, vol 27, no 1, pp 24-49.

CIC (Commission on Integration and Cohesion) (2007a) *Our interim statement*, London: CIC/DCLG.

CIC (2007b) *Our shared future*, London: CIC/DCLG.

Clarke, T. (2001) *Burnley speaks, who listens…? A summary of the Burnley Task Force report on the disturbances in June 2001*, Burnley: Burnley Task Force.

Collins, M. (2004) *The likes of us: A biography of the white working class*, London: Granta Books.

Commission on the Future of Multi-Ethnic Britain (2000) *The future of multi-ethnic Britain: The Parekh Report*, London: Profile Books.

Community Cohesion Unit (2005) *Community cohesion: SEVEN STEPS: A practitioner's toolkit*, London: Home Office/ODPM.

Council of the European Communities (2007) *Third annual report on migration and integration*, Brussels: Council of the European Communities, http://ec.europa.eu/justice_home/fsj/immigration/docs/com_2007_512_en.pdf

Council of the European Union (2007) *Handbook on integration*, Brussels: European Commission, Council of the European Union, www.consilium.europa.eu/ueDocs/cms_Data/docs/pressdata/en/jha/94682.pdf

CRE (Commission for Racial Equality) (2006) *30: At the turning of the tide*, London: CRE.

CRE (2007) *A lot done, a lot to do: Our vision for an integrated Britain*, London: CRE.

DCLG (Department for Communities and Local Government) (2005) *Improving opportunity, strengthening society*, London: DCLG.

DCLG (2006a) *Managing for diversity: A case study of four local authorities*, London: DCLG.

DCLG (2006b) *Improving opportunity, strengthening society: One year on, a progress report*, London: DCLG.

DCLG (2007) *Improving opportunity, strengthening society: Two years on, a progress report*, London: DCLG.

DCLG (2008a) *Communicating important information to new local residents*, London: DCLG.

DCLG (2008b) *The government's response to the Commission on Integration and Cohesion*, London: DCLG.

DCLG (2009) *Improving opportunity, strengthening society: A third progress report on the government's strategy for race equality and community cohesion*, London: DCLG.

EUMC (European Monitoring Centre of Racism and Xenophobia) (2005) *The impact of 7 July 2005 London bomb attacks on Muslim communities in the EU*, Vienna: EUMC.

Fekete, L. (2009) *A suitable enemy: Racism, migration and Islamophobia in Europe*, London: Pluto.

Flint, J. and Robinson, D. (2008) 'Introduction', in J. Flint and D. Robinson (eds) *Community cohesion in crisis? New dimensions of diversity and difference* (pp 1-13), Bristol: The Policy Press.

Gifford, Lord (et al) (1986) *The Broadwater Farm Inquiry*, London: Karia Press.

Gough, J., Eisenschitz, A. and McCulloch, A. (2006) *Spaces of social exclusion*, London: Routledge.

Hall, J. (2006) "'Race' and silence: the discourse of reticence', Unpublished PhD thesis, University of Warwick.

Home Office (2001a) *Community cohesion: A report of the independent review team*, London: Home Office.

Home Office (2001b) *Building cohesive communities: A report of the Ministerial Group on Public Order and Community Cohesion*, London: Home Office.

Home Office (2004) *The end of parallel lives? The report of the Community Cohesion Panel*, London: Home Office.

Home Office and Vantagepoint (2003) *Community Cohesion Pathfinder Programme: The first six months*, London: Vantagepoint/Home Office.

Home Office, Commission for Racial Equality, Local Government Association, Office of the Deputy Prime Minister and Neighbourhood Renewal Unit (2003) *Building a picture of community cohesion*, London: Home Office.

Kalra, V. (2003) 'Police lore and community disorder: diversity in the criminal justice system', in D. Mason (ed) *Explaining ethnic differences: Changing patterns of disadvantage in Britain* (pp 139-52), Bristol: The Policy Press.

Kalra, V.S. and Kapoor, N. (2009) 'Interrogating segregation, integration and the community cohesion agenda', *Journal of Ethnic and Migration Studies*, vol 35, no 9, pp 1397-415.

Kearns, A. and Forrest, R. (2000) 'Social cohesion and multilevel urban governance', *Urban Studies*, vol 37, no 5-6, pp 995-1017.

Kearns, A. and Parkinson, M. (2001) 'The significance of neighbourhood', *Urban Studies*, vol 38, no 12, pp 2103-10.

Kundnani, A. (2007) *The end of tolerance? Racism in 21st century Britain*, London: Pluto.

Laurence, J. and Heath, A. (2008) *Predictors of community cohesion: Multilevel modelling of the 2005 Citizenship Survey*, London: DCLG.

Lawrence, D. (1974) *Black migrants: white natives. A study of race relations in Nottingham*, Cambridge: Cambridge University Press.

Lester, A. (1998) 'From legislation to integration: twenty years of the Race Relations Act', in T. Blackstone, B. Parekh and P. Sanders (eds) *Race relations in Britain: A developing agenda*, London: Routledge.

Levitas, R. (1996) 'The concept of social exclusion and the new Durkheimian hegemony', *Critical Social Policy*, vol 46, no 16, pp 5-20.

Levitas, R. (1999) *The inclusive society: Social exclusion and New Labour*, Basingstoke: Macmillan.

LGA (Local Government Association) (2005) *Leading cohesive communities: A guide for local authority leaders and chief executives*, London: LGA.

LGA et al (2002) *Guidance on community cohesion*, London: LGA.

McGhee, D. (2005) *Intolerant Britain? Hate, citizenship and difference*, Maidenhead: Open University Press.

Macpherson, W. (1999) *The Stephen Lawrence Inquiry: The report of an inquiry by Sir William Macpherson of Cluny*, London: The Stationery Office.

Morris, L. (1994) *Dangerous classes: The underclass and social citizenship*, London: Routledge.

Orton, M. and Ratcliffe, P. (2008) 'From single to multidimensional policy approaches to equalities? The example of contract compliance', in D. Schiek and V. Chege (eds) *European Union non-discrimination law: Comparative perspectives on multidimensional equality law* (pp 163-84), Abingdon: Routledge Cavendish.

Patterson, S. (1965) *Dark strangers: A study of West Indians in London*, Harmondsworth: Penguin Books.

Phillips, A. (1999) *Which equalities matter?*, Cambridge: Polity Press.

Phillips, M. and Phillips, T. (1998) *Windrush: The irresistible rise of multi-racial Britain*, London: Harper/Collins.

Putnam, R.D. (1993) 'The prosperous community: social capital and public life', *The American Prospect*, vol 4, no 13, pp 35-42.

Putnam, R.D. (2000) *Bowling alone: The collapse and revival of American community*, New York, NY: Simon & Schuster.

Ratcliffe, P. (1996) *'Race' and housing in Bradford: Addressing the needs of the South Asian, African and Caribbean communities*, Bradford: Bradford Housing Forum.

Ratcliffe, P. (2004) *'Race', ethnicity and difference: Imagining an inclusive society*, Maidenhead: McGraw-Hill/Open University Press.

Rex, J. and Moore, R. (1967) *Race, community and conflict: A study of Sparkbrook*, London: Institute of Race Relations/Oxford University Press.

Ritchie, D. (2001) *Oldham Independent Review: One Oldham, one future*, Oldham: Oldham Independent Review.

Rowe, M. (1998) *The racialisation of disorder in twentieth century Britain*, Aldershot: Ashgate.

Sanders, P. (1998) 'Tackling racial discrimination', in T. Blackstone, B. Parekh and P. Sanders (eds) *Race relations in Britain: A developing agenda*, London: Routledge.

Solomos, J. (2003) *Race and racism in Britain* (3rd edition), Basingstoke: Palgrave Macmillan.

Wallace, T. and Joshua, H. (1983) *To ride the storm*, London: Heinemann.

West Midlands County Council (1986) *A different reality: An account of black people's experiences and their grievances before and after the Handsworth rebellions of September 1985*, Birmingham: WMCC.

TWO

Evaluating social cohesion

Helen Sullivan

Introduction

This chapter is concerned with the evaluation of social cohesion. It begins by identifying some key evaluation challenges posed by the proposed definition of social cohesion. It situates these challenges in ongoing debates about the merits of different approaches to evaluation and highlights the potential contribution of recent developments in 'theory-based evaluation'. Drawing on 'theories of change' – a popular example of theory-based evaluation – the chapter explores how these challenges may be met and the implications for evaluators.

This book argues for a reappraisal of the value of policies based on 'community cohesion' and their replacement by a policy programme aimed at 'social cohesion'. As Ratcliffe argues in Chapter One (p 000):

> Social cohesion is a more fundamental concept than *community* cohesion. It effectively acknowledges the presence of intra- as well as inter-'community' divisions. Social cohesion refers to a situation where these internal divisions (based, for example, on age/generation, gender and socioeconomic background) have also been addressed successfully. Here, 'success' is judged by sustainable, lasting stability based on the firm foundation of *achieved* equality targets.

Equality is also understood in a particular way,

> not confined to global comparisons between groups defined in terms of ethnicity and/or faith ... [but involving] a substantial narrowing of differentials between those from diverse social backgrounds *within* ethnic and faith groups. This implies that the integration/cohesion agenda needs to be set within a broader social policy agenda driven by a

> concern with universal human rights. (Ratcliffe et al, 2008,
> p 16, emphasis in original)

This book sets out what it considers to be the key components of a social policy agenda for social cohesion. In terms of policy areas, education, the labour market and housing are identified as central to the material conditions experienced by all communities. In addition, the complex and often contradictory nature of 'community' will influence the likely impact of policy interventions. This impact needs to be considered in a number of ways: in relation to intergenerational dynamics, in the exchanges and relations between settled and 'new' migrant groups, in the context of the neighbourhood conditions that 'communities' inhabit and in the influences of wider 'communities' and places on each other and on neighbourhoods. Also, overlaid on the policy/community/neighbourhood canvas is the role of political institutions, cultures and practices, the interface between the national and the local and the interface between the representative and participative modes of democratic engagement.

The agenda for change outlined in this book poses a number of important challenges to evaluators, four of which are highlighted here.

First is the challenge of defining and describing the outcome that is being sought; what would 'social cohesion' look like? Reference is made throughout the chapters of this book to a number of possible descriptors, including sustainability, stability, inclusion, equality and reduction in differentials (material and other). Each of these terms is complex, containing multiple components that are themselves in need of further elaboration to be made tangible and measurable for evaluation purposes. In addition, these terms need to be considered in relation to each other, that is, is the achievement of 'sustainability' contingent on the achievement of other 'outcomes', which are they and what is the relationship between them? This offers complexity of a different but no less challenging kind.

This raises the issue, second, of causality or how we know that the policy interventions being implemented are making a contribution to the objective that is being sought? The various chapters of this book offer examples of possible interventions in education, housing, employment and work with communities. In each case, evaluators need to be able to assess both the relationship between the specific intervention and its immediate goal, for example improving access to social housing, reducing worklessness or addressing underachievement, and also the contribution it makes to the overall outcome of social cohesion. Establishing causality is all the more difficult in dynamic social systems, where contextual factors, including history, institutions and agency, interact to shape the potential impact of any proposed intervention.

Third, in addition to conceptual clarity, making progress towards understanding causality necessitates the availability of reliable and relevant data. Sometimes this data will be available as part of a wider dataset recording the performance of particular policies or the quality of life of local communities. Often, however, the data that are available are inadequate, either because they measure the wrong things or measure them in the wrong way for them to be useful in assessing progress towards social cohesion (see Chapter Three for a more in-depth discussion of this in relation to 'performance indicators'). Consequently, evaluators will tend to find themselves having to collect new data. Given the complexity of 'social cohesion', identifying which data to collect, how to collect them and then how to analyse them is likely to be time consuming and costly, and possibly beyond the budgets available to commissioners.

Lastly, a key, but often implicit, component of this policy agenda is the co-production of policy – the generation of services or interventions through processes of negotiation with relevant constituencies, including politicians, professionals and 'the public'. This more deliberative approach to policy design and delivery is frequently evoked in democratic societies where ideas about what to do may not be self-evident, but vary depending on the identities and interests of different groups. Evaluators need to be able to acknowledge this diversity, accessing different ways of understanding both the problem and any potential solution(s) and taking account of them in constructing assessments of both process and outcomes.

The challenges outlined above are fundamental to the epistemology of social science, but have gained significance as expressions of the particular difficulties facing policy makers and evaluators in the 21st century. Powerful forces such as globalisation and neoliberalism have challenged the power and capacity of the nation state, while the New Public Management agenda has changed its nature, fragmenting its operations across sites and stakeholders (Pierre and Peters, 2000). At the same time, the state has faced new challenges from within as complex issues such as social exclusion, community safety and environmental sustainability have exceeded the capacity of traditional approaches to public policy making and required the state to develop a new role as an enabler – working with other actors to achieve positive outcomes (Richards et al, 1999). Policy interventions in turn have become as dynamic, complex and diverse as the social, economic and political conditions they are required to operate within (Kooiman, 1993). In relation to evaluation, these developments have led some to question whether established evaluation approaches are sufficient, or whether different approaches are required to provide what Chen (1990, p 293) terms 'an adequate conceptual framework' for evaluation. The next section explores these issues and describes one approach to evaluation that supporters consider can address the identified challenges.

Debates in evaluation

Three important debates have dominated evaluation research and practice. They concern the approach to evaluation, the methods used in evaluation and the relationship between the evaluator and those being evaluated. Each of these debates is interconnected and contributes to a wider discussion about the purpose and value of evaluation, and each is important to an understanding of how social cohesion might be evaluated.

In the United Kingdom (UK), evaluation has tended to be methods led, typified by the approach of the Treasury, which emphasises output and outcome evaluation, and looks to principles of additionality, displacement and substitution in assessing programme effectiveness. Evaluations of UK programmes have been predominantly *ex post* in their application and have consequently found it difficult to assess matters of attribution or 'added value'. This dominant evaluation paradigm is associated with a hierarchy of methods that regard randomised controlled trials (experiments in which treatments are randomly allocated to subjects and compared with control groups in receipt of a placebo) as the 'gold standard' of evaluation methods, and with an evaluation stance that sees the evaluator maintaining a clear distance from the evaluation 'subject' in order to protect objectivity and independence. This evaluation paradigm is rooted in medical science with its concern for evaluating change in individuals following the running of clinical trials for a drug or other 'treatment'.

This dominant evaluation paradigm began to be questioned as public policy makers developed a different perspective on how policy 'worked' and how it could be evaluated. Public policy, particularly that concerned with addressing key challenges such as social exclusion, regeneration or environmental sustainability, was rarely focused just on change in individuals. Instead, policy was designed to make change in multiple ways, for example in individuals, populations, communities, services and systems. Working out whether and how change happened in such multifaceted contexts opened up discussions about:

- when to evaluate – should the focus be on *ex ante* rather than *ex post* in order to try and frame the potential links between action and outcome?;
- what to evaluate – in a crowded policy environment, how should key lines of enquiry be established for evaluation, and on what basis?; and
- how to evaluate – are randomised controlled trials possible or even desirable in such complex policy contexts, or might other methods including qualitative ones be more appropriate?

These discussions also raised questions about the respective roles and relationship between evaluator and the evaluation 'subjects' – what roles did evaluators need to be able to play, and how might 'subjects' relate to them in these different roles? Finally, in environments with multiple actors, there were likely to be multiple views about what any given policy was for and how progress might be demonstrated – how could evaluators draw out those different perspectives and then draw on them to make judgements about progress.

One approach to evaluation that appeared to fulfil the demands made by multi-stranded policy initiatives is the 'theory of change' (ToC) approach (Aspen Institute, 1997). This is defined as 'a systematic and cumulative study of the links between activities, outcomes and contexts of the initiative' (Connell and Kubisch, 1998, p 15) or 'a theory of how and why an initiative works' (Judge, 2000, p 2). It is a hybrid of process and outcomes analyses that is used without a comparison group to explore behaviours and outcomes that are not easily measurable. It requires the specification of short- and long-term goals, the interventions that will give rise to specified consequences to make progress towards these goals, and the assumptions and rationales that underpin the selection of particular interventions for particular contexts.

ToC was devised to meet the need for an evaluative approach that could accommodate the multilevel and many dimensional impacts of developing social and public policy interventions in North America, the so-called 'comprehensive community initiatives' (CCIs) (Aspen Institute, 1997). CCIs aimed to promote positive change in individual, family and community circumstances through the development of a variety of mechanisms to improve social, economic and physical circumstances, services and conditions in disadvantaged communities. In doing this, CCIs placed a strong emphasis on community building and neighbourhood empowerment.

Policy makers and evaluators in the UK were attracted by the potential of ToC because of its apparent capacity to accommodate multiple perspectives and contributions (diversity), its explicit concern with the relationship between interventions, processes and outcomes (dynamics) and its emphasis on wholesale change at individual, organisational and system levels (complexity) (Connell and Kubisch, 1998). Its focus on systematically analysing the links between the activities, outcomes and contexts of an intervention over time suggested one route towards generating credible evidence of 'what works, for whom, in what circumstances'. This proved attractive to both academics and policy makers, and ToC subsequently informed numerous national evaluations including the national evaluation of Health Action Zones, of the New Deal for Communities and of Local Strategic Partnerships (Sullivan and Stewart, 2006).

Central to a ToC evaluation is the requirement that the evaluator 'surface' the implicit theory of action inherent in a proposed intervention in order to delineate what *should* happen if the theory is correct and to identify short-, medium- and long-term indicators of changes, which can provide evidence on which to base evaluative judgements. Conventionally, a ToC approach begins by examining the needs and resources of a local community, identifying long-term goals that will meet these needs, specifying a range of interventions (activities, processes, projects) that will lead to these goals, articulating the rationale for each of these interventions and then prospectively specifying short-, medium- and long-term milestones on the way to goal achievement (see Figure 2.1).

Figure 2.1: Developing a ToC

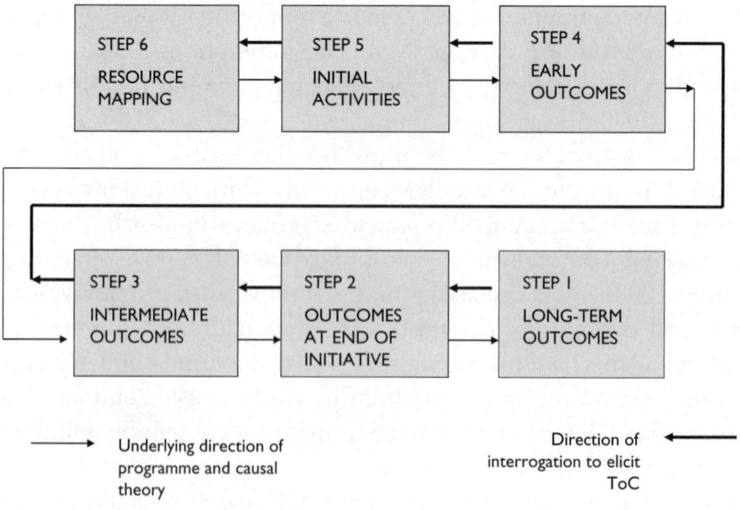

Source: adapted from Mackenzie and Benzeval (2005)

The relationship between the stages of the ToC is a dynamic one as expectations about the achievement of outcomes may change in view of available resources and the ToC itself may be modified over time following initial implementation.

At each stage, the measurement of change needs to be facilitated by the delineation of:

- the key *indicators* of change;
- the target *populations* for change;
- the *threshold* for change, that is, how much change is enough; and
- the *timelines* for change.

Supporters of the ToC approach argue that it has a number of benefits. The ToC emphasis on the prospective specification of goals, targets and activities is argued to facilitate measurement and data collection by clearly indicating which elements are important for the evaluation, thereby also enabling the targeting of scarce evaluation resources. The ToC focus on context supports stakeholder learning about what works in what circumstances, so producing more useful policy learning. The close involvement of stakeholders in the processes of prospective specification reduces problems of attribution, facilitating greater confidence in the subsequent evaluation findings (Judge, 2000).

ToC has strong linkages with other well-known approaches to evaluation as well as complementing developments in the field that emphasise the conceptual (eg Chen, 1990) and practical (eg Funnel, 1997) contribution of theory-driven approaches. Sullivan et al (2002) identify three important aspects of evaluation practice that ToC can be aligned with:

Process–outcomes evaluation

Process–outcomes evaluations combine an assessment of progress made towards anticipated outcomes with an examination of how far the intervention or programme has been implemented in line with policy expectations. These approaches have become increasingly common in evaluations of public policy following policy makers' awareness that programmes or interventions are not always (or perhaps ever) implemented in ways that are consistent with policy makers' intentions (Owen with Rogers, 1999). Understanding what happens and why in a programme can be vital in helping to examine why particular objectives were or were not achieved (Imrie and Thomas, 1995). ToC adds value to this approach by requiring the link between process and outcomes to be articulated at the beginning of the process.

Responsive/interactive evaluation

The involvement of particular stakeholders in the process of designing and undertaking evaluation is most obviously exemplified by action research or empowerment evaluation (Fetterman et al, 1996). However, there are numerous other ways in which stakeholders' perspectives can be included in evaluation. The purpose of evaluations of this type is to be flexible so as to ensure that factors important to the evaluation are not excluded by predetermined evaluation questions, approaches and methods. Increasingly popular in public policy as a way of building learning into the process of policy implementation, responsive evaluation has been used with staff groups and with community members (eg Hart and Bond, 1995; Everitt and Hardiker, 1996; Sullivan and Potter, 2001). ToC adds value to these approaches by linking the participation of all relevant stakeholders with the maximisation of learning, and also by making explicit the different value bases that underpin the perspectives of more or less powerful stakeholders.

Realistic evaluation

For Pawson and Tilley (1997), evaluations enable judgements to be made about what works, where, for whom and why. To secure these judgements, evaluators need to understand the relationships that exist between specific contexts, the intervention or programme and its outcomes and, specifically, to understand the mechanisms by which an intervention leads to certain outcomes within certain contexts. Mechanisms are important because they provide the 'reasons and resources to change behaviour' (1997, p 36). This is partly because social programmes tend not to be unified wholes but rather are loose configurations of plans, policies and activities.

Context is important because it offers a range of influences over how programmes may operate. Programmes will be implemented differently in different areas and there will be conflicting theories about the mechanisms by which they will be thought to impact on key outcomes. Realistic evaluation, therefore, shares with ToC a concern for both context and the testing of theory, although they have different conceptions of theory and of the scale of the programmes within which they operate. A ToC approach highlights the dynamic nature of context, particularly the policy context and the way in which a programme may have to adapt over time as a result of changes in the national policy context, as well as locally generated changes consequent on early activities.

The next section considers the application of a ToC approach to the evaluation of social cohesion, paying particular attention to the issues and challenges identified in the introduction to this chapter.

ToCs and social cohesion

Complexity and outcomes

A ToC approach pays close attention to the prospective specification of outcomes. To achieve desired change, stakeholders must be clear about the outcomes that are sought and the appropriateness of the interventions designed to achieve those outcomes in the prevailing context. This implies two distinct but linked activities in relation to social cohesion. First, there needs to be investment of resources early on in the policy design process to define and describe the outcomes associated with social cohesion at the strategic, meso and micro levels. This requires going beyond statements of outcomes that are so broad and abstract as to be unhelpful or inhibiting, for example 'sustainable communities'. Rather, attention needs to be paid to describing more tangible manifestations of change that can combine to create the conditions for social cohesion, for example improvements in educational attainment of 'underachieving groups'. Second, stakeholders need to be confident that the interventions that are being proposed to help create the conditions for social cohesion are necessary and appropriate for the prevailing conditions. This implies a sound appreciation of the relevant contextual conditions and discretion over the kinds of policy instruments that may be applied (in terms of authority to act and the resources to support action). Stakeholders need to be able to access evidence in relation to the *need* for the interventions, the *pertinence* of the chosen interventions above others and the intended *consequences* of the interventions in terms of short-, medium- and long-term goals. This helps to elaborate the nature of the data needed to support evaluation and it also helps to demonstrate the linkages between action and outcomes.

Determining causality in dynamic contexts

A key claim of the ToC approach is that the combination of prospective specification and the need for evidence provides a means of addressing the 'attribution dilemma' associated with evaluating complex initiatives: that is, the approach helps establish causal links between policy interventions and outcomes. The potency of the ToC's capacity to limit 'the attribution dilemma' is derived from the Aspen Institute Roundtable's insistence on the direct involvement of key stakeholders in the development of the ToC. By drawing stakeholders together and involving them in a dialogue about how and why proposed actions will lead to desired outcomes, advocates of ToC argue that these stakeholders will have greater confidence in attributing subsequent changes to the previously specified actions. Involvement in the process of theory generation instils ownership among stakeholders that extends beyond action to evaluation. What this should imply for practice is that '[a]lthough this strategy cannot eliminate all alternative explanations for a particular outcome, it aligns the major actors in the initiative with a standard of evidence that will be convincing to *them*' (Connell and Kubisch, 1998, p 18, italics in original).

This approach is helpful in relation to social cohesion as it allows for the fact that there may be multiple ways in which to pursue social cohesion, but requires policy designers to make informed judgements about which may be the most productive interventions in any given context, and then to specify the evidence necessary to support or negate the validity of these judgements. It also requires all of those involved to take ownership of the priorities, interventions and sources and standards of evidence required. This again focuses attention on processes of policy design but also draws attention to the need to involve all relevant stakeholders. This is considered further below.

Specifying data

As indicated above, elaborating a ToC requires designers to specify and justify why and how their proposed actions will lead to the desired outcomes. This close specification and justification gives confidence to those involved in supporting the interventions. It also helps focus on the kinds of data needed to demonstrate that the intervention is having the desired effect.

As outlined on page 47 this requires designers to agree on the indicators, populations, thresholds and timelines for change.

Becoming adept at making tangible (but not necessarily quantifiable) the various dimensions of change requires investing sufficient time and skill. Failure to do so can result in generating data that are neither robust nor useful as the discussions in the Part Two of this book illustrate. Despite this strict framework, evaluators have considerable freedom to identify those kinds of data – qualitative and quantitative – that might provide the evidence required to assess the extent to which the ToC is having the desired impact, and where it might be falling short. So, for example, while there may be some emphasis on the measurement of the numbers of people securing access to new services, the evaluation will also want to collect narrative data from those accessing new services about their experiences, to find out what exactly it is about the new interventions that made a difference to them and what could still be improved. Likewise, evaluators will be paying attention to the experiences of those who do not access new services, even if eligible, to find out why, and to consider these experiences against the ToC with a view to refining it.

Acknowledging diversity (and difference) in plural communities

A ToC approach privileges the engagement of all relevant stakeholders, including the representatives of communities affected by proposed policy interventions. Engagement with this potentially diverse group of stakeholders also requires that they reach a consensus about the ToC to be applied. Like broad stakeholder involvement, the achievement of consensus is considered key if widespread ownership of subsequent action and evaluation are to be assured. For Weiss (1995), there is an important distinction between the need to generate consensus as to the overarching theory, and programme or initiative theories that point to different routes to the desired ends. In her view, while the achievement of consensus in the former is essential, it is not necessarily desirable in the latter where 'until better evidence accumulates, it would probably be counterproductive to limit inquiry to a single set of assumptions' (1995, p 35). In their development of the ToC approach, Connell and Kubisch (1998, p 31) clarify this distinction by suggesting that while multiple strategies are both inevitable and may be even desirable, there must be some limits, namely that if ToCs 'are to be implemented (doable) they cannot be contradictory'.

Sullivan and Stewart (2006) have suggested that this feature of ToC is more problematic in the UK than the United States (US) due to the nature of the policy context. This is partly a result of the more intense role played by the UK state as a direct service provider, but also of the continuing centralised nature of UK public administration. While the devolution of powers to Northern Ireland, Scotland and Wales has created the opportunity for more consensual approaches to policy making, there remains a strong reminder of the principal-agent model of government, which has been debated over the past 40 years

(Gamble, 2000). Sullivan and Stewart (2006) argue that this centralising tradition has led to organisation among many communities *in opposition* to state action/inaction. In this context, the consensual paradigm may prove rather elusive. Tensions between communities and the state may be compounded by tensions between different agents of the state whose previous behaviour has been characterised by the absence of shared experience, by institutional fragmentation, by inter-agency competition and sometimes by interest group conflict. These may be experienced most acutely at the local level where communities interact with local actors such as local government who have discretion in policy areas such as community cohesion. Sullivan and Stewart (2006) conclude that the use of the ToC in a UK context needs to be particularly sensitive to the unequal power relations in operation between stakeholders, which may allow some to shape – dictate even – both the ToC to be adopted and the rules by which an intervention must run.

Drawing on a range of UK evaluations with which they were involved, Sullivan and Stewart (2006) argue that 'ownership' of the ToC may rarely achieve the Aspen Institute's ideal of 'total ownership', that is, that all stakeholders have an equal say and stake in the emergent ToC. Rather, ToCs are more likely to be 'owned' by one or other of the stakeholders involved: an elite, the principal funder of an initiative, the evaluators themselves or in some cases a community. Multiple ToCs can co-exist and so there are likely to be instances in which dominant ToCs, for example those of an elite or principal, are contested by a community alternative. In such cases, evaluators may find themselves having to mediate between competing ToCs and/ or making a judgement about the relative merits of the competing theories. In Chapter Eleven, Mayo et al highlight the particular values that underpin work with communities and non-governmental organisations to develop meaningful evaluation that acknowledges the importance of conflict as well as consensus in community interactions and engagement.

These caveats are apposite in relation to evaluations of social cohesion where power relations between decision makers and 'beneficiaries' are likely to be very unbalanced and considerable investment of resources (time, skill, money) may be needed to build the capacity of all stakeholders to engage productively with each other. Productive exchanges do not necessarily imply consensual exchanges and there may be circumstances in which the pursuit of multiple strategies is essential in order to keep all of the stakeholders engaged, and to build the evidence base about which interventions work, in which circumstances and for whom.

Contributors to the Aspen Institute Roundtable suggest that emergent ToCs need to be assessed by evaluators and other stakeholders to ensure that they are 'fit for purpose'. They propose judging the quality of a ToC against the following criteria:

- how *plausible* it is – the extent to which stakeholders are convinced of the logic of the theory underpinning the proposed policy and interventions in pursuit of social cohesion;
- how *doable* it is – the degree to which necessary resources are available to deliver the necessary interventions;
- how *testable* it is – how far it is possible to collect evidence that will demonstrate the validity of the theory; and
- how *meaningful* it is – the importance attached to the outcomes by stakeholders and their consequent preparedness to make the necessary changes to achieve them. This last is particularly important in a political context where the pursuit of social cohesion may be perceived to be in tension with other political priorities, for example economic growth. (Judge, 2000)

The implications for evaluators and evaluation

The application of a ToC approach in different settings in the UK has raised a number of issues related to its wider utility (Sullivan et al, 2002; Barnes et al, 2005; Sullivan and Stewart, 2006).

The Aspen Institute Roundtable emphasises the importance of an intensive relationship between evaluator and 'subject' in ToCs. This involves the evaluator working with 'subjects' to elicit and elaborate the ToCs in play, contributing to the process of negotiation that may lead to consensus about the agreed ToCs, or that may reveal differences likely to constitute barriers to effective action. This has implications for evaluation commissioners, as the use of ToCs requires a significant commitment to evaluation resources – time and money.

The use of ToCs also has specific implications for the role of the evaluator (Brown, 1998). Experience from the US and the UK suggests that evaluators involved in ToCs need to be practiced evaluators but also to have skills in relation to group processes, for example facilitation, negotiation and conflict resolution. They will need knowledge of the substantive area under examination (social cohesion) and will also need to be experienced at working with communities. Evaluators are also likely to require sound political skills in order to manage the tension that will be created by the utilisation of ToCs, to generate and maintain the necessary commitment to the process by key stakeholders and to manage the evaluator/technical assistance/learning roles. The emphasis that ToCs place on consensus and the need for all stakeholders to agree may paradoxically result in fewer stakeholders being engaged in the process of deliberation about rationales for intervention and outcomes. In practice, it almost certainly prefers those stakeholders who are involved early on, have an established place at the table and understand the 'rules of the game', to those who are less well organised, less well served by current arrangements and more likely to be disadvantaged as service users and communities. This highlights the difficulty of balancing the long-term investment needed to build the necessary capacity among stakeholders to participate effectively, with the commissioners' imperatives (often political) to generate 'early wins' from policy interventions.

The ToC demands that for developments to be sustainable they have to emerge from the interaction of the stakeholders with ownership of the process. In pursuing social cohesion, these stakeholders will include community members. This presents a challenge to the evaluator for it implies that the theory-building process needs to be completed before specific questions can be addressed to the ToC. Underlying this is uncertainty about the extent to which evaluators can make use of, or draw on, existing evidence and lessons that pertain to the area under investigation. The emphasis on bottom–up theory building risks limiting the explanatory possibilities available from broader theoretical perspectives. Additionally, by emphasising local strategies and activities, there is a risk of marginalising wider systemic factors that may influence significantly the local capacity to pursue social cohesion. This has been recognised by the Aspen Roundtable in its later work, which advises on engagement with stakeholders that have interests in, and possible influence over, wider systemic forces (Kubisch et al, 2002).

Engagement of a wide range of relevant stakeholders is also important in securing an understanding of the similarities and differences between ToCs in operation at different levels – for example national, local, neighbourhood – and among user groups. ToCs privilege the application of local ToCs but in centralised policy regimes it is likely that national-level ToCs will be significant in shaping what is possible locally. The risk here is that it becomes more difficult to accommodate different perspectives and ownership will be both limited and potentially fragmented.

Experience of using ToCs has also highlighted the tendency for some aspects of the ToC approach to become dominant at the expense of others. There are two issues here. The first pertains to the tendency to reconceptualise the ToC as a linear process with progress from the baseline towards a specified outcome. Often, the way the ToC is represented visually aids this representation of it as a merely linear process (Figure 2.1 provides an example of this). It is important to hold on to the idea of the ToC as a dynamic framework, one that sets out desired routes and pathways across multiple levels, but which acknowledges that these may be interrupted at any time as context changes, policy shifts or interactions between key actors move in unexpected ways. Capturing these influences on the ToC is an important aspect of the evaluator's role, not least because it may result in the ToC being revised to accommodate new conditions and circumstances.

The second issue concerns the way in which, in the UK context, policy makers have a tendency to privilege the 'doable' and 'testable' elements of the ToC, which can be represented in hard, quantifiable terms, over the 'plausible' and 'meaningful' elements, which are more discursive and subject to regular contestation. This emphasis is entirely in keeping with a tradition of evaluation that has emphasised 'hard' evidence in the form of quantifiable data, but it undermines the more rounded framework offered by the ToC approach.

Conclusion

This chapter began by highlighting the challenges to evaluators posed by the concept of social cohesion and situated these in the broader context of governing complex societies. It reviewed developments in evaluation and offered the ToC as a potential approach to evaluation that could accommodate some of the challenges posed by social cohesion, specifically delineating outcomes, attributing causality, specifying data and engaging with a diverse and unequal set of stakeholders. Drawing on a range of evaluations, the chapter then considered the ways in which ToCs have been applied in the UK, identifying some of the challenges faced by evaluators and reflecting on the implications for evaluation and evaluators.

Under New Labour, evaluation's profile was raised and it was acknowledged as a key element in the government's focus on 'evidence-based policy making'. Significant funding was allocated to evaluation and policy makers sought out much closer relationships with evaluators (academic and other) as part of the process of developing policy that 'worked'. New developments in evaluation were sought in order to complement the government's interest in formative evaluation and the ToC approach was one evaluation approach that fitted well, combining an emphasis on formative evaluation with a focus on stakeholder engagement in the process of evaluation design. It was perhaps inevitable that policy makers and evaluators would find the experience of working in this way and with new evaluation instruments less rewarding than they expected. Policy makers found themselves frustrated at evaluators' inability to tell them categorically 'what worked' and evaluators became disillusioned by policy makers' inability to see a policy through. In relation to ToCs, the resources required to operationalise the approach were rarely made available to evaluation teams and over time the penetration of 'performance management' began to distort ToC frameworks, rendering them less like the model of the Aspen Institute, and consequently less able to generate the kind of evaluation that the model promised. These experiences influenced a shift in New Labour policy on evaluation towards the end of its time in government, away from formative approaches and ToCs and back to cost-benefit and value-for-money studies with an increasing emphasis on econometric approaches.

Current circumstances present a particular challenge to policy makers and evaluators. Budget cuts in the delivery of public services make it very unlikely that resources will be protected for evaluation, particularly evaluation that is as costly as ToCs. At the same time, however, the challenges faced by UK society remain as complex and challenging as those faced by New Labour in 1997. Whether and how the current government addresses these policy challenges and the role that evaluation might play in supporting them is as yet unknown. The remaining chapters in this book provide valuable insights into the strengths and limitations of existing practice in terms of evaluation, performance management, data collection and evidence, while also engaging with the possibilities of a ToC approach.

References

Aspen Institute (1997) *Voices from the field: Learning from the Early work of comprehensive community initiatives*, Washington, DC: Aspen Institute.

Barnes, M., Bauld, L., Benzeval, M., Judge, K., Mackenzie, M. and Sullivan, H. (2005) *Building capacity for health equity*, London: Routledge.

Brown, P. (1998) 'Shaping the evaluator's role in a theory of change evaluation: practitioner reflections', in K. Fulbright-Anderson, A.C. Kubisch and J.P. Connell (eds) *New approaches to evaluating community initiatives: Volume 2: Theory, measurement and analysis* (pp 70-85), Washington, DC: Aspen Institute.

Chen, H.T. (1990) *Theory driven evaluations*, London: Sage Publications.

Connell, J.P. and Kubisch, A.C. (1998) 'Applying a theory of change approach to the evaluation of comprehensive community initiatives: progress, prospects and problems', in K. Fulbright-Anderson, A.C. Kubisch, and J.P. Connell (eds) *New approaches to evaluating community initiatives: Volume 2: Theory, measurement and analysis* (pp 15-44), Washington, DC: Aspen Institute.

Connell, J.P., Kubisch, A.C., Schorr, L.B. and Weiss, C.H. (eds) (1995) *New approaches to community initiatives: Volume 1: Contexts, methods and contexts*, Washington, DC: Aspen Institute.

Everitt, A. and Hardiker, P. (1996) *Evaluating for good practice*, London: Macmillan.

Fetterman, D.M., Kaftarian, S.J. and Wandersman, A. (1996) *Empowerment evaluation: Knowledge and tools for self-assessment and accountability*, Thousand Oaks, CA: Sage Publications.

Funnel, S. (1997) 'Program logic: an adaptable tool for designing and evaluating programs', *Evaluation News and Comment*, July, pp 5-17.

Gamble, A. (2000) 'Policy agendas in a multi level polity', in P. Dunleavy, A. Gamble and I. Holliday (eds) *Developments in British politics 6*, Basingstoke: Palgrave.

Hart, E. and Bond, M. (1995) *Action research for health and social care*, Buckingham: Open University Press.

Imrie, R. and Thomas, H. (1995) 'Changes in local governance and their implications for urban policy evaluation', in R. Hambleton and H. Thomas (eds) *Urban policy evaluation* (pp 123-38), London: Paul Chapman.

Judge, K. (2000) 'Testing evaluation to the limits: the case of English Health Action Zones', *Journal of Health Services Research and Policy*, vol 5, no 1, pp 1-3.

Kooiman, J. (1993) 'Governance and governability: using complexity, dynamics and diversity', in J. Kooiman (ed) *Modern governance* (pp 35-50), London: Sage Publications.

Kubisch, A.C., Auspos, P., Brown, P., Chaskin, R., Fulbright-Anderson, K. and Hamilton, R. (2002) *Voices from the field II: Reflections on comprehensive community change*, Washington, DC: Aspen Institute.

Mackenzie, M. and Benzeval, M. (2005) 'Evaluating policy and practice: designing the national HAZ evaluation', in M. Barnes, L. Bauld, M. Benzeval, K. Judge, M. Mackenzie and H. Sullivan (2005) *Building capacity for health equity* (pp 43-66), London: Routledge.

Owen, J.M. with Rogers, P.J. (1999) *Program evaluation, forms and approaches* (international edition), Sydney, Australia: Allen & Unwin.

Pawson, R. and Tilley, N. (1997) *Realistic rvaluation*, London: Sage Publications.

Pierre, J. and Peters, G. (2000) *Governance, politics and the state*, London: Macmillan.

Ratcliffe, P., Newman, I. and Fuller, C. (2008) *Community cohesion: A literature and data review*, Warwick: Warwick Business School, University of Warwick, http://www2.warwick.ac.uk/fac/soc/wbs/research/lgc/latest/community_cohesion_-_a_literature_and_data_review_.pdf

Richards, S., Barnes, M., Coulson, A., Gaster, L., Leach, B. and Sullivan, H. (1999) *Cross-cutting issues in public policy and public services*, London: Department of the Environment, Transport and the Regions.

Sullivan, H. and Potter, T. (2001) 'Doing "joined-up" evaluation in community based regeneration', *Local Governance*, vol 27, no 1, pp 19-31.

Sullivan, H. and Stewart, M. (2006) 'Who owns the theory of change?', *Evaluation*, vol 12, no 2, pp 179-99.

Sullivan, H., Barnes, M. and Matka, E. (2002) 'Building collaborative capacity through theories of change: early lessons from the evaluation of Health Action Zones in England', *Evaluation*, vol 8, no 2, pp 205-26.

Weiss, C. (1995) 'Nothing as practical as good theory: exploring theory-based evaluation for comprehensive community initiatives for children and families', in J.P. Connell, A.C. Kubisch, L.B. Schorr and C.H. Weiss (1995) *New approaches to community initiatives: Volume 1: Contexts, methods and contexts* (pp 32-50), Washington, DC: Aspen Institute.

Part Two
Community cohesion to social cohesion: evaluation and data – methodological issues

THREE

Measuring performance in community cohesion

Crispian Fuller

Introduction

This chapter examines national indicators that attempt to measure performance in cohesion interventions. The importance of such an issue lies in the critical significance of performance management in what has been termed the 'managerial state', and which has been a key element of New Labour's approach to centralising control and devolving responsibility for delivery. On the one hand, such performance management systems seek to control the actions of delivery agencies; on the other hand, and as suggested by governmentality scholars, they represent processes of social construction as government creates and frames social realities through performance indicators (PIs), which often go on to inform future policy choices (Power, 1999; Stone, 2002). This chapter will engage with the literature on performance management, social identity and 'place', with the purpose of evaluating the impact of the on community cohesion performance management arrangements.

Performance management, identity and place

The 'managerial state' and rise of performance management

Notwithstanding its uneven and incomplete nature, neoliberal tendencies have been notably dominant within governing systems over the last 30 years. This has led to processes of privatisation and marketisation of public services, and the widespread but uneven adoption of principles of New Public Management (NPM), as well as the transition to what has been described as a 'managerial state', 'regulatory state' or 'audit society'. There are differences between these perspectives but their broad argument states that the transition from hierarchical structures has been accompanied by the proliferation of state and quasi agencies at multiple geographical sites, decentralised responsibility for delivery to the private sector and civil society, and the growth in the importance of networks. Within such an environment the nation state has sought to implement new forms of control and management to ensure compliance from these heterogeneous bodies in the absence of trust, most notably through the enactment of the 'audit society' (Power, 1999). This involves the state working through formal regulations and regulatory bodies to control state and quasi-autonomous bodies, ensuring bureaucratic and political accountability, as well as utilising a range of auditing and performance management mechanisms. This is what Dean (1999, p 6) has termed the 'governmentalization of government', with the state folding back the ends of government upon its instruments. Within this framework, there is a belief that subjective reality can be verified and, through quantified rationalised decision-making frameworks, brought under control and surveillance (Talbot, 2008).

Within this framework, accountability systems work at a number of levels, including financial, managerial (achievement of policy objectives while attaining the three Es of economy, efficiency and effectiveness) and political (decisions justified in terms of stewardship of public services). There are four specific functions for PIs: giving strategic direction by informing objectives; governing resource allocation (who gets what); a means of exercising control; and a means of encouraging learning. Despite the positive manifestations of performance management, there is widespread recognition in the United Kingdom (UK) that performance management is used to control (Pollitt et al, 2004).

A considerable literature has emerged on performance management systems and indicators, encompassing both academic studies and management handbooks. Jackson (1988) argues that for PIs to have validity they must include the characteristics listed in Table 3.1.

But this rational framework poses considerable challenges to performance management regimes. Such regimes are influenced by who constructs systems and PIs, and who does the measuring. They are rarely apolitical and rationalised frameworks, but embedded within political aims and the politics of accountability. Governments create and frame complex social realities through PIs that reduce such complexity to a singular definition, with the purpose of bringing such objects under perceived rational decision-making control (Enticott and Entwistle, 2007). It is therefore the case that PIs are only ever incomplete representations of broader social processes, and thus any measurement of cause and effect is potentially dubious, particularly as there are many intervening variables. PIs also obviously 'fix' social

Table 3.1: Characteristics of performance indicators

Type of validity	Explanation
Consistency	Definitions are consistent over time and between units
Comparability	Need to be able to compare like with like
Controllability	Only measured under their control
Contingency	Performance is not independent of the environment within which decisions are made
Comprehensiveness	PI reflecting those areas of behaviour important to decision making
Boundedness	Concentration on a limited number of key PIs as giving biggest payoff
Relevance	Whether applications require specific PIs relevant to special needs and conditions
Feasibility	The extent to which targets are based on unrealistic expectations

Source: Jackson (1988)

relations in temporal terms and thus potentially do not take account of changes to society, the economy and so on, which can make PIs obsolete. A further issue is the political impetus placed on short-term measures and accompanying PIs, due largely to political expediency.

Performance management arrangements are key mechanisms within the policy implementation, monitoring and auditing/evaluation process, and thus they are a critical element of any theory of change (ToC). The rationale and assumptions underpinning any policy approach is typically embedded within quantified output or outcome targets and PIs. However, this is a paradoxical situation. On the one hand, the ToC seeks to determine causal processes within complex environments by examining, for example, the motives of key policy makers and deliverers; on the other hand, performance management rationales and systems are the antithesis of such an approach given their concern with 'Taylorist' segmentation of the policy process, the encompassing of complex environments into singular variables, and in the causal attribution between these variables and particular organisational factors (encompassed within the three Es) (Pollitt, 1990). This then leaves us with a chapter that has to critique performance management systems on their own terms, rather than those of the ToC.

Social identity and place

At the basis of performance management is an understanding of uniformity in not just social relations, but also the social identity of individuals. Performance management arrangements, as a governmental technology, typically seek to transform the subjectivities of individuals into self-regulating subjects that adhere to political aims (Endicott and Entwistle, 2007). However, such arrangements do not appreciate the historical and cultural creation of social identity within particular social sites. As Hall (1987, p 50) argues, identities are heterogeneous and emergent, constantly produced within specific historical and cultural sites and in relation to other actors and numerous social practices, often in contradictory and conflictual ways.

Of critical importance therefore is to appreciate the importance of place in producing particular social identities and community relations. A strong 'relational' perspective has developed in the examination of place. This approach has come to see place as unbounded territories, characterised by networks of virtual and material social relations that work through both proximate and distant interactions, but where the historical contingency of territory still has some role to play (Massey, 2005). This produces places of many different networks, encompassing disparate actors and objects and covering heterogeneous spaces. For Amin (2002), this means that communities should be understood as diverse entities located within similarly heterogeneous networks and spaces. Their attachment to place is thus complex and open as they live through multiple networks that stretch within and beyond place, and encompass diverse cultural, social, economic and political practices. Importantly, Amin (2002, p 976) argues that the 2001 riots in towns and cities in Northern England highlighted the 'problematic nature of attempts to build community and local consensus, and the limitations of seeing "difficult" areas as places of fixed identities and social relations'.

There is also a great deal of contingency within the production of 'place'. For Barnes (2008), the social relations producing practice and power relations are intrinsically created through interwoven and spatially differentiated forces that happen to converge in particular places. The production of practice and power within place are therefore highly fortuitous and typically conditional. Massey (2005) argues that place is produced through both deliberate and fortuitous circumstances. Deliberate actions can often be accompanied or subordinated by actions producing unintended and fortuitous consequences.

What this suggests is the importance of moving beyond a fixed notion of place to understand how communities live through multi-spatial networks, in which they do not necessarily relate to a fixed notion of place such as a 'neighbourhood'. This obviously has important implications for efforts to create PIs that possess national comparability but are locally sensitive, to fully understand distinctiveness in the construction of community relations. In reality, performance management systems produce spatial ambiguity in that they create geographical definition of areas such as neighbourhoods, set within a wider policy approach focused through a national conceptual lens and interpretation. Such performance management systems largely follow broader policy discourses and practices that seek to frame social inequality in terms of spatial factors, such as the role of 'neighbourhood effects', rather than recognising the role of broader structural processes (Imrie and Raco, 2003).

Community cohesion and performance management

In this section we examine the nature of the PIs that have been utilised by government, and thus we are able to decipher the rationale and assumptions underpinning approaches to community cohesion. Many of these indicators are monitored through the Citizenship Survey, carried out bi-annually since 2001 on behalf of the Home Office and subsequently the Department for Communities and Local Government (DCLG).[1] Since 2008, this has been supplemented by the Place Survey, which collects data on 18 national indicators for local government and provides information on people's perceptions of their local area and the local services they receive.

Performance management indicators

The Home Office community cohesion indicators, 2003

The Home Office's community cohesion indicators, set out in *Building a picture of community cohesion* (Home Office, 2003), represents the first major effort to quantify community cohesion. The framework includes 10 indicators for use by local authorities and their partners:

Headline outcome
CC01: The percentage of people who feel that their local area is a place where people from different backgrounds can get on well together

Common vision and sense of belonging
CC02: The percentage of respondents who feel that they belong to their neighbourhood/town/county/England/Wales/Britain

CC03: Key priorities for improving an area

CC04: The percentage of adults surveyed who feel they can influence decisions affecting their local area

The diversity of people's backgrounds and circumstances are appreciated and positively valued
CC05: The percentage of people who feel that local ethnic differences are respected

CC06: The number of racial incidents recorded by police authorities per 100,000

Those from different backgrounds have similar life opportunities
CC07: Local concentration of deprivation

CC08: The percentage of pupils achieving five or more GCSEs at grades A*-C or equivalent

CC09: The percentage of unemployed people claiming benefit who have been out of work for more than a year

Strong and positive relationships are being developed between people from different backgrounds in the workplace, schools and neighbourhoods
CC10: The percentage of people from different backgrounds who mix with other people from different backgrounds in everyday situations

The explicit purpose of these indicators is to establish a baseline from which to monitor progress against outcomes, based on the belief that the measurement of community cohesion will have long-term benefits around assessment of the effectiveness of various interventions.

The headline PI (CC01: The percentage of people who feel that their local area is a place where people from different backgrounds can get on well together) works on the basis of what the Home Office considers to be the essence of community cohesion. The other nine PIs are based on the definition of community cohesion provided to local authorities through 2002 guidance (LGA, 2009):

- there is a common vision and a sense of belonging for all communities;
- the diversity of people's different backgrounds and circumstances are appreciated and positively valued;
- those from different backgrounds have similar life opportunities; and
- strong and positive relationships are being developed between people from different backgrounds in the workplace, in schools and within neighbourhoods.

It is important to note that indicators based on perception are open to a range of problems. This can include the more commonsensical issues around survey completion, to the more complex issues around definition of 'background' and 'getting along'. In relation to the former, there is an 'acquiescent response set' problem, whereby individuals agree with a statement regardless of its content (Dillman, 1978). This is in effect related to the second, more complicated issue, around people's perception of both terminology and their environment, which is discussed below in relation to the national indicators.

The headline outcome seeks to move beyond ethnicity to encompass a broadly defined 'background' of individuals, where cohesion increases as more people agree within this statement. Such a broad definition dilutes the attribution of causal factors to any one variable, such as ethnicity, age and gender, with 'background' becoming a potentially 'catch-all' term. For instance, it is possible for an individual to understand background as being a spatial issue in which they make judgements based on individuals who have moved into the area from other areas or parts of the country. This would potentially reduce any reference by a participant to issues around ethnicity, age, gender and class.

The first of the *common vision and sense of belonging* indicators is designed to measure residents belonging to individual areas (CC02). As before, there is no explicit reference to the individual constituting community, nor is there an agreed understanding of 'belonging' when such a concept makes reference to a diverse number of spatial scales (for example, neighbourhood, local area), and can extend beyond national boundaries. There must be an understanding that belonging is likely to vary and thus be in conflict between these scales. For example, a neighbourhood with concentrations of older people may well produce high levels of local belonging, but this may differ significantly with the perception of the broader local area, which could be constituted by young families. What this illustrates is the importance of a concrete understanding of spatial definitions within indicators.

The indicator CC04, with its focus on citizen influence, works on the basis that cohesion is positively correlated with strong levels of perceived influence. While it is true to say that greater involvement and influence can foster a strong sense of local belonging, relating this to developing stronger cohesive communities has important caveats. Not least is the role of community leaders in certain ethnic communities representing these groups through legitimate means, whereby there is a tacit and tangible belief in the role of these individuals in making correct decisions on behalf of local ethnic groups. Similarly, a sense of belonging typically relates to neighbourliness and respect for the liveability of place, which is different from seeking to influence actual decisions. One is an everyday practice undertaken through tacit and tangible means, the other takes place within a broader realm that encompasses the decisions taking place within polity.

The third grouping relates to positive views among citizens of different *backgrounds and circumstances*. The first indicator – CC05 – looks at the percentage of people who feel that local ethnic differences are respected. But the concept and definition of respect is related to negative elements of ethnic relations (tension and community disturbance), and is not associated with the role of more positive elements. It is therefore possible to measure the most negative features of ethnic diversity and get positive results based on the lack of incidents, but this adds little insight into measurements based on a more robust criteria relating to the many other factors constituting positive relations between different ethnic groups. It is also important to note that 'respect' is conceptually different from 'tolerance', with the former not necessarily related to the latter.

As highlighted in Chapter One, the second indicator (CC06: The number of racial incidents recorded by police authorities per 100,000) reflects the reporting of incidents, but within a context where it is difficult to predict how many incidents are not reported. Such an indicator therefore relies on considerable individual (broadly defined), community and spatial contingency in the way reporting incidents to the police is viewed.

A fourth strand examines *different backgrounds and life opportunities*. Examination of deprivation relates to much broader issues. It was the case for New Labour that deprivation is related to community cohesion. Built on the principles of communitarianism, this is based on the assumption that prosperous and 'responsible' communities have high levels of social trust (Imrie and Raco, 2003). This rests on the argument that community cohesion (here defined through such criteria as a lack of antisocial behaviour or high levels of volunteering) is produced within more affluent communities, or where there is a mix of incomes. In such arrangements there are strong levels of social control, ensuring norms of behaviour among individuals geared towards reciprocal relations with regard to respect for other citizens (Aber et al, 1997). Such arrangements contribute to cohesion, but are indirect in nature as they work through the broader processes underpinning affluence.

This is a PI that relies on the Index of Multiple Deprivation (IMD) by examining whether particular minority ethnic or religious groups are concentrated in areas of high deprivation. It is descriptive in nature with no reference to variance between domains within the IMD, nor to the causal factors underlying deprivation in relation to ethnicity and faith. Similar factors are obviously important in regard to the other two PIs for General Certificate of Secondary Education (GCSE) attainment (using PLASC data) and unemployment (using NOMIS data). It is important to note that the claimant count makes no reference to ethnicity.

The final PI (CC10) is related to *relations between people from different backgrounds in the workplace, schools and neighbourhoods*. This is based on the following PI definition: 'In which of the following situations, if any, would you say you regularly meet and talk with people of a different ethnic origin to you?'. The focus is clearly on regular interaction, working with an assumption that cohesion is related to regularly meeting one another and talking. Major issues with this PI include the causal weight placed on contact and close spatial proximity always producing positive results, and there is also no reference to the nature of discussions between different communities (Amin, 2002). One must accept that interaction is highly variable in nature, from a simple 'hello' in which it is difficult to differentiate everyday politeness from strong ethnic relations, to in-depth discussion around local, community or family issues between citizens from different backgrounds.

These Home Office indicators have influenced many different aspects of public policy. For example, the indicators were suggested to be an important measure of the success of area-based initiatives in the joint Home Office and ODPM guidance *Community cohesion and area based initiatives: guide for residents and practitioners* (Home Office and ODPM, 2004). The guidance suggests adopting the community cohesion indicators in monitoring the impact of area-based initiatives on community cohesion. It acknowledges that the term 'community cohesion' may well need adapting to localities. On the one hand, this is important in recognising the significance of local diversity; on the other hand, it reduces the scope for national comparison. More importantly, adaptation of identified key concepts within national guidance has the potential of actually undermining such indicators, since the adopted PIs have definitions that are transient rather than fixed.

The discussion above has indicated some of the weaknesses with these indicators. Similar problems are outlined in relation to the subsequent indicators discussed below.

The Audit Commission's quality of life indicators

Advice to local authorities on community cohesion PIs has typically included reference to the Audit Commission's quality of life indicators. In regard to community cohesion this includes the indicators of:

- the percentage of residents who think that people being attacked because of their skin colour, ethnic origin or religion is a very big or fairly big problem in their local area; and
- the percentage of residents who think that for their local area, over the past three years, community activities have got better or stayed the same.

As this suggests, the first is largely concerned with the most negative features of community disharmony, leaving little possibility of inferring community cohesion where a low frequency result for the indicator is recorded. More importantly, this is in essence an indicator concerned with a criminal act, rather than a perceptual judgement based on social relations. The first PI also ignores other motivations for attacks, such as sexuality, physical disability and mental health. The second indicator is largely a contextual factor that provides evidence of community cohesion as part of a 'bundle' of indicators.

The national indicator set

More recently, the initial national performance indicator (NI) set included community cohesion NIs that were focused on Public Service Agreement 21 (PSA21) ('Build more cohesive, empowered and active communities') and that were monitored through the Place Survey:

- NI1: that percentage of people who believe that people from different backgrounds get on well together in their local area; and
- NI2: the percentage of people who feel that they belong to their neighbourhood.

The second NI was subsequently removed in April 2010 following a budget announcement. Nonetheless, it is important to note that these indicators built on the Home Office's community cohesion indicators by focusing on broadly defined concepts of 'background' and 'belonging', which make no reference to the heterogeneous sociocultural and economic processes working through and within place. This has important implications for the results. One must remember that just because an individual identifies similarities with other local residents does not represent evidence of community cohesion. Just because they may identify similarities in terms of perceived social class and identities does not mean that they act with or for other residents in such processes as informal social control mechanisms.

There are major tensions between the high percentage of people believing that people from different backgrounds get on together (80%), compared with just under half of people believing that racial prejudice is greater than it was five years ago. There is a tension here in terms of geography. It is important to understand the perceived spatial imaginary of respondents when answering these survey questions. Such issues cannot be clarified through correlation with other survey questions that reveal participants' spatial imaginaries, as such issues would need to be resolved in direct reference to particular variables. Thus, when asking about racial prejudice it is important to ask whether they are including the local area in their definition of 'Britain overall'.

Around half of respondents did not have friends that were from a different ethnic group, raising concerns around their actual ability to make judgements on other people from different backgrounds getting on, and on their area being an area where people respected ethnic differences. One must question the ability of citizens who do not have friends from different ethnic backgrounds to make such judgements when they do not experience everyday lived interaction with citizens from different backgrounds. Thus, there is incongruence between knowing different ethnic groups and the far greater number of people presenting a positive picture of ethnic relations. This returns us to the discussion of the difference between making informed judgements based on experience (such as having friends from different groups) versus observation alone (what one observes in everyday life). This also applies to the indicator based on income, which is largely a perceptual indicator that is based on individual judgement and with no direct reference to their possession of material objects (which can be a proxy for income).

The positive results for different backgrounds and ethnic relations do not fit adequately with participants believing that they belong to their neighbourhood (32%). While this is a different type of indicator, with belonging relating to a range of causal factors, there is a significant difference with the results for background and ethnic relations. Issues of semantics within surveys are obviously critical in these results, but there are issues around the difference between individuals with different backgrounds getting along, and how much they belong to their neighbourhood. One could suggest that respondents believe that people get along by not actually being in conflict, rather than there being more positive features of community cohesion, which are then reflected in the low frequency results for the response to belonging to their community. Furthermore, it is important to note that an individual believing that they do not belong to their local community does not inevitably lead to negative consequences for their quality of life (as suggesting by the results of other PIs), particularly for affluent, mobile citizens.

There is a further issue at this point, which builds on observations around the validity of actually asking survey questions on local communities. For Amin (2002), government fails to understand that communities are heterogeneous entities, where conformity to underlying social values is often lacking because individuals are engaging in multi-temporal and spatial social, cultural and economic networks that stretch beyond a given spatially defined scale. In essence, government has potentially fallen into a 'naïve pursuit of a unitary sense of place' (Amin, 2002, p 14), as represented in the poor results for a sense of belonging to their neighbourhood. Discrepancies with these results are further reinforced through the much higher frequency results for people believing that they 'definitely enjoyed' living in their neighbourhood (65%).

The results for levels of trust also present interesting findings that display the differences between differing ethnic groups. Around 49% of respondents believe that their neighbours could be trusted, with the figure increasing to 51% for White people, but falling for Asian people (30%) and Black people (21%). The problem with the results is that they make no reference to the actual socioeconomic make-up of the environments of respondents. So, for example, the local levels of trust in neighbours by Black people (21%) could be based on high levels of crime experienced in their neighbourhoods, compounded by other elements of poverty. Alternatively, responses for White people could be based on environments such as periphery council estates with low levels of out- and in-migration. It must also be noted that only 30% of people feel safe walking alone after dark and that while such issues relate to differing dynamics around criminal behaviour and broader European-wide trends with regard to fear of crime, they compound issues around a lack of trust in neighbours.

This is obviously related to broader issues around equality. For it may well be the case that Black respondents have experienced higher levels of societal and institutional racism, reducing their levels of trust in general. What this demonstrates is the failure of the 'social capital' perspective (see, for example, Putnam, 2007), and that of communitarianism, to understand the critical role of power in its diverse forms (for example from infrastructural power within the state). Further discrepancies are evident in the differences between people feeling very strongly that they belong to their neighbourhood (32%) and the 68% of respondents who believe that their neighbourhood pulled together to improve it. As before, there are important issues around semantics and a need for further information on how respondents understand and define the terms 'pulled together' and 'improve'. It may well be the case that there is a difference between respondents believing that a group acted to improve the area, and the actual larger population of the neighbourhood, many of which may well not have been involved.

In terms of social networks around 50% of respondents have friends from different ethnic groups to themselves, increasing to 90% for Black people, compared with 47% for White people. The nature of place has a potentially important role in this process as Black respondents may well be concentrated in urban locations with access to a diverse population. The further role of place is evident in people in London being more likely to have friends from different ethnic groups (77%), compared with just 32% for the North East.

Moving forward

It is clear that many PIs rely on snapshot perceptual and attitudinal responses from participants, within a framework where there is a conceptual reliance on ambiguous terms such as 'background' and 'belonging'. These rely on respondents perceiving questions in the way that policy makers believe they would do, but in reality they are so broad as to permit person- and community-centred meanings of these indicators. A potential danger within this framework is for there to be insufficient reference to the many elements constituting community cohesion, including the various features of ethnicity, faith, gender, age and economic class.

It is also the case that certain performance indicators are focused on particularly negative features of community cohesion, thereby removing the possibility of actually exploring many other more positive features. Furthermore, these indicators are not sensitive to the types of social networks that government believe characterise cohesive communities, such as robust bridging and bonding social capital. These issues relate to a need to be more sensitive to 'place'. This is critical to understanding the nature of community cohesion or disharmony, since it is a site where citizens experience everyday life through a multitude of networks.

The weakness of all these indicators has been recognised in the *What works in community cohesion* (DCLG, 2007) report. It is understood that the complex nature of communities reduces the effectiveness of indicators to a level where they should only inform strategy and interventions, rather than monitoring the success of organisations *per se*. However, the report does not suggest elimination of indicators, arguing that these are important in accountability and ensuring suitable interventions, particularly in regard to mainstream services. More generally, there is concern that the central government recommended that indicators were too narrow in focus as they tended to be concerned with outputs rather than outcomes (DCLG, 2007). Other issues related to the concern that there is too much emphasis on easily measurable harder targets that marginalise softer measures that provide important perceptual data.

Improving opportunity, strengthening society: Race equality in public services – statistics (DCLG, 2006) provides data for a range of indicators for reporting on the government's strategy to improve race equality and community cohesion, with particular focus on reporting against PSA7 – 'To reduce race inequalities and build community cohesion'. The report covers five different government areas with PSA targets related to race inequality and community cohesion, including education; the labour market; housing; health and personal social services; and the criminal justice system. This is a set of indicators that offers the potential for a broad range of factors to be explored, which have a direct and indirect (or contextual) relationship with community cohesion. While it is possible to measure relationships between these variables and ethnicity, gender, age and class, the role of place is obviously critical. While not directly relating to community cohesion, if one works on the theoretical basis that 'place', as a discursive expression and material reality of everyday lived experience (that is, a citizen believes that a neighbourhood includes streets a, b and c, and the communities within those streets, based on their everyday cognition), is produced through heterogeneous social relations (encompassing a range of citizens and institutions that work through diverse spatial networks), then it is important to take full account of these when examining community cohesion (Casey, 1997). This suggests the need, first, for a bundle of indicators to give a contextual reading of community cohesion and, second, for community cohesion indicators to go beyond simple descriptors such as 'background' and 'belong', as well as seeking to define 'place' since this is likely to vary between citizens, organisations and other actors.

Beyond central government, organisations concerned with performance management, such as the Local Government Association (LGA), have sought to propose PIs. The *Action guide on community cohesion* (LGA, 2004) recommends the development of a range of local indicators that are both objective and perception based, and build on the definition of 'community cohesion' established by the LGA and its partners, which was first published in the 2002 guidance (LGA, 2002). The guide suggests the use of a cross-section of indicators from the *Building a picture of community cohesion* (Home Office, 2003) document, the Citizenship Survey, quality of life indicators and neighbourhood statistics. The guide understands that perception and objective indicators rely on local context, and the interpretation of public officials within this context. This includes interpreting results in reference to local knowledge and an understanding of local issues, as well as using them as a platform for discussion. The guide also reiterates the importance of utilising a bundle of indicators that is sensitive to local issues and has the ability to measure change. While such an account represents sensitivity to the importance of context, and the limitation of PIs, it still follows the belief that social relations and community cohesion can be quantified.

Reflections on the theory of change

Given the importance of place contingency and the multifaceted nature of the sociospatial networks in which actors and communities function, how can this be operationalised as a means in which to evaluate social cohesion?

First, it is important for evaluators to critically analyse performance management regimes during the process of evaluation, following the approach of eliciting their theoretical and practical ToCs. This is because such regimes, including accompanying PIs, derive largely from the perspectives, values and beliefs of policy makers and politicians, rather than being objective, rational, value neutral or apolitical. What is being monitored and measured are therefore typically biased and incomplete representations of social reality. A key issue for evaluators is therefore to critically engage with the motives of policy makers and the qualitative incompleteness and dissonance with reality of performance management regimes, including tensions with complex social reality and the consequences of such processes on the outcome success of programmes.

Second, it is possible to critically examine official programme PIs from the perspective of understanding the complex and subjective nature of the 'real world' as outlined in this chapter. At the core of such an approach is an understanding that evaluators should base any examination of the theories of policy makers in the context of the historical and cultural contingency and specificity of place, and the important role of such processes in the (re)creation of social cohesion. This understands that actors work through complex social networks that can go beyond administrative boundaries and sovereign powers of nation states. Any examination of the theories of policy makers has to therefore take account of the complexity of place and the 'stretched' social networks of actors.

This obviously has important implications for the utilisation and deployment of indicators as a means in which to evaluate the impact of policy. If we understand generically orientated PIs to be reductionist, seeking uniformity across disparate places and communities, then they have no major role to play in evaluation. Any indicators that can be utilised for evaluation are those developed endogenously *within* and *with direct regard to* place. The strength of such indicators derives from their internal validity in that they are able to accurately examine causality, but where there is an appreciation that external validity in the form of generalisation across communities and place is not possible or desirable. The power of internal validity comes not just from the place specificity of PIs, but the possibility to undertake temporal analysis, measuring change over time. Of course, this does highlight the critical issue of where communities and places begin and end. Despite the centrality of the policy makers in creating bounded space for a particular programme, evaluators should seek to *create* place from the empirical observation and analysis of the lived experiences and perceptions of actors within places.

Operationalising these complexities into indicators for the purposes of evaluation is a potentially problematic task given the dissonance with official programme PIs. One possible answer lies in a scenario where actual 'outcomes' provide the comparative dimension between the evaluators and official programme PIs. While this has the potential for reducing the ability to evaluate the PIs relating to 'mechanisms', it facilitates the examination of the outcomes. A second approach is one in which it is possible to undertake comparison of the actual causality of policy 'mechanisms' (and thus the ToCs of policy makers) with the causality produced through place specificity and complex social networks. This would involve examining official PIs and those of evaluators in a longitudinal analysis of change over time arising from these mechanisms. There is an issue of the longitudinal analysis being influenced by the actual programme, and therefore it is important to use a policy-off comparator or include a broader hinterland for the evaluators' PIs.

Conclusion

From the above analysis it is clear that indicators and datasets on community cohesion have tended to concentrate on rather vague concepts, such as 'neighbourhood', 'community' and 'sense of belonging', and the perception of citizens at particular points in time. The broad-brushed nature of these concepts reduces difference and local complexity to simple and generic semantics. Issues of faith, gender, age and socioeconomic class can thus be subsumed within simple descriptors, which in turn reduce the actual effectiveness of contextual data that helps in the analysis of causal processes, such as relating to health (for example Employment and Support Allowance claimants) and worklessness. This relates to much broader ambiguity regarding the geographical definition of areas such as neighbourhoods, set within a broader policy approach focused on a national conceptual lens and interpretations. The indicators rely on respondent citizens understanding concepts within survey questions in ways that are coterminous with the way they were designed by policy makers. For instance, a respondent may well judge 'background' to be based on incomers versus existing residents within a neighbourhood (as a physical space), rather than other criteria such as age, gender and ethnicity.

Ultimately, there is a failure of many indicators to fully encompass causal processes, particularly with regard to the role of place and the uneven and heterogeneous nature of communities. What this suggests is the importance of moving beyond a fixed notion of place, as evident within performance management rationales, to understand how communities live through multi-spatial networks, in which they do not necessarily relate to a fixed notion of place such as a 'neighbourhood'. In the examination of the ToCs of policy makers, this relies on evaluators constructing place-specific PIs in which to examine mechanisms and outcomes.

Note
[1] This led to various reports on cross-cutting themes, including race, faith and community cohesion; active communities and community cohesion; collective efficacy – perceptions of communities; and regional characteristics. The cross-cutting report examines the relationships between: racial and religious prejudice/discrimination and community cohesion; participation in voluntary activities and civil renewal and perceptions of the community; and regional comparisons for distinctive areas.

References

Aber, J.L., Gephart, M., Brooks-Gunn, J. and Connell, J. (1997) 'Development in context: implications for studying neighbourhood effects', in J. Brooks-Gunn, G. Duncan and J. Aber (eds) *Neighbourhood poverty volume 1: Contexts and consequences for children*, New York, NY: Russell Sage Foundation.

Amin, A. (2002) 'Ethnicity and the multicultural city: living with diversity', *Environment and Planning A*, vol 34, no 6, pp 959-80.

Barnes, T.J. (2008) 'American pragmatism: towards a geographical introduction', *Geoforum*, vol 39, no 4, pp 1542-54.

Casey, E. (1997) *The fate of place*, Berkeley, CA: University of California Press.

DCLG (Communities and Local Government) (2006) *Improving opportunity, strengthening society: Race equality in public services – statistics*, London: DCLG.

DCLG (2007) *What works in community cohesion*, London: DCLG.

Dean, M. (1999) *Governmentality: Power and rule in modern society*, London: Sage Publications.

Dillman, D.A. (1978) *Mail and telephone surveys: The total design method*, Chichester: Wiley-Interscience.

Enticott, G. and Entwistle, T. (2007) 'The spaces of modernisation: outcomes, indicators and the local government modernisation agenda', *Geoforum*, vol 38, no 5, pp 999-1011.

Hall, S. (1987) 'Minimal selves', in L. Appignanesi (ed) *Identity: the real me* (pp 45-52), London: ICA.

Home Office (2003) *Building a picture of community cohesion: A guide for local authorities and their partners*, London: Home Office.

Home Office and ODPM (Office of the Deputy Prime Minister) (2004) *Community cohesion and area based initiatives: Guide for residents and practitioners*, London: Home Office and ODPM.

Imrie, R. and Raco, M. (2003) *Urban renaissance? New Labour, community and urban policy*, Bristol: The Policy Press.

Jackson, P. (1988) 'The management of performance in the public sector', *Public Money & Management*, vol 8, no 4, pp 11-16.

LGA (Local Government Association) (2002) *Guidance on community cohesion*, London: LGA.

LGA (2004) *Action guide on community cohesion*, London: LGA.

Massey, D. (2005) *For space*, London: Sage Publications.

Pollitt, C. (1990) *Managerialism and public services*, Oxford: Blackwell.

Pollitt, C., Talbot, C., Caulfield, J. and Smullen, A. (2004) *Agencies: How governments do things through semi-autonomous organizations*, London: Palgrave Macmillan.

Power, M. (1999) *The audit society: Rituals of verification*, Oxford: Oxford University Press.

Putnam, R.D. (2007) 'E Pluribus Unum: diversity and community in the twenty-first century', The 2006 Johan Skytte Prize Lecture, *Scandinavian Political Studies*, vol 30, no 2, pp 137-74.

Stone, D. (2002) *Policy paradox: The art of political decision making*, New York, NY: W.W. Norton & Co.

Talbot, C. (2008) 'Performance management', in E. Ferlie, L. Lynn and C. Pollitt (eds) *The Oxford handbook of public management* (pp 491-520), Oxford: Oxford University Press.

FOUR

Migration, race and population dynamics

Ludi Simpson

Introduction

This chapter reviews the available approaches to understanding and interpreting local population change, in the context of government policy for community cohesion and this book's emphasis on social cohesion. There is some agreement among academics and government that the ethnicity of residential patterns and friendship networks should not be given prominence when identifying targets for social policy. But indicators of population change are nonetheless essential contextual information for social programmes. Furthermore, claims that residential segregation is dangerous and friendship networks are polarised are still so commonplace that they require addressing in the first part of this chapter. The second part reviews existing advice on local demographic monitoring and provides further practical guidance to assist policy makers to develop the necessary contextual information for the evaluation of local initiatives.

Claims

Since 2001, Britain's ethnic geography has been seen as threateningly polarised. The contexts in which the policies of community cohesion developed early in the 2000s have been rehearsed already in this book. 'Parallel lives', 'communities living in fear' and 'the challenge of diversity' were threads that ran riot through local policy. Largely as a response to the disturbances in the Asian areas of northern towns of England in 2001, to the radical Islamist terrorist attacks on the United States (US) in the same year and to the United Kingdom (UK) military invasions of Afghanistan and Iraq, common thoughts about what makes a viable, safe community have been racialised, internationalised and Islamified.

By 2004, the government's review of its community cohesion programmes chaired by Ted Cantle decried official statistics for not providing the means to measure local residential segregation, which needed to be 'broken down' (Cantle, 2004). A year later, the chair of the Commission for Racial Equality (CRE) responded to the London terrorist bombings in a speech entitled 'Sleepwalking to segregation' (Phillips, 2005). He identified the emergence of 'fully fledged ghettos', residential segregation and narrow ethnic friendship networks as encouragements to terrorism. Others made a further link from ethnicity and segregation to immigration, insisting that levels of immigration were too high to allow successful integration, including the high-profile examples of the academic Mike Poulsen (2005), the political campaign MigrationWatch UK (2006) and the government minister Phil Woolas (quoted in *The Times*, 2006).

In contrast, the statistics show that Britain is becoming more ethnically diverse, but not more ethnically polarised. A greater proportion of Britain's residents tick a box other than 'White British', but such citizens are increasingly found in all parts of Britain, and are not stuck in ghettos.

In the latter part of the 2000s, the language of government tempered somewhat. The Commission on Integration and Cohesion warned in 2007 that: 'Excessive coverage about residential segregation, for example, serves to spread a view that the whole of England is spatially segregated. It overstates and oversimplifies the problem and leaves us "sleepwalking into simplicity"' (COIC, 2007, p 3).

The ethnic composition of neighbourhoods and friendship networks still taxes the popular image of successful communities, and stimulates academic and government concerns.

The nature of changing ethnic composition

Using the categories of 'ethnic group' collected in official statistics in Britain, with all their uncomfortable drawbacks and idiosyncrasies (Aspinall, 2009; Finney and Simpson, 2009, chapter 2), it is clear that in most major cities of Britain the number of White residents has decreased in the past two decades and the number of minority residents, taken as a whole or individually, has increased. This is not, however, a result of White and other residents 'pulling apart', seeking parallel lives or ethnic comfort zones as commentators referred to above have suggested. Evidence on migration presented later in this chapter shows very clearly that moves out of areas of immigrant settlement, often near the centre of cities, are made in very similar proportion by White and other residents. It is also not the case that minority residents tend to move to live in areas where others of their own ethnic group are a greater proportion than their current area of residence. The opposite is the case: Bangladeshis are leaving Tower Hamlets, Pakistanis are leaving Bradford, Indians are leaving Leicester and Caribbeans are leaving Lambeth (for example as analysed in Simpson and Finney, 2009). How is it then that the White population in those same areas is becoming smaller as a proportion of the total?

Figure 4.1 presents the local population dynamics of most cities with a settled immigrant population in one of its neighbourhoods. Areas of cheap inner-city housing, where minority immigrants often settle, thereby creating an ethnically diverse area, fill up as the young immigrants have families.

Although the settlement area loses minority population to other areas of Britain as individuals and families 'get on and get out', this loss is more than compensated by further immigration and by *age momentum*. Age momentum is the natural growth (excess of births over deaths) that can be expected in any young population. This natural growth through age momentum is a larger source of population growth than high fertility rates or immigration. Simpson (2007a) quantifies this phenomenon for Birmingham as a whole, but it is a general phenomenon: analyses later in this chapter show that minority births outstripped minority immigration in most settlement neighbourhoods in Britain.

Both White and minority populations move further out, aspiring to better housing and a better environment and responding to the lack of available housing in the growing diverse area. The suburbanisation for minorities remains mostly within the city, while the White population

Figure 4.1: The growth of minority populations and movement to the suburbs

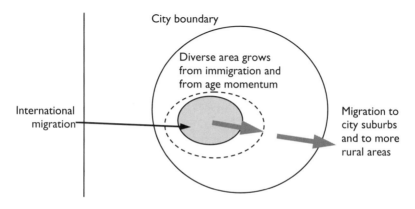

generally already lives closer to the city boundary and crosses it more often during suburbanisation. The patterns of migration and natural growth that result in changing ethnic composition described here and in Figure 4.1 are not unique to one city, nor to the recent past. While there is diversity in the rates of change and the nature of the local housing markets, the directions of change and the factors at play are to be expected in all urban areas with significant past immigration; they derive from the youth of immigrants coupled with suburbanisation. Suburbanisation, and longer distance counter-urbanisation to more rural areas, preceded immigration and indeed made space for immigration (Finney and Simpson, 2009, p 128).

It is these dynamics of natural growth and migration that explain why the White population is becoming a smaller proportion in most cities, at the same time as segregation is decreasing. Once this growth is recognised as mainly internally driven by age momentum rather than by opposite streams of migration, then its negative and false association with segregation is broken. It becomes easier to recognise the growing minority population of Britain as a natural development and as a growing diversity rather than a growing apart.

Friendship, social networks and trust

In the politics of integration and cohesion, focus shifts regularly between where people live and who people mix with, not always recognising that the two are not the same. Social networks usually involve a small minority of the local neighbourhood but also people from wider networks based on work, education and earlier residential locations.

One can ask why public policy should concern itself with who are friends with whom. A circle of friends is a rather narrow measurement of interaction between social groups, which will also involve work, shopping and neighbourly contact. If friendship groups express a preference to spend time with people they feel most affinity towards, it should not be surprising that many people, especially those who state small friendship circles, name only those of their own ethnic background.

If we do accept friendship networks as something relevant to public policy, we need to be alert to misleading reports as the following example shows. When the CRE commissioned a YouGov poll, the poll 'showed that young people from ethnic minorities were twice as likely to have a circle of friends exclusively from their own community as were older ethnic minority folk.... It must surely be the most worrying fact of all that younger Britons appear to be integrating less well than their parents' (Phillips, 2005).

However, the evidence does not support the threatening narrowness reported by the Commission's quote above, which was based on the results from a non-random sample with fewer than 1,000 respondents. Even then, more than half of most minority respondents' friends were White, which would be hard to accept as a worrying result. The Citizenship Survey, using standard methods to ensure a representative sample, and interviewing several thousand individuals and thus much more robust than the YouGov poll, finds that minorities born in Britain are *less* likely to have exclusively minority friends than those born outside Britain (Heath and Li, 2007, p 22).

The report on 'meaningful interactions' from the most recent survey (2007-08: CLG, 2009, chapter 7) shows that minority adults are more likely to have friends from a different ethnic group (81%) than White adults (49%), and that this is largely because White people usually live in areas where there are few minority residents. Young minorities are more likely to have friends from a different ethnic group than older minorities (directly contradicting the YouGov poll), and minorities born in the UK are more likely to have friends from other ethnic groups than minorities born outside the UK.

The implications of this approach are that a mixed circle of friends indicates integration, and that friends who come exclusively from one's own community indicate a lack of integration. Yet, 'People who agreed that their local area was cohesive' (54%) were as likely to have friends from different backgrounds as people who disagreed that their local area was cohesive (52%; CLG, 2009, table 71). Regression analysis to take into account other factors (such as age, sex and area deprivation) showed a possible but unclear relationship between perceptions of cohesion and having friends from different ethnic backgrounds but this relationship is not proved.

So friendship circles are neither threateningly narrow, nor narrowing, nor more narrow for minorities than for the White population, nor directly related to cohesion and integration and so perhaps are not particularly relevant. There are similar reasons, laid out in Finney and Simpson (2009), to reject notions that either immigrants or minorities contribute to dangerous overcrowding of Britain, or competition for resources, or are unwilling to integrate, or that cities are gripped by fear and ethnic rivalries or that parental choice of school creates segregation by race more than it does segregation by class. This series of unsupported claims by their repetition constitutes a *litany* that is itself divisive. An unfair linguistic sliding between 'immigrants' and 'minority ethnic groups' makes the act of immigration last not just a year or two, nor for only a lifetime, but for generations. An equation of immigrants and minorities is plainly unhelpful: half of Britain's minority ethnic people were born in Britain, and half of all immigrants are White.

The purpose of this chapter so far has been first to clarify that it would be difficult to establish a desired level or direction of change for the ethnic composition of a neighbourhood or of social networks, and by extension the same goes for religious or linguistic composition. Second, that a collection of popular linked claims suggesting a dangerous aspect of ethnic composition is not supported by evidence, which on the contrary shows that the possible indicators of segregation and friendship groups are moving in directions away from the supposed danger.

The consequence is not simply a satisfied sigh of relief that segregation has been over-egged. It is also to focus on the components of population change, births, deaths and migration, and the reasons for the changes that are observed. The next section of the chapter reviews existing resources for demographic analysis, before the final section turns to some specific examples of helpful analyses.

Existing resources to measure population diversity

Statistics of segregation have been developed but are generally considered to lend themselves to misleading comparisons between areas, and to falsely equate residential composition with social interaction and integration. An initial report commissioned by the Institute for Community Cohesion (ICoCo) on the availability of data for monitoring community cohesion (Johnson, 2007) reviews existing data sources on immigration and segregation, with a warning discussion about segregation indices that have 'serious flaws'.

However, residential segregation still gets a regular airing in the press and is the topic of a vast academic literature, which often assumes that any level of segregation indicates a malaise. A recent example of some pitfalls into which a focus on segregation may lead is provided by 'Measuring Diversity', a website launched in 2010 at Bristol University, which offers comparisons of ethnic composition and ethnic segregation over time and the ability to compare areas within England. 'Taken together, all the statistics give a representation of the level of ethnic segregation in each Local Authority (LA) in England.... The two formal measures of segregation, the dissimilarity index and index of isolation we present have intuitive appeal, and are the two most widely used in academic research' (www.measuringdiversity.org.uk/data).

However, one of the two indices of segregation is far from being 'widely used in academic research', but is a severe modification of the much-used Index of Isolation. The design of the original Index of Isolation allows it to be interpreted directly as an answer to the question: 'How likely is it that members of a certain minority group come into contact with members of the same group, rather than other ethnic groups?'. But although this is the description given for the Bristol index, the modifications invalidate this interpretation and no other is offered.[1] The ICoCo report also argued that the results of segregation indices 'were not independent of the absolute size of individual populations (or their relative size), and also the size of the areas used to measure and compute the index … [and that] the "Isolation Index" does assume … that geographical propinquity – even, sharing the same physical space, is the same as social interaction' (Johnson, 2007, p 50).

How does the 'Measuring Diversity' website justify such a focus on a topic that has been said to be distracting to the point of 'sleepwalking into simplicity'?

> One of the big questions of our times is how well individuals from different ethnic groups get along together. Schools are an important place where this interaction takes place. It is a common saying that individuals' attitudes are strongly influenced by their school days. So the peer groups that children play with, talk to and work with are important factors moulding their perspectives on society. The extent of ethnic diversity in schools is an important issue of public debate. This website provides some facts to enlighten this debate. (www.measuringdiversity.org.uk/)

Thus, the composition of a school is taken to represent the interactions within it. The fact of public debate on Britain's diversity has become sufficient reason to measure the variation of diversity and to compare indices of segregation for one area against others. No advice is given on the well-known thorny issues in comparing areas' ethnic diversity using these indices, some of which are mentioned in the ICoCO report (Johnson, 2007). The boundary of a local authority will also affect its value on the Bristol measures. Bradford local authority includes many rural, mainly White, villages to the north and west of the city, bringing its percentage of minorities down and its indices of segregation up. So the fact that Bradford's measures of segregation are higher than Manchester's, for example, is partly because Manchester is more tightly bounded by an urban boundary. There is no fair way of evaluating for any policy purpose the comparison of two local authorities' indices of segregation.[2]

The ICoCo report also looked at the theory of a 'tipping point' between the minority and majority populations in an area 'after which majority "flight" takes place and the area (at least in theory) becomes predominantly or wholly dominated by the hitherto subordinate group'. The report concludes: 'No study has ever actually been able to establish this popular theory in practice, or to identify this mythical point, but it has remained a popular political device' (Johnson, 2007, p 50).

ICoCo has provided a 'Toolkit for population dynamics' since its inception in 2005, in response to 'a growing volume of evidence that our local populations are changing rapidly as a result of both international migration and movement within the UK' (www. cohesioninstitute.org.uk/Resources/Toolkits/PopulationDynamics). It provides references to national studies on immigration, and local studies claiming inadequacy of estimates from the Office for National Statistics (ONS).

However ICoCo has not pursued its toolkit to monitor local population change. While it has identified population data as necessary, and its commissioned investigation has rejected segregation as a useful summary measure, no alternative has been found. Demographic change is neither a topic of discussion in ICoCo's online forum nor a priority of current ICoCo project work.

Nonetheless, most would agree with ICoCo that where people live is essential contextual information. The Department for Communities and Local Government (DCLG) publishes 'tools' to encourage good practice in local authorities. The *Community cohesion impact assessment and community conflict prevention tool* (Broadwood and Sugden, 2008, p 5) stipulates that its users 'will need current and detailed information on who lives in the area in which the activity will take place'. But its advice on where to get local knowledge of ethnic composition is less advanced than the ICoCo preliminary report described above. The DCLG tool suggests use of the ONS Neighbourhood Statistics databases, but these have no information on ethnicity more recent than the 2001 Census for areas within local authorities.

Similarly, the Equality and Human Rights Commission (EHRC) has commissioned reports on measurement of equalities more generally, which implies measurement of population composition in order to gauge rates of participation in employment, education and so on. As yet the EHRC has not made progress in this direction nor does it have plans to do so.

—

Other reports have emphasised the understanding that can be gained from partial or qualitative intelligence from businesses, police, housing agencies and national insurance statistics (Audit Commission, 2007; IDeA, 2007). A report from Coventry University (Thunhurst et al, 2007, p 6) provides a review of promising datasets in relation to local health monitoring of ethnically diverse areas but laments that 'the outstanding data vacuum relates to our knowledge of the current population base'.

In summary, the importance of monitoring population composition in order to understand change has been repeatedly claimed but remains a gap in practice. Very little advice exists to help the practitioner to quantify the size and ethnic composition of local population, or to quantify migration to and from local neighbourhoods.

Monitoring population diversity and dynamics

Following the dictum of theories of change, as well as common sense, one should ask what do we want, how much, by when? Any target of a particular ethnic mix would not only be difficult to achieve and thus lead to disappointment, but would also be philosophically and politically questionable. It is no longer acceptable to judge the worth of an individual by the colour of his or her skin, so why should it be sensible to judge the success of a neighbourhood by its colour? Instead of targeting ethnic mix, one should name the issues that need improvement, whether these are neighbourhood development, social equality, participation or interaction.

This is not to say that people's place of residence is not affected by race relations or social policies. Resident induction schemes that firmly deal with racial harassment have helped to attract minority families to areas that were previously seen as hostile (Phillips et al, 2008). Sensitive planning consents and affordable housing have helped to attract minority families to areas in which they previously could not live. Because of the limited housing in most ethnically diverse areas, it is in the suburbs where ethnic mix may be most likely to be responsive to social policy. These examples themselves support the point being made that social equality, and in particular equality in the housing market, are the keys to allowing people to move more freely, rather than existing residential patterns or residents' willingness to move.

The remainder of this chapter treats demographic change not as a policy target but as a neighbourhood characteristic whose understanding can helpfully underpin the development, implementation and evaluation of social policy. The composition of a population according to its age, its formation of families and households and its patterns of migration directly affect the mix of services required, and provides the baseline denominator for social indicators of educational success, employment and housing. Ethnicity, as a dimension of population change, is intended as one aid to understanding change, not as an evaluative indicator. Three analyses that can be repeated in most neighbourhoods of Britain are suggested in this section.

Some of the most useful analyses are based on the national Census, which gives detailed population statistics for each area of the UK. Occasional tainting criticisms that the Census misses so many people that nothing in it can be trusted are very wide of the mark. The total missed in 2001 was 6%, far less than in social surveys. A survey following the Census estimated the number and characteristics of those missed, which were then included in all Census output. Extensive study estimated that only a further 0.5% was missed altogether from Census output (ONS, 2004). Only in the areas where the Census failed to directly count a substantial proportion of the population (for example more than a quarter of four inner boroughs of London), is it fair to take the results very cautiously. A bigger drawback is that the Census is taken only once every 10 years in the UK. Neighbourhood evaluation studies will make valuable use of the updates from the 2011 Census when its tables for small areas are published in 2013.

What is the population of the neighbourhood(s) and is it changing?

Government's annual population estimates give an age structure for males and females and each ethnic group for every local authority and health area in England and Wales (www.statistics.gov.uk/StatBase/Product.asp?vlnk=14238). These areas are too big to interest most neighbourhood interventions. For small areas in Britain, the age and sex structure of population is updated annually, but without an ethnic group dimension.[3]

The annual estimates give a picture of change over time. In Table 4.1, Oldham is chosen only to exemplify an analysis that can be made for the small areas within any district of Britain. While the population of Oldham District rose only slightly between 2001 and 2008, sizeable areas of over 5,000 residents within Oldham increased or decreased by up to 11%.

The ethnic composition of a neighbourhood is not updated annually in government statistics and is best indicated by the last Census. Supplementing the Census outputs, a complete estimate of the 2001 population by age, sex and ethnic group, including allowances for all

Table 4.1: Population change within Oldham, 2001–08

	Areas	2008 Population	Change since 2001	
All areas	34	219,717	+1,180	+1%
Greatest increase	1	7,602	+764	+11%
Increase more than 100	12	82,373	+4,138	+5%
Change of up to 100	9	59,299	+94	0%
Decrease more than 100	13	78,045	–3052	–4%
Greatest decrease	1	5,333	–567	–10%

Notes: 34 Middle Super Output Areas of Oldham, varying in population between 5,000 and 10,000. The 2008 estimates are expected to be revised by the ONS by 2011.

Source: www.statistics.gov.uk/StatBase/Product.asp?vlnk=14357

non-response, is available for every Census Output Area in England and Wales (www.ccsr.ac.uk/research/PopulationEstimates.htm). The population in the Census year can be 'rolled forward' so that after five years, 10-year-olds have become 15-year-olds and so on. Young children can be added using a ratio of children to adults.

The most useful additional updated statistical information is provided by the annual School Census. Although only referring to children of school age and in state schools, it records ethnicity and language and may be used to identify local change. Access to the School Census for population estimation is at present restricted, but may be feasible for research purposes by local authorities. The ONS is currently investigating its use for population estimates, using the version in England, which has been established longest in the UK and is part of the National Pupil Database. The School Census can also provide estimates of migration, as in the third example analysis below.

Population change: the Census of Population

Table 4.2, from the 2001 Census, takes the 20 districts in Britain with electoral wards that have the highest percentage of minority ethnic residents, in this case defined as those who recorded themselves with an ethnic group other than White. It demonstrates several key explanatory facts about population change in these areas.

The number of minority births tends to be more than the number of minority immigrants in a year, a result not of high fertility so much as a relatively young adult population. As discussed above, the source of growth in the minority populations is more from an excess of births over deaths than from immigration.

Table 4.2: Indicators of diversity and population change in local areas from the 2001 Census

	Ward in the district with most minority ethnic residents	Minority ethnic residents	Minority ethnic residents as %	Largest minority ethnic group in ward	Number of residents in the largest minority group	Number of minority births in one year	Number of minority immigrants in one year	Migration in UK, White residents	Migration in UK, minority ethnic residents
Ealing	Southall Broadway	11,500	88	Indian	7,050	431	401	–99	–1,438
Newham	Green Street East	11,150	84	Indian	3,950	588	436	–160	–931
Leicester	Latimer	9,550	83	Indian	8,600	486	508	+35	–816
Birmingham	Handsworth	21,100	82	Pakistani	6,550	1411	718	–786	–1,320
Blackburn and Darwen	Bastwell	6,000	81	Pakistani	3,100	284	112	–148	–193
Brent	Wembley Central	8,650	79	Indian	4,350	119	146	–128	–348
Bradford	University	16,650	74	Pakistani	12,450	403	302	+185	–444
Redbridge	Clementswood	8,050	71	Indian	2,900	159	103	–210	–155
Pendle	Whitefield	2,950	70	Pakistani	2,800	70	33	–23	–120
Tower Hamlets	Spitalfields	5,850	70	Bangladeshi	4,850	116	49	–50	–240

Continued...

Ward in the district with most minority ethnic residents		Minority ethnic residents	Minority ethnic residents as %	Largest minority ethnic group in ward	Number of residents in the largest minority group	Number of minority births in one year	Number of minority immigrants in one year	Migration in UK, White residents	Migration in UK, minority ethnic residents
Southwark	Peckham	7,700	68	African	4,050	165	67	–13	–384
Luton	Dallow	8,800	67	Pakistani	4,450	214	172	–150	–89
Burnley	Danehouse	4,050	66	Pakistani	2,550	115	78	–30	–159
Hounslow	Heston East	6,950	65	Indian	4,500	106	132	–139	–114
Croydon	West Thornton	10,500	64	Indian	3,250	193	215	–184	–27
Harrow	Kenton East	6,350	64	Indian	4,500	81	87	–181	+17
Sandwell	St. Pauls	7,300	64	Indian	3,550	137	67	–78	–84
Slough	Central	6,350	63	Pakistani	2,900	107	126	–89	–141
Wolverhampton	Blakenhall	6,900	61	Indian	5,150	100	66	+3	–139
Oldham	Werneth	6,800	58	Pakistani	4,600	190	99	–170	–50
Total of all 20 wards		173,150	73			5,475	3,917	–2,415	–7,175

Note: All figures are given directly in the Census except the number of births, which is estimated as one fifth of the number of children aged under five. The final four columns refer to the year before the Census, 2000-01, extracted from Finney and Simpson (2009, p 130)

Source: 2001 Census, tables ST101, KS06 and KS24.

The last two columns of Table 4.2 show how the area interacts with the rest of the UK through migration. For all but one of these areas there was, on balance, movement out by minority residents, reinforcing the message that the increases in established minority populations are driven largely by an excess of births over deaths. The exception is Harrow's diverse area of Kenton East, which received movement from Inner London to this relatively prosperous borough.

When comparing the migration of White and minority residents, the net out-migration from these 20 'least White' neighbourhoods was not the White flight taken as fact by some senior politicians. The balance of movement out by minority residents was greater than that of the White population for most of these wards, and by a ratio of three to one overall. In Bradford, Leicester and Wolverhampton, three of the districts most often parodied as having 'ghettos', the balance of White movement was *in* to their least White wards.

The use of statistics to examine myths of race and migration is the focus of Finney and Simpson's (2009) book, but here the message is more that these particular indicators of demographic change tell a strong story that is a helpful context when evaluating social change in neighbourhoods.

The movement out of these areas is selective, however: those who move out are the families who can afford to do so and have aspirations to move to better surroundings. The combined use of population statistics like these together with intelligence from qualitative interviews was the key, for example, to understanding change in Oldham and Rochdale's Housing Market Renewal areas (Phillips et al, 2008; Simpson et al, 2008).

Population change: the School Census

The School Census has been mentioned already as a useful source to estimate the ethnic and linguistic composition of local areas. It has also been used to measure migration. For international migration, pupils who arrive in state school after age five whose first language is not English are likely to be immigrants to the UK. Internal migration within the UK is indicated by a change of residential postcode identified in successive annual School Censuses. These migration measures have been validated against official estimates of migration from the Census, from patient re-registration and from the allocation of new National Insurance numbers (Simpson et al, 2010, 2011).

Figure 4.2 shows an analysis of migration in Leicester for 2006. Again, Leicester is chosen only to exemplify an analysis that can be repeated for the small areas of any district. In this case there is outward movement by families of Indian ethnic origin, away from the inner-city wards. This is confirmation that the pattern shown in Table 4.2 from the 2001 Census continued later in the decade.

The School Census is particularly useful because it also indicates families' economic circumstances through the pupils' assessed eligibility for free school meals, only awarded to children in households with low income. The movement of families in areas with social programmes can be described and compared with those in other areas. The movement for any area can be monitored before, during and after an initiative. Jivraj (2008) provides an example for Neighbourhood Management Pathfinder areas.

Figure 4.2: Net impact of migration within England, children aged 5–15 of Indian ethnic group origin, Leicester City wards, 2006

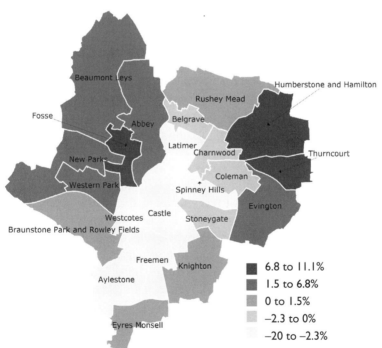

Notes: Net migration with the rest of England during the year January 2006 to January 2007, as a percentage of all Indian pupils aged 5–15 in January 2006. Negative values indicate net out-migration, positive values indicate net in-migration.

Source: Jivraj and Marquis (2009)

Analytical challenges in population statistics

Two challenges are discussed in this section: it may not be plain sailing to find statistics for the precise area of a new neighbourhood programme; and differences between ethnic groups may not be easily interpreted. The main strategy recommended to confront such challenges is to discuss and seek advice from a range of perspectives: those who are familiar with the statistics and their manipulation as well as those in the communities involved, and staff from community programmes that may be concerned with the area.

Statistics that do not match neighbourhoods

Statistics about population are often published only for standard official areas such as electoral wards or statistical output areas. It is fortunate if these standard areas match the boundary of a local cohesion programme, and it is more likely that they do not. It may be that statistics are provided for a larger area that contains more than all of the target area, or that the statistical areas overlap the target area and match it only approximately. In either case, there are several rules to help analysis.

First, percentages and rates for an approximate area are more likely to apply to the target area than counts of people. The former will be wrong only to the extent that the people in the target area have different characteristics, and not simply because there are more or less of them.

Second, maps are essential to understand how statistical areas approximate to the target area. The difference between the areas that the statistics apply to and the target area may be small or large and may contain different types of housing and people: the extent to which this matters often comes down to a judgement that the researcher with local knowledge will have to make. Sometimes those familiar with geographical coding and databases will be able to help allocate statistics to the target area according to the numbers in each overlap.

Finally, different statistics are sometimes available for *different* areas that contain or approximate the target area: for example employment data for one area and population data for another. The interpretation of such disparate approximate views of the area of interest is fraught with difficulty and should be avoided or only undertaken with a clear eye to the dangers of misinterpretation.

Interpreting ethnic differences

When ethnic groups have different demographic outcomes – migration or household size for example – the interpretation of the differences is as challenging as it is for socioeconomic indicators. The challenge is to specify the mechanism that creates the differences. It is highly unlikely to be related directly to general cultural differences labelled under the heading of 'ethnicity', except when racism is involved. In that case, *other people's* attitudes are affected by their view of your ethnicity and race, and those attitudes affect their behaviour and therefore their own outcomes and those of the people they perceive as different.

Often there will be other mechanisms that explain differences in outcomes between ethnic groups, which may relate to the different age or social composition of each group. Earlier in this chapter the young age of most immigrants was seen to explain much of the growth of minority populations, simply because younger women are more likely to have children than older women. The higher fertility of some groups – when comparing women of the same age – is largely explained by the family building that is highly associated with recent immigration. Fertility rates have fallen for all established ethnic groups in Britain during the past two decades because the proportion of recent immigrants has fallen. Similarly, the higher migration rate of some minority ethnic groups is also largely explained by their younger age structure. These are all non-ethnic explanations that partly account for ethnic differences.

In fact, Indian, Pakistani and Bangladeshi young adults have *lower* rates of migration than others of the same age (Finney and Simpson, 2008). This is likely to relate to traditions and customs of young adults living with parents until creating a new family unit through marriage, and sometimes for a while after. This pattern, evident across otherwise quite different ethnic groups, again specifies a non-ethnic mechanism by which population dynamics can be understood to play out in the particular contexts of a neighbourhood and particular histories of immigration and subsequent internal migration.

Conclusions

The dynamic nature of Britain's ethnic diversity can be traced to the longer-term consequences of immigration, which include the momentum for growth within any young population through an excess of births over deaths, continued immigration from existing and new origins, and the movement away from immigrant settlement areas of

White and minority ethnic groups as a result of limited housing capacity and a common aspiration for good living environments.

Social policies may wish to influence family and individual decisions of where to live, by making various parts of the housing market more equally accessible. However, it would be wrong to imagine that such influence could be so great as to be easily measured by changing residential patterns or changing migration patterns. These are for the most part determined by much larger economic and demographic pressures.

The focus on ethnic composition, in particular the percentage of each ethnic group in local areas, and indices of segregation based on those percentages, is a largely sterile pursuit, first because the indices are regularly misinterpreted and over-interpreted and second because, being the result of a mix of components of population change that are largely predetermined, they are not easy to influence through social policy.

Neighbourhood population studies do provide an essential context for policies of social cohesion, and suffer from a lack of updated information between Censuses of Population. Nonetheless, analyses of government estimates, of the Census of Population and of the School Census provide basic insights that complement qualitative intelligence and can go much further than common existing practice.

Chapter Five explores further the potential of statistical analysis of administrative records. Chapter Eight provides evidence of the racialisation of spatial analysis in the context of cohesion policies in housing.

Notes

[1] The modifications involve a partial standardisation for population size, which removes the index's mathematical equivalence to probabilities of living in the same neighbourhood as others of the same group; for technical details of this criticism, see White (1986) and Simpson (2007b).

[2] See Simpson (2007b) for a review of segregation indices and their lack of comparability across areas. Comparisons are valid over time for the same area, if area boundaries do not change.

[3] In England and Wales, for Lower Super Output Areas, population 1,000-2,000 (www.statistics.gov.uk/about/methodology_by_theme/sape/default. asp). In Scotland, for Datazones, population 500-1,000 (www.gro-scotland. gov.uk/statistics/theme/population/estimates/special-area/sape/index.html). In Northern Ireland (less often than annually), for Super Output Areas, population 1,300-2,800 (www.nisra.gov.uk/demography/default.asp125.htm).

References

Aspinall, P. (2009) 'The future of ethnicity classifications', *Journal of Ethnic and Migration Studies*, vol 35, no 9, pp 1417–36.

Audit Commission (2007) *Crossing borders: Responding to the local challenges of migrant workers*, London: Audit Commission.

Broadwood, J. and Sugden, N. (2008) *Community cohesion impact assessment and community conflict prevention tool*, London: CLG, www.communities. gov.uk/publications/communities/communitycohesiontool

Cantle, T. (ed) (2004) *The end of parallel lives? The report of the Community Cohesion Panel*, London: Home Office.

CLG (Communities and Local Government) (2009) *2007-08 Citizenship Survey: Community cohesion topic report*, London: DCLG.

COIC (Commission on Integration and Cohesion) (2007) *Our shared future*, London: DCLG.

Finney, N. and Simpson, L. (2008) 'Internal migration and ethnic groups: evidence for Britain from the 2001 Census', *Population, Space and Place*, vol 14, no 1, pp 63–83.

Finney, N. and Simpson, L. (2009) *'Sleepwalking to segregation'? Challenging myths about race and migration*, Bristol: The Policy Press.

Heath, A. and Li, Y. (2007) 'Measuring the size of the employer contribution to the ethnic minority employment gap', Unpublished paper prepared for the Business Commission of the National Employment Panel, available from authors at Nuffield College, Oxford University OX1 1NF.

IDeA (Improvement and Development Agency) (2007) *Good practice guide for local authorities: New European migration*, London: IDeA.

Jivraj, S. (2008) *Migration selectivity and area-based regeneration in England*, University of Manchester CCSR Working Paper 2008-22, Manchester: University of Manchester, www.ccsr.ac.uk/publications/working/2008-22.pdf

Jivraj, S. and Marquis, N. (2009) 'The Pupil Level Annual School Census: a new approach to measuring internal migration of school-aged pupils in England', Presentation at the conference 'Migration, Community and Ethnicity', 2 April, CCSR, University of Manchester, www.ccsr.ac.uk/erm/2009-04-02/documents/PLASC_ERMpresentation_020408.pdf

Johnson, M. (2007) *COHDMAP: Cohesion mapping of community dynamics: Availability of data for monitoring community cohesion: Report of the scoping study*, Coventry: Institute for Community Cohesion.

MigrationWatch UK (2006) *The effect of immigration on the integration of communities in Britain,* Briefing Paper 9.19, Guildford: MigrationWatch UK.

ONS (Office for National Statistics) (2004) *2001 Census based local authority population studies*, Newport: ONS, www.statistics.gov.uk/census2001/cn_111.asp

Phillips, D., Simpson, L. and Ahmed, S. (2008) 'Shifting geographies of minority ethnic settlement: remaking communities in Oldham and Rochdale', in J. Flint and D. Robinson (eds) *Cohesion in crisis? New dimensions of diversity and difference* (pp 81-97), Bristol: The Policy Press.

Phillips, T. (2005) 'After 7/7: sleepwalking to segregation', Speech to the Manchester Council for Community Relations, 22 September.

Poulsen, M. (2005) 'The "new geography" of ethnicity in Britain?', Paper presented to the 'Annual Conference of the Institute of British Geographers and the Royal Geographical Society', London, 31 August–2 September, available from the author.

Simpson, L. (2007a) *Population forecasts for Birmingham, with an ethnic group dimension*, Birmingham: Birmingham City Council.

Simpson, L. (2007b) 'Ghettos of the mind: the empirical behaviour of indices of segregation and diversity', *Journal of the Royal Statistical Society: Series A (Statistics in Society)*, vol 170, no 2, pp 405-24.

Simpson, L. and Finney, N. (2009) 'Spatial patterns of internal migration: evidence for ethnic groups in Britain', *Population, Space and Place*, vol 15, no 1, pp 37-56.

Simpson, L., Gavalas, V. and Finney, N. (2008) 'Population dynamics in ethnically diverse towns: the long-term implications of immigration', *Urban Studies*, vol 45, no 1, pp 163-83.

Simpson, L., Jivraj, S. and Marquis, N. (2011: in press) *International and internal migration of ethnic minorities, measured from the National Pupil Dataset*, London: DCLG.

Simpson, L., Marquis, N. and Jivraj, S. (2010) 'International and internal migration measured from the School Census in England', *Population Trends*, vol 140 (summer), pp 106-24, www.statistics.gov.uk/StatBase/Product.asp?vlnk=6303

The Times (2006) 'Suspect in terror hunt used veil to evade arrest', 9 October, www.timesonline.co.uk/tol/news/uk/crime/article666149.ece

Thunhurst, C., Lawrence, A., Gilchrist, M. and Jordan, S. (2007) *Measuring the health of urban populations: A small area study in Coventry and Leicester*, Coventry: Coventry University.

White, M. (1986) 'Segregation and diversity: measures in population distribution', *Population Index*, vol 52, pp 198-221.

FIVE

Using local administrative data to evaluate social and community cohesion

John Eversley and Les Mayhew

Introduction

This book argues that an analysis of social cohesion needs to focus on whether people from different backgrounds have similar life opportunities as well as assessing interaction, interdependence and conflicts of interests of people from different backgrounds. Whatever the vision of a cohesive society is, there are important questions to answer about where we stand now, and how we can measure change. This chapter focuses on the measurability of social cohesion. We argue that use of flawed data, often analysed inadequately, misleads us as to where we are and where we are going. This is not inevitable, however, because better data and better analytical techniques are already out there.

We note that many existing measures of cohesion emphasise and critique perceptions and 'cultural' explanations of problems in cohesion, rather than providing material explanations of competition and exclusion and ideas of social cohesion (Phillips, 2005, 2006; Broadwood and Sugden, 2008; DCLG, 2008a; Ratcliffe et al, 2009). Administrative data not only help to correct that emphasis but, when coupled with survey data, can be used to look at attitudes, behaviour and status.

Building on the previous two chapters by Fuller and Simpson respectively, this chapter begins with a short discussion about the existing measures of cohesion and the limitations with current, and most frequently used, sources of data. The following section considers how the present state of the science could be greatly improved by using a system called 'Neighbourhood Knowledge Management' (branded as *nkm*) applied to normal local authority level administrative data and case studies. We then turn our attention to the practical and ethical issues involved in using such data and how they can be managed.

The problems with existing measures of cohesion

There are a number of problems with existing measures of cohesion. The problems are of three kinds:

- what is being measured;
- the sources of data; and
- how the data are analysed.

What is being measured

Fuller has already argued that a negative approach to measuring cohesion fails to value or measure the benefits that stem from extensive interaction and positive relationships. Both Fuller and Simpson argue that physical proximity is neither a necessary nor a sufficient condition for positive interaction or wellbeing and both highlight problems of confusing statistical association with causality. The problems with measuring perceptions of cohesion have also been thoroughly explored by Fuller. Inequality between people or groups in relation to cohesion has typically been expressed in terms of either ethnicity or religion. Associations between poverty and ethnicity or religion are often implicit in studies or not explored through evidence (Phillips, 2005; Broadwood and Sugden, 2008).

The sources of data

Many of the sources of measurement that Fuller refers to rely on official statistics derived from the Census and national surveys commissioned by government such as the Labour Force Survey or Health Survey for England. As the government elected in 2010 abolished the Comprehensive Area Assessment regime (HM Government, 2010), some surveys and other datasets used to support assessments may be discontinued or cut back. However, this may actually increase or sustain the need for local-level analysis.

There are other potential sources of data that are not adequately used, often through lack of knowledge of their existence or how to access them, and, unfortunately, rarely do these datasets reference dimensions such as ethnicity.

Examples include:

- area administrative counts published by national, regional and local statutory agencies – for example numbers of people on benefits, recorded crime, admissions to hospital;
- one-off local or specific surveys commissioned by local authorities, the National Health Service (NHS) and other agencies, which are essentially qualitative or attitudinal;
- private sector data, for example on retail consumption, credit ratings and house purchases, which are usually proprietary and commercially marketed.

Simpson's chapter deals with a number of problems associated with the use of existing data. Here we note some additional problems:

Out-of-date data

It is not only the Census that is out of date. The fieldwork for the last major survey of race discrimination was carried out in 1994 (Modood et al, 1997, p 3). Even annual surveys can be rapidly overtaken by events impacting on status (unemployment during the recession) or attitudes (following local, national and international events). Sources that appear up to date may be based substantially on out-of-date data – for example nearly 40% of Mosaic data[1] comes from the 2001 Census (Experian, 2010b). Also, some ethnic density studies use 1991 data (Boydell et al, 2001).

Flaws in the original surveys

Problems with the 1991 and 2001 Censuses in not capturing specific populations are well known (see, for example, Statistics Commission, 2003; ONS, 2004; House of Commons Treasury Select Committee, 2008a, 2008b; UK Statistics Authority, 2009).

Imputed or synthesised data

As a result of missing data or relatively small national samples, data are often synthesised to the local level. What is a legitimate interpretation at a national or regional level may not be justified at the local level. This is true of some of the assertions based on the Citizenship Surveys (DCLG, 2009) and the economic data derived from the Labour Force Survey. Mosaic data that is not from the Census relies to a significant extent on synthetic imputation to the local level and is therefore particularly contentious (Experian, 2010a).

Use of rigid and aggregate classifications

The area classifications that exist, such as Mosaic or Acorn, characterise areas by their dominant characteristic. That means that minority populations within the areas may remain invisible. When the characterisation is significantly based on consumer data or marketing data derived from large retailers and financial institutions, there may be issues about not reflecting users of specialist goods and services used by specific communities (Experian, 2010b).

Another problem occurs in relation to cohesion when aggregate categories are used. The Census category of 'Black African' includes a huge range of communities. The experience and socioeconomic status of Somalis and Zimbabweans are very different, but they are often analysed as part of a single group (Mitton and Aspinall, 2009).

Gaps

As Tuke (2008) and the Equality and Human Rights Commission (EHRC, 2009) show, major gaps result from the focus on ethnicity in work on inequality and cohesion and other dimensions are neglected, including:

- disabled people;
- lesbian, gay, bisexual and transgender people;
- carers;
- specific areas of wellbeing;
- objective measures of health;
- physical and legal security; and
- post-school information about young people.[2]

How the data are analysed

As a result of underlying problems, pragmatic 'fixes' have been used that perversely can cause other problems; these include using data that are not 'fit for purpose', using data inappropriately and making unjustified inferences from the data:

Flawed analytical techniques

The way the data are analysed is often flawed; for instance the presence of high proportions of Somali young people and high levels of recorded crime are assumed to mean that Somalis are victims or perpetrators of crime.[3] As Simpson shows, the size of a geographical area determines the result you get; it follows that inferences must necessarily be conditioned by the geography selected.[4]

Using qualitative data as a substitute for robust quantitative data

Qualitative research and bespoke local surveys overcome some of these problems and they have immense value in their own right. However, they are often small-scale and (one-off) snapshots. Much of the research on smaller or more recent Black, minority ethnic and refugee communities has been qualitative – often as a result of the invisibility of such communities in official statistics. A review of research on the Somali community (published as long ago as 2004) illustrates this over-reliance on qualitative and one-off surveys (Harris, 2004). This is also true in relation to lesbian, gay, bisexual and transgender communities (Tuke, 2008).

One-dimensional and static categories that homogenise people

As Fuller and Simpson both note, complex multiple and dynamic identities are ignored, for example 'race' may have dimensions of ethnicity, faith, migration, appearance and language as well as intersections with age, sex, disability, income and wealth.

The consequences

The result of all these problems is that planning and analysis are seriously hindered and possibly incorrect in the detail. Resources and initiatives may be poorly targeted and wasted as a consequence. What constitutes success and failure of interventions in policy terms may be contested, but even if that were not an issue, what is being measured may not be relevant or valid. In the absence of robust data on needs, impact or mechanism, agencies may simply not act (Audit Commission, 2008, 2009).

Can the situation be improved?

Most of the flaws identified in previous sections are well known, but there is a widespread assumption that they are unavoidable – that there is no alternative. We argue that there are opportunities to address many (but not all) of these challenges. Our methodology – called Neighbourhood Knowledge Management (*nkm*) – has been in development and use for over 10 years and has been employed by numerous local authorities and the NHS.

The Neighbourhood Knowledge Management approach

nkm uses the following:

Local administrative data at household level

Administrative data are the data collected by councils, primary care trusts and other public agencies in order to operate public services. As almost all of these datasets have addresses for individuals, it is possible to use the Local Land and Property Gazetteers (LLPGs), which all English and Welsh local authorities are required to maintain (Scotland and Northern Ireland have separate arrangements), to assign a unique geo-referenced identifier to every household – a barcode based on Eastings and Northings.[5] Although conceptually simple, there may be technical, legal and ethical issues in using such data, depending on the context and the data owner.

A wide variety of indicators of economic and social wellbeing

There are literally thousands of data fields contained in local administrative datasets that could be better used. They include items such as age, sex, ethnicity, languages spoken, migration status, disability, household status, proxies for wealth (Council Tax band) and poverty (free school meal take-up and Council Tax benefits) and housing tenure.

Contemporary data

Most of the datasets are updated annually but some more frequently, for example the General Practitioner (GP) Register is updated quarterly and the School Census is updated three times a year.

A data-linking arrangement that can be added to and updated

Because data-linking is done through geo-referencing, data can be added or removed as new information becomes available: for instance, if someone moves, their status changes or an event happens. It is therefore also possible to do time-series analysis or to change the units of analysis such as age group, neighbourhood definition, time period or population denominator.

New analytical techniques

Handling millions of data items and many variables requires sophisticated data handling techniques. These cover the basic integration of datasets, an operation that requires address- and person-matching algorithms, through to techniques to measure the 'penalty' endured by different population groups experiencing similar events for an Equality Impact Assessment. One of the most useful tools we have developed is the 'risk ladder'. This measures the probability of events occurring either with different combinations of specific factors and/or by the number of factors that are impacting, although it does not imply causality. Risk ladders can be applied with total flexibility to any meaningful geographical unit so that inequalities both between and within communities can be compared.

Examples include the probability of events occurring such as being a victim or accused of a criminal offence, being on benefits, or differences in levels of access to services (for example distance from a GP practice, waiting times, opening hours and cost of a journey). Using such techniques one can, for example, examine groups of people that are similar in all other respects apart from, say, ethnicity or poverty, and then explore whether their access to, or take-up of, services differs or if they are more prone to certain outcomes such as low school attainment and so on. Where outcomes differ they may provide the springboard for further queries and analyses, for example are the differences simply a spatial phenomenon due to where people live or is it more fundamental than that, perhaps indicative of exclusion (for example imposed, self-imposed or institutional) or suggestive of a lack of cohesion within or between groups?

Mapping risk

Geographic Information Systems (GIS) is used to map risk at the household, neighbourhood or other geographical level. Knowing the spatial distribution of risk and exposure to risk is valuable for estimating need and targeting resources, identifying gaps and so on. Maps, risk ladders and other visualisation techniques provide valuable tools for synthesising, simplifying and hence interpreting local data with timely accuracy to any-sized geographical shape or unit.

Administrative data and cohesion

In 2009, the *nkm* team were commissioned by a consortium of London local authorities to assist them in developing their work on cohesion using administrative data in a project called *London Excels*. The idea, conceived by the Government Office for London and funded by the Department for Communities and Local Government (DCLG), is to help the authorities better tell their 'story of place', recognising that many areas are unable to counter myths or offer robust information on how areas are changing, who exactly lives there and how different populations interact with each other and with public services. Each local authority is receiving resources to help with a case study as well as support in setting up or extending structures and processes to further the use of administrative data for work on cohesion, equalities and human rights. Only one of the boroughs has an integrated *nkm* database already in existence, so the project is demonstrating what can and cannot be done without such a database.

Below we illustrate work done by the *nkm* team both for *London Excels* and in other projects to show what can be done with administrative data to support work on cohesion.

Accurately estimating population flows

One of the more challenging tasks in measuring populations is to encompass migration (international and internal). Births data contain country of birth of both parents as well as information on occupations. They are therefore potentially an important source of administrative data, allowing migration and socioeconomic data to be looked at together. Death registration also contains data on country of birth, and occupation.

However, there can be barriers to gathering the necessary data at the local level (ONS, 2008) with sufficient accuracy and granularity (Finney and Simpson, 2009). New National Insurance numbers and GP registration can provide useful data on international migration (ONS, 2009a, 2009b; DWP, 2010b). National Insurance information is not available below local authority level but GP registration is. (For a comparison of what they show at district level, see LGA, 2008.) Von Ahn (2006) and Mayhew and Waples (2009) show how GP registration data can be used to estimate total populations incorporating migration. Overall, the *nkm* study showed a confirmed population of Newham of 270,091 at 30 June 2007, 20,491 more than the equivalent Office for National Statistics (ONS) mid-year estimates. It also looked at the 'unconfirmed' population of about 15,000 who are people living at 'addresses' that were not recorded in Newham's Local Land and Property Gazetteer but who appear on other databases, particularly the GP Register, and showed that many of the unconfirmed population were international migrants using 'Flag 4' on the GP Register. This is a marker used in the Patient Register Data system to identify individuals, on their first registration with a GP, whose previous address was outside the UK and who have spent more than three months abroad (ONS, 2009a, 2009b). By confirming their residency in the borough with other administrative data, the study identified that between 4 and 5% of the population (12,000 people) came into the borough from abroad each year but only just over 40% remained resident in the borough after one year, equating approximately to an average stay of around 14 months. The *London Excels* project has also given advice on using administrative data to identify 'landing zones' within boroughs where international migrants arrive and also the type of properties in which migrants live (tenure, Council Tax band and whether [always] designated 'Residential').

Identifying 'hidden' communities

There are many groups that self-identify or who are identified as distinct but are not generally visible in official statistics such as the Somali, Turkish, Greek (and whether either are Cypriot), Irish or Charedi (Ultra Orthodox Jewish) communities. The needs of such communities may be overlooked, particularly when resource allocation or performance indicators are centrally driven (as in the NHS).

This issue was tackled by the *nkm* project to estimate the size of the population in the London Borough of Hackney. The council was concerned that the 2001 Census did not count or identify separately the Charedi community in Hackney. As a community that does not generally live in social housing or send their children to state schools, two major sources of administrative data (landlord databases and the School Census) could not be used. However, a telephone and address directory of the Charedi community was publicly available. By combining this with the GP Register and Council Tax Benefit data, the study was able to provide an overall Charedi population figure (about 7% of Hackney's population), its age, sex and household structure (Mayhew and Harper, 2008).

Multiple identities and affiliations

As Finney and Simpson (2009, p 30) state, '[i]t is rare in statistical practice to measure the richness of multiple affiliations'. Commentators frequently equate migration, ethnicity and religion. Administrative data can be used to reflect multiple identities encompassing, for example, ethnicity, migration status, household status (for example single parent or three generation), income and wealth, educational attainment, languages spoken and religion.

In one authority we have been able to look at patterns of where children live and go to school in relation to the religion, language and ethnicity of their school pupils. We were able to analyse whether these three constructions of 'identity' converge or diverge and also the degree to which schools are more or less segregated than where the pupils live. Based on primary school pupils attending state schools, it appears that children are more segregated at school by religion than they are by language or ethnicity or by where they live (unpublished). Burgess et al (2003) and the Department for Children, Schools and Families (2008) have also used Pupil Level Annual School Census data to look at school integration but neither has been able to look at the religion of the pupils.

Data about ethnicity, language and religion are not available or easily imputable for most adults who do not live in a household with children attending state schools. For this population, name algorithms can provide an adequate but imperfect substitute. There are a number available: *Nam Pehchan, Sangra,* Experian *Origins, Distinctive Jewish Names* and *Origins* from CASA/Experian (Cummins et al, 1999; Warwick Medical School, 2005; Macfarlane et al, 2007; Cheshire et al, 2009). Identification based on names has been shown to have a high degree of accuracy, although there are some errors, with more false positives than false negatives. *nkm* uses name recognition in conjunction with datasets in which ethnicity, language or religion is stipulated or partly stipulated. This works either in broad groups or at specific country of origin level depending on the degree of uniqueness of individual names: 80-90% accuracy is typically achievable by these methods

Understanding population dynamics

Change and the perception of change are central to many of the tensions in local communities. What demographers call population 'churn' is part of that change. Administrative sources such as the School Census, National Insurance registrations and the use made of translation and interpretation services can give 'early' indications of communities arriving or departing. Triangulation of sources is often necessary and may show different patterns (LGA, 2008).

Quantitative and 'geological' approaches to demography that characterise 'phases' of settlement are problematic, often with groups not counted until long after they have settled and are assumed to have 'flown'. In East London, Huguenot, Jewish and Bangladeshi 'ages' are very frequently identified. Thus, Bangladeshis are generally reported as having settled in East London from the 1950s and 1960s, with only stories of individuals before that. The availability of the 19th-century Census online allows the documentation of early settlers more easily (Ullah and Eversley, 2010). However, it is not straightforward to use individuals' names or place of birth, as national boundaries have changed as individuals' legal status has changed or attitudes to and conventions about names within and outside the community have changed. Work using *nkm* in the London Borough of Brent in 2007 studied the change in population by small area and household at two points in time. The results showed areas of high and low churn, rising and falling population, demographic and income characteristics of leavers and joiners, and the balance between internal and external migration.

Looking at the interaction of material and social factors

Much of the analysis of cohesion that has been carried out categorises people by their ethnicity, religion or migration status. Factors such as poverty/wealth, housing tenure or type of housing and household size are not taken into account. However, as Finney and Simpson (2009, p 80) point out, the degree to which the UK is 'overcrowded' depends on how we choose to live: in single-person households, in houses or in flats. If we are to understand why there may be competition, or perceptions of competition, for social goods, administrative databases that provide wider socioeconomic information are invaluable.

Equalities Impact Assessment

Public authorities are required to assess the equalities impact of major policy initiatives before enacting them. Administrative data are very valuable for doing this. In the London Borough of Barking and Dagenham, the *nkm* team were asked to do an Equalities Impact Assessment (EIA) on regeneration proposals for the Gascoigne estate. Being able to look at the population at household level was necessary because ward and Super Output Area boundaries would have included dwellings not affected by the regeneration proposals and would have prevented a comparison of the impact of different phases of the proposals. It was also essential to use very up-to-date information about the population (age, sex and numbers in households). The perception that 'official' figures do not reflect the numbers of recent migrants or where they live has been an important part of the local political discourse. It was important to have ethnicity information and information about disabled people. The results of the EIA suggested that generally the regeneration plan would be fair to all sections of the community. However, it threw up some suggestions that some services to disabled people might not be accessed equally by all sections of the community (Neighbourhood Knowledge Manager, 2010).

Issues and barriers

Administrative data can be used in a number of ways, including those outlined above, but there are challenges in using the data.

Confidentiality and information governance: freedom of information

The basic permission required to use administrative data for the kinds of purpose outlined here is contained in the Data Protection Act 1998, section 33 (OPSI, 2010), which says that data can be used for research purposes and that:

> This includes statistical or historical purposes provided:
>
> (a) that the data are not processed to support measures or decisions with respect to particular individuals, and
> (b) that the data are not processed in such a way that substantial damage or substantial distress is, or is likely to be, caused to any data subject.

There are legal restrictions on the use of specific datasets. NHS data are discussed below but there are also rules on sources such as the births and deaths figures (ONS, 2008a), the Council Tax Register (ICO, 2007a) and the Electoral Register (ICO, 2007b). There is an argument that the state (in all its forms) holds a great deal of data about people living in the UK, which people have a right to expect to be used positively for the benefit of the community and to inform the best use of resources, while making sure that the data are not used in relation to decisions on individuals. Some people have used a freedom of information argument to obtain aggregated information about populations and public services (Brooke, 2008). The coalition government's programme includes a new 'right to data', so that government-held datasets can be requested and used by the public and then used on a regular basis, and also a plan to extend the scope of the Freedom of Information Act 2000 (HM Government, 2010).

One of the difficulties with the legal situation on sharing data is that the decision to share information is frequently left to the council and NHS officials responsible, who may not have any tested legal advice. In a situation where case law is evolving, officials will err on the side of caution.

National datasets

So far it has not been possible to obtain datasets concerning benefits administered by central government at person-identifiable level (they are available at Super Output Area level) although the situation is evolving (eg DWP, 2010a). The Statistics and Registration Service Act 2007 is creating opportunities for data sharing and data linkage, which makes the possibility of obtaining national datasets for local data linkage more likely.

Specific issues with NHS data

The structures, processes and legislative framework for using NHS data have been changing over the last few years. The present position is that the use of personal data is covered by the Health and Social Care Act 2008, section 251. The administration of the rules, since January 2009, is by the National Information Governance Board for Health and Social Care (NIGB) through its Ethics and Confidentiality Committee.

Section 251 support is required if you wish to access patient-identifiable information without the patient's consent. Section 251 approval is *not* required for local clinical audit as long as:

- the audit is conducted by one of the organisations that have delivered the patient's care or treatment;
- the audit is carried out in accordance with clinical governance guidelines; and
- it has been approved by the NHS trust's medical director and Caldicott guardian.[6]

The reason for using the information has to be for the purpose of improving patient care or in the public interest; it has to be for a medical purpose that cannot be achieved using de-identified data and used in a situation where seeking consent for the use of identifiable data is not practicable. 'Medical purpose' is broadly defined as activities carried out for the purposes of preventative medicine, medical diagnosis, medical research, the provision of care and treatment, and the management of health and social care services. Patient identifiers include the name, address, postcode, date of birth, date of death and NHS number (NIGB, 2009).

nkm projects are generally approved by medical directors and Caldicott guardians because they are for the purposes of preventative medicine (public health) and the management of health and social care and it is not feasible to get consent from the individuals. Person-identifiable data are pseudonomised before they are matched with other datasets and the integrated dataset is anonymised. The NHS organisation (usually a primary care trust) is normally a partner in the project and often the member of the *nkm* team responsible for pseudonomising the data is made an honorary consultant at the trust.

Integrating administrative and other data

Data derived from administrative datasets can be compared with that derived from official statistics and surveys. In the population estimations that the authors have done for various local authorities, we have compared mid-year estimates produced by the ONS (and the Greater London Authority). In work on access to public services, we have been able to combine data from a household survey with administrative data. In the cohesion context, a desirable goal would be to integrate information from Place surveys (DCLG, 2008b) into a database compiled from administrative data. Whether it is possible or not will often depend on the conditions under which permission to collect the survey data was given by the participants and by agencies that supplied, for example, names and adsdresses.

Reliance on quantitative data

The quantitative data available from administrative data frequently focus on spatial proximity, not on whether positive or negative relationships exist. It is not clear that having a neighbour, colleague or fellow pupil from a different background necessarily leads to (positive) interaction or that not having such a person excludes the possibility of (positive) interaction. However, geography is always a factor at some scale. The work on ethnic diversity described earlier tries to address this by combining perception data from survey and Census material (Bécares et al, 2009; Stafford et al, 2009).

Conclusion

Cohesion policy and practice – particularly when cohesion within, as well as between, communities is to be addressed – needs good evidence to support interventions. As Lang and Heasman (2004) say in the context of food, policy is frequently made in the absence of evidence or despite the evidence. Whatever the aims of policy in relation to cohesion are, there is a need for data to understand:

- needs;
- drivers;
- mechanisms (how interventions actually work); and
- the impact of interventions.

Administrative data have been identified as a major tool for the future of sociology and social policy (Savage and Burrows, 2007, 2009; Webber, 2009). The example of Neighbourhood Knowledge Management shows that this is an immediate and practical possibility for addressing important issues.

Notes
[1] Mosaic is a commercially produced dataset, which categorises people, households and areas into almost 70 types.

[2] Note: there are gaps in pre-school information too.

[3] The ecological fallacy: assuming that individuals necessarily reflect the characteristics of an area, for example that if an area has poverty and high crime, poor people are the victims or perpetrators.

[4] The modified areal unit problem: associations between factors can appear or disappear according to the size of the spatial unit being analysed.

[5] Like an Ordnance Survey grid reference or points on a graph, Eastings are often called 'x' coordinates and Northings 'y' coordinates.

[6] Caldicott guardians are senior staff in the NHS and social services appointed to protect patient information (DH, 2008).

References

Audit Commission (2008) *Equalities Impact Assessment of Comprehensive Area Assessment: Joint inspectorate proposals for consultation – summer 2008*, London: Audit Commission, www.audit-commission.gov.uk/SiteCollectionDocuments/Downloads/EIAofCAA.pdf

Audit Commission (2009) *Comprehensive Area Assessment: Equalities Impact Assessment of the second trial stage of Comprehensive Area Assessment*, London: Audit Commission, www.audit-commission.gov.uk/SiteCollectionDocuments/Consultation/200902CAAEIAOfTheTrialStage.pdf

Bécares, L., Nazroo, J. and Stafford, M. (2009) 'The buffering effects of ethnic density on experienced racism and health', *Health & Place*, vol 15, no 3, pp 700-8.

Blair, T. (2006) Speech on multiculturalism and integration, 8 December, www.number10.gov.uk/Page10563

Boydell, J., van Os, J., McKenzie, K., Allardyce, J., Goel, R., McCreadie, R.G. and Murray, R.M. (2001) 'Incidence of schizophrenia in ethnic minorities in London: ecological study into interactions with environment', *British Medical Journal*, vol 323, no 7325, p 1336.

Broadwood, J. and Sugden, N. (2008) *Community cohesion impact assessment and community conflict prevention tool*, London: DCLG.

Brooke, H. (2008) 'Met keeps crime statistics under lock and key', *The Guardian*, 17 July, www.guardian.co.uk/technology/2008/jul/17/freeourdata.privacy

Burgess, S., Johnston, R. and Wilson, R. (2003) *School segregation in multi-ethnic England*, Working Paper Series No 03/092, Bristol: CMPO, www.bristol.ac.uk/cmpo/publications/papers/2003/wp92.pdf

Cheshire, J., Mateos, P. and Longley, P. (2009) *Family names as indicators of Britain's changing regional geography*, Working Papers Series 149, London: UCL, www.casa.ucl.ac.uk/working_papers/paper149.pdf

Cummins, C., Winter, H., Cheng, K.K., Maric, R., Silcocks, P. and Varghese, C. (1999) 'An assessment of the Nam Pehchan computer program for the identification of names of South Asian ethnic origin', *Journal of Public Health Medicine*, vol 21, no 4, pp 401-6.

DCLG (Department for Communities and Local Government) (2008a) *National indicators for local authorities and local authority partnerships: Handbook of definitions*, www.communities.gov.uk/publications/localgovernment/finalnationalindicators

DCLG (2008b) *The Place Survey Questionnaire*, London: DCLG, www. communities.gov.uk/documents/localgovernment/doc/880053.doc

DCLG (2009) *2007-08 Citizenship Survey community cohesion topic report*, London: DCLG, www.info4local.gov.uk/documents/ publications/1320061

Department for Children, Schools and Families (DCSF) (2008) *The composition of schools in England*, Statistical Bulletin, London: DCSF.

DH (Department of Health) (2008) *NHS Caldicott guardians*, London: DH, www.dh.gov.uk/en/Managingyourorganisation/ Informationpolicy/Patientconfidentialityandcaldicottguardians/ DH_4100563

DWP (Department for Work and Pensions) (2010a) *Access to non-disclosive DWP data and guidance on data sharing with DWP*, London: DWP, http://research.dwp.gov.uk/asd/data_guide.asp

DWP (2010b) *National Insurance number allocations to adult overseas nationals entering the UK to September 2009*, London: DWP, http:// statistics.dwp.gov.uk/asd/asd1/tabtools/nino_alloc_summ_tables_ feb10.xls

EHRC (Equality and Human Rights Commission) (2009) *Data gaps table – England*, Manchester: EHRC, www.equalityhumanrights.com/ uploaded_files/emf/datagaps_england.xls

Experian (2010a) *Case study: Tower Hamlets PCT: Encouraging more efficient use of A&E services*, Nottingham: Experian, www.experian. co.uk/www/pages/downloads/case_studies/Tower_Hamlets_V4.pdf

Experian (2010b) *Mosaic United Kingdom*, Nottingham: Experian, http://strategies.experian.co.uk/Products/Demographic%20 Classifications/~/media/Files/Brochures/Mosaic%20UK%20 2009%20brochure.ashx

Finney N. and Simpson, L. (2009) *'Sleepwalking into segregation'? Challenging the myths about race and migration*, Bristol: The Policy Press.

Harris, H. (2004) *The Somali community in the UK: What we know and how we know it*, London: ICAR.

HM Government (2010) *The coalition: Our programme for government*, London: Cabinet Office, www.cabinetoffice.gov.uk/media/409088/ pfg_coalition.pdf

House of Commons Treasury Committee (2008a) *Counting the population: Written evidence, House of Commons 183-Vol II*, London: The Stationery Office, www.parliament.the-stationery-office.com/ pa/cm200708/cmselect/cmtreasy/183/183ii.pdf

House of Commons Treasury Committee (2008b) *Eleventh report: How the population is counted*, London: The Stationery Office, www. parliament.the-stationery-office.com/pa/cm200708/cmselect/ cmtreasy/183/18305.htm#a17

ICO (Information Commissioner's Office) (2007a) *Technical guidance note: The use of personal information held for collecting and administering Council Tax*, Wilmslow: ICO, www.ico.gov.uk/upload/documents/ library/data_protection/detailed_specialist_guides/use_of_personal_ information_held_for_collecting_and_admini%E2%80%A6.pdf

ICO (2007b) *Your personal information and the electoral register*, Wilmslow: ICO, www.ico.gov.uk/upload/documents/library/data_protection/ practical_application/sale_of_the_electoral%20register_its_%20 your%20information.pdf

Lang, T. and Heasman, M. (2004) *Food wars: The global battle for mouths, minds and markets*, London: Earthscan.

LGA (Local Government Association) (2008) *Where have recent in-migrants gone?*, London: LGA, www.lga.gov.uk/lga/aio/1098476

Macfarlane, G.J., Lunt, M., Palmer, B., Afzal, C., Silman, A.J. and Esmail, A. (2007) 'Determining aspects of ethnicity amongst persons of South Asian origin: the use of a surname-classification programme (Nam Pehchan)', *Public Health*, vol 121, no 3, pp 231-6.

Mayhew, L. and Harper G. (2008) *Estimating and profiling the population of Hackney*, London: Mayhew Harper Associates.

Mayhew, L. and Waples, S. (2009) *The London Borough of Newham: Counting the confirmed and unconfirmed population*, London: Mayhew Harper Associates.

Mitton, L. and Aspinall (2009) UPTAP workshop, Leeds, 24-25 March, www.uptap.net/project26.html

Modood, T., Berthoud, R., Lakey, J., Nazroo, J., Smith, P., Virdee, S. and Beishon, S. (1997) *Ethnic minorities in Britain: Diversity and disadvantage: The fourth national survey of ethnic minorities*, London: PSI.

National Information Governance Board for Health and Social Care (NIGB) (2009) *ECC frequently asked questions*, London: NIGB, www. nigb.nhs.uk/ecc/eccfrequently

Neighbourhood Knowledge Management (2011) *Equality impact assessment for the Gascoigne Estate in the London Borough of Barking and Dagenham*, www.nkm.org.uk/flyers/BDequalityassessment.pdf

ODPM (Office of the Deputy Prime Minister) (2005) *State of the English cities report*, London: ODPM.

ONS (Office for National Statistics) (2004) *2001 Census, local authority population studies: Full report*, London: ONS, www.statistics.gov.uk/ downloads/theme_population/LAStudy_FullReport.pdf

ONS (2005) *International Passenger Survey – UK*, www.statistics.gov. uk/STATBASE/Source.asp?vlnk=348&More=Y

ONS (2008) *Briefing note: ONS policy on protecting confidentiality within birth and death statistics* (revised 2008), London: ONS, www.statistics. gov.uk/downloads/theme_health/ConfidentialityBirth&Death.pdf

ONS (2009a) *Flag 4 GP registrations by local authority*, London: ONS, www.statistics.gov.uk/downloads/theme_population/Background_ notes.doc

ONS (2009b) *Flag 4 GP registrations by local authority 2001-2008 data tables*, London: ONS, www.statistics.gov.uk/downloads/theme_ population/Flag4_GP_Registration_by_local_authority.xls

OPSI (Office of Public Sector Information) (2010) *Data Protection Act 1998 section 33*, London: OPSI, www.opsi.gov.uk/Acts/Acts1998/ ukpga_19980029_en_5#pt4-l1g33

Phillips, D. (2006) '"Parallel lives"? Challenging discourses of British Muslim self-segregation', *Environment and Planning D: Society and Space*, vol 24, no1, pp 25-40.

Phillips, T. (2005) 'After 7/7: sleepwalking to segregation', Speech at the Manchester Council for Community Relations, 22 September.

Ratcliffe, P., Newman, I. and Fuller, C. (2009) *Community cohesion: A literature and data review*, Warwick: Business School, www2.warwick. ac.uk/fac/soc/wbs/research/lgc/latest/community_cohesion_- _a_literature_and_data_review_.pdf

Savage, M. and Burrows, R. (2007) 'The coming crisis of empirical sociology', *Sociology*, vol 41, no 5, pp 885-99.

Savage, M. and Burrows, R. (2009) 'Some further reflections on the coming crisis of empirical sociology', *Sociology*, vol 43, no 4, pp 762-72.

Stafford, M., Becares, L. and Nazroo, J. (2009) 'Objective and perceived ethnic density and health: findings from a United Kingdom general population survey', *American Journal of Epidemiology*, vol 170, no 4, pp 484-93.

Statistics Commission (2003) *The 2001 Census in Westminster: Interim report: Report no 15*, Newport: Statistics Commission, www.statscom. org.uk/uploads/files/reports/Census%202001.pdf

Tuke, A. (2008) *Measuring equality at a local level*, London: IDA, www. idea.gov.uk/idk/aio/8873228

Ullah, A.A. and Eversley, J. (2010) *Bengalis in London's East End*, Swadhinata Trust, www.swadhinata.org.uk/files/Bengalis%20in%20 London%27s%20East%20End%20Book.pdf

UK Statistics Authority (2009) *Monitoring report 4: Interim report: Migration statistics*, Newport: UK Statistics Authority, www.statisticsauthority. gov.uk/reports---correspondence/reports/migration-statistics--interim-report.pdf

von Ahn, M. (2006) *Newham's population and the Office of National Statistics mid-year estimates*, www.coventry.ac.uk/researchnet/content/1/c4/17/99/Newham%20Pop%20and%20MYE%27s.pdf

Warwick Medical School (2007) *Identifying ethnicity: Comparison of two computer programmes*, Warwick: Warwick Medical School, Warwick University, www2.warwick.ac.uk/fac/med/research/csri/ethnicityhealth/aspects_diversity/identifying_ethnicity/

Webber, R. (2009) 'Response to "the coming crisis of empirical sociology": an outline of the research potential of administrative and transactional data', *Sociology*, vol 43, pp 169-78.

SIX

Assessing the impact of social cohesion initiatives in a media age: methodological and theoretical considerations

Roger Grimshaw and Kate Smart

Introduction

The main aim of this chapter is to develop methodological and theoretical thinking about how to assess cohesion initiatives in an age of heightened and diverse media communications. It will discuss how the concept of 'community' can be socially understood within a global and local social context in which complex communication systems shape its meanings. It will use an illustrative case study, drawing on the methods and findings of a specific research project concerned with aspects of cohesion in a large metropolis – London. The study showed how newspaper representations of asylum constructed images of migration that were differently received by members of communities and how particular groups were vulnerable to the influence of negative press images. The conclusions indicate that any assessment of strategies for increasing cohesion must take into account the ways in which communication flows influence perceptions and attitudes.

Assessment of a social initiative will always depend on adopting a defensible framework of assumptions about its possible impact: using metaphors of 'healing', for example, these would include an understanding of the 'sickness', the nature of the 'patient', the ways in which 'remedies' take effect, and of the indicators of improvement. In Chapter Two, the theory of change was seen as a key point of departure for reflections on evaluation. Without a robust and valid set of such assumptions, an evaluation will be little more than a collection of data that readers will have to interpret for themselves. The methods of assessment must be directed by an interpretive framework that tells the researchers where to seek information, how to construct measures and what to make of the responses. In particular, the framework should take account of an initiative's full social context and its meanings to the various publics for which it has importance and relevance.

Critical thinking about 'community'

The policy agenda associated with community cohesion initiatives has been pragmatic in the sense that it derived its understanding of communities from the experience of overt problems, chiefly manifest through 'extremism', disorder and conflict. It then sought to identify the boundaries and constitution of communities that to a lesser or greater degree could be situated near or around the problems. The aim of policy was therefore to effect some kind of reconciliation or healing process that in engaging communities would avert the likelihood of conflict. Initiatives were designed to promote common values, to improve mutual understanding, and – in their social aspects – to create stronger shared bases for social participation and therefore for greater common interests to evolve.

However, the problematic nature of the 'community cohesion project' is revealed by three fundamental dimensions of the social nexus that it seeks to address. These have to do with the geopolitical aspect of community, the structural contexts of community relations and the embedding of community in diverse communication systems.

Connecting the local and the geopolitical

A community is not necessarily, or only, a geographical entity. It is not realistic to conceive of 'communities' in the United Kingdom (UK) as simply 'neighbours' occupying a common space; they appear as distinctive groupings existing in a network of identities, which goes beyond local or even national boundaries (Vertovec, 2002). Descriptions of groups frequently speak of boundaries not tied to locality, but to nations, regions, ethnic affiliations and transnational forms of identity such as religion. The localisation of community can be misleading in tracing problems only to their local manifestations and diverting attention to their wider, geopolitical significance – a point emphasised in Chapter Three of this volume by Crispian Fuller.

In the case study that forms a major reference point for our discussion, it was a geopolitical issue – the question of asylum – and its implications for the UK that ultimately led to expressions of anxiety about cohesion and raised fears of social conflict among officials.

The structural contexts of community relations: markets, states and households

Relations between groups defined as communities are embedded in the ever-more fluctuating workings of markets across regions and nations. The flows of migration are linked to the operation of unequal markets that demand types of labour and prescribe how these will be met. At the same time, the regulation of residence and nationality by states prioritises citizens over visitors and other incomers in accessing opportunities and resources. The reproduction of children and families is affected by markets that privilege the young and able worker, and by regulations that exercise influence and control over family unity and affiliations across national boundaries (Cohen, 2001).

The combined effect of markets, state and reproductive controls produces a shifting hierarchy of inequalities in which a range of incomers with widely differing resources share a contested terrain with the gradations of more or less established citizens. It is arguably this jostling competitive dynamic that underlies deeper social anxieties running through all kinds of social encounters. Although anxiety can be felt by incomers, any anxieties of established citizens tend to command greater attention. This is a result of power inequalities that accord precedence to existing residents (even by small degrees), not as a result of any factual undermining of their position by immigration (Dustmann et al, 2003). In a diverse urban context, a history of immigration produces a sedimentation or layering of power, reflected in research showing how, among many sections of the population, despite differences in the times of their 'arrival', attitudes towards the most recent migrants carry common currents of anxiety and concern (Barrow Cadbury Trust, 2008). In the case study, we will go on to see in what ways the perceived distribution of resources and services in localities played a part in influencing attitudes to asylum.

Communications and communities

Communities can be defined in terms that suit policy makers, as entities with characteristics that make political or administrative sense for a time, but are later changed. Thus, in time, we have seen a substantial revision of the Census categories to include a range of British identities, with reference to a cluster of originating communities and regions in the world. It is evident that the introduction of such terms arises from a political context in which identity is recognised to be complex and, at least potentially, self-defined. However, the degree to which any such categorisation will be acceptable remains problematic: evolving identities may be resistant to ready-made classifications, however sensitively defined (Ipsos MORI, 2007).

The dependence of terminology on context and on political language brings out another fundamental dimension of the problem – the embedding of 'community' in multiple systems of communication that are not necessarily shared or aligned.

As well as not necessarily being shared, the communication systems that refer to community are distinct and uneven. First, there is a key distinction between 'public forums' and 'media' activity. While the former engage parts of the population in direct discussions, the latter is more frequent, more widely accessible and by its nature a matter of record. Public forums can include state and official communications, discussions in civil society organisations, campaigning activity (for example around immigration) and everyday talk in places where community members congregate or make contact. Media activity encompasses commercial media (press, radio and television), community media (newsletters and so on), advertising and internet 'chat'. It is possible to produce a basic matrix of communication systems as in Table 6.1.

Table 6.1: Communication systems

Public forums	Media
State and official communications	Corporate and commercial media
Civil society – faith and voluntary sector	Community media
Campaigns	Advertising
Everyday talk	Internet 'chat'

The sheer diversity of all these communications is evident: it suggests that the divergent structures and accessibility of such communication systems pose a problem for understanding what their outputs mean for an assessment of community or social cohesion. How do all these different processes affect something that might be called cohesion? Do these systems themselves contribute to a singular or agreed definition of cohesion – or are they helping to reproduce incommensurate or contradictory definitions?

Communication systems

The communications domains are unequal in several respects. The large-scale and typically commercial media form a dominant communications system in respect of other media, notwithstanding the rise of the internet. The media, and in particular the press, has been influential in constructing the community cohesion field, especially in producing widely consumed images of changing communities and their connections with a wider international context.

The press takes on a major role in the sense-making process because its information is widely and regularly disseminated. Moreover, the process of change has been dramatised by imagery that reproduces itself through the prioritisation of news items according to an editorial agenda and vision. The sight of 'militancy' or 'extremism', for example, becomes familiar through headlines and photography as well as repeated descriptive terms.

National press outlets are important because community changes are widespread and the issues are perceived to have implications for national identity. The local press also plays a key part because it is one of the few means by which we find a body of information relevant to particular community changes. In this sense, the press has been a major conduit for making sense of community identities and relations. Community media, such as newsletters, will be unable to challenge the reach of the corporate and commercial media, although the growing significance of the internet has opened up a new frontier in communication activity. Websites and social media, such as Twitter, have created innovative structures for networking communications.

A recent illustration shows the press's role in framing social cohesion issues. In a newspaper report about the recent banning of Islam4UK (*The Daily Telegraph*, 2010), an organisation allegedly linked to the controversial figure of Omar Bakri Mohammed, it becomes clear how the internet is perceived as an opportunity for 'extremists' to rally support. While noting that the Al-Muhajiroun organisation had been banned, the paper went on:

> Islam4UK soon sprang up in its place and offers Bakri a platform to deliver his lectures over the internet…. One article on the site even calls for Buckingham Place [sic] to be turned into a mosque once this goal is achieved, showing a mock-up picture of what it might look like.

We do not need to discus the merits or otherwise of particular political organisations to see how important can be the role of widely circulated newspapers in constructing and disseminating a vivid image of 'extremism'. An organisation that uses the internet to spread its alternative message can be regarded as challenging not simply a policy establishment but also by implication the hegemony of dominant communications media. Hence, cohesion strategies in an era of diffuse technological media have to take account of complex communication processes that will influence the reception of messages about cohesion.

Statements by politicians and officials are accorded authority in the public forums, and while discussions in civil society organisations can be significant in drawing together group members, they are not especially accessible to the broad mass of the population. Everyday talk in public forums (leisure venues, pubs, places of work and so on) functions at a low level of visibility but crystallises commonsense public discourses that will vary across social categories of class, gender and so on. Everyday talk is also a vehicle that not only reflects personal and social experiences but also serves as a vehicle for generalisation that can form the basis of 'gossip' and 'rumour'. Everyday conversations may well draw on material disseminated by the media but the assumptions and concerns expressed in conversation 'filter' the impact of media representations in ways that we go on to demonstrate.

For evaluators and for community members alike, making sense of this new communications field has been challenging because it requires a shift in the organisation of communication and perceptual faculties. For all members of society, the question is posed: where do we go to update our information about the shape of communities, to discuss those issues and arrive at conclusions? For evaluators, the question becomes: how does the changing landscape of communications affect the methods and focus of research?

From theory to method

The outcomes of a communication strategy are defined within the terms of its aims and objectives, for example to increase accurate knowledge about communities and to reduce hostility. The evaluator seeks evidence of changes in levels of inaccurate knowledge or of hostile attitudes or intentions. Outcome evidence should be obtained by research with samples of the key audiences segmented in terms of their significance as representative of communities, by age, gender and so on.

At the same time, the outcome evidence should be plausibly linked to the public consumption of messages generated by the strategy; these messages may be directly produced as 'authorised' outputs, by local authorities, for example, or indirectly as part of local dialogues that have been facilitated through strategic support.[1] Without a clear assessment of the size and shape of available messages on a particular topic, it is impossible to determine where a particular message fits into the daily flow of communications accessible to the public.

The impact of communication strategies should be evaluated in terms of the extent to which they take into account the structure of relationships among the elements of communication systems. Thus, a particular communication can garner a wide audience if it is inserted in a widely consumed media outlet or a major public forum. In particular, media outlets speak to differentiated audiences that accord them degrees of credibility, and approach them with different sets of assumptions. It is crucial that the attitudes of consumers to those media outlets themselves are researched. Otherwise it becomes possible to overestimate the impact of a particular communication simply because it has been widely consumed.

The analysis of impact should therefore be conducted according to a model of message consumption that clearly establishes the extent of differentiated responses to widely disseminated messages and seeks to account for them through the audiences' evaluations of media and forums, and through eliciting their background assumptions.

The main case study of news media impact that follows illustrates these principles by developing a model of how press reports affected attitudes in London boroughs. It is important to recall that similar analysis can be conducted among smaller groups and communities; however, these should be conducted with reference to all the significant forms of message consumption and exchange among a particular community in order to locate precisely the influence of any particular message. Hence, a number of features should be included in the evaluation, as follows:

- strategic aims and objectives;
- messages described and located in the context of communication systems;
- audiences – reception, attitudes to media and forums, and assumptions;
- outcomes – knowledge, hostility and so on; and
- an interpretive model of message impact.

Measuring and evaluating information from communications media

Press structure

In order to monitor the major public communication processes, an evaluation should incorporate samples of the press and news media that stretch from the national to the city-wide and the local press. Once the sheer number of media outlets is appreciated, consideration of what constitutes a sufficient sample becomes challenging. In our national study of compliance with press guidelines (Smart et al, 2007), a total of 50 newspapers were studied, comprising 20 nationals (and Sunday equivalents), 22 regional and eight minority newspapers, reflecting the higher circulation press. However, the same study also showed some of the diversity within the press that may present some basis for purposive sampling on the basis of hypotheses.

Because the 'top circulation' press achieves the most population reach, national papers with the highest circulation should be included. Another reason for prioritising the national press would be the assessment that among them are newspapers that are more likely to publish significant coverage of cohesion issues. In our national study, the top six circulation dailies were the most frequent publishers of articles on asylum (Smart et al, 2007, p 56). Any understanding of a community's views could not be undertaken without a good sense of what the majority press was saying.

However, the regional, local and minority press are also important segments of the picture, with significant agendas that are influenced by editorial perspectives on the community readership. The local and regional press are likely to have an image of readers as members of communities. As one editor expressed it:

> "We are printing what we think is news and what our readers are interested in. I don't have a personal or political agenda; and nobody here does. If we wanted just to appeal to all the racist, right-wing bigots in the area, it wouldn't be a good policy because we'd alienate ourselves from most readers. We wouldn't survive. We want our readers to be everybody."

In our London study of press impacts on public attitudes, we sampled five national daily newspapers and their Sunday equivalents, two London-wide newspapers, two publications with minority ethnic group interest and a total of eight local papers (four for each borough where attitudes were studied in detail).

Monitoring

The period of monitoring should be selected according to the frequency of coverage that is expected. For example, in the London study, 137 articles were analysed over a three-week period. The purpose of the media monitoring element of the study was to provide detailed information on stories published about asylum seekers and refugees in a wide range of newspapers for the core period of the study – August and September 2003.

In particular, the media monitoring element explored the hypothesis that:

> Newspapers often present images of asylum seekers and refugees that contain language, photographs and graphics likely to give rise to feelings of fear of and hostility towards asylum seekers and refugees among their readers. This effect is compounded by inaccurate and unbalanced reporting.

At the same time as recording the content of information, our hypothesis demanded that we assessed this information for accuracy and balance. Where information was known to be accurate or inaccurate, this was highlighted by the researchers. Where accuracy could be established without additional research, an assessment was made of whether the information was provided by named sources, whose accuracy could be checked by readers. In the context of newspaper reporting, our view was that balance does not require neutrality; an article may express an opinion without being unbalanced, but balance does require that alternative views receive due coverage and background information is provided.

Given the volume of material generated in the monitoring period, we analysed the newspaper sample in two ways:

- a headline 'timeline' – a series of tables that listed headlines from all the relevant articles that appeared in the sample papers over two months; and
- content analysis of articles from a three-week period in August.

Findings

Using the criteria as carefully as possible, the study found clear evidence of negative, unbalanced and inaccurate reporting, most significantly in the national press that reported on asylum and refugee issues far more frequently than either the local or Black and minority ethnic press.

The main political parties – Labour and Conservative – dominated the political sources quoted in news stories, with the Liberal Democrats rarely quoted.[2] There was little reference made to information contained in UK asylum law or international instruments such as the Convention on the Rights of Refugees 1951, and nowhere was the Office of the United Nations High Commissioner for Refugees quoted.

The frequency of negative language was notable in the following examples.

- The words 'bogus', 'false', 'illegal', 'failed' or 'rejected' appeared five times in the headlines and 103 times in the text: 'arrested', 'jailed' or 'guilty' appeared 14 times in the headlines and 35 times in the text; 'criminal' (violent, non-violent or unspecified) appeared 12 times in the headlines and 53 times in the text; while 'scrounger', 'sponger', 'fraudster' or 'robbing the system' appeared five times in the headlines and 30 times in the text.
- There was evidence that statistics were often poorly presented: in the three-week sample, on over a third of occasions where numbers were cited (58 out of 144), sources were either not given or were highly unspecific – 'official statistics say' and so on.
- The imagery of asylum was constructed visually in ways that had negative connotations: for example, 15 of the 37 photographs showing asylum seekers or refugees presented them as criminals.

It is important to place the results of the study in context. It is not expected that one issue will be reported in similar ways all the time and a study of the whole press, like a study of every public forum, will deliver results that may differ in detail or proportion from those of a sample. What becomes clear, however, is that public media representations are able to develop a substantial body of images and interpretations that goes beyond the capacity of single publications, and possesses the collective reach to address a large number of readers.

Eliciting community-based responses

Localities, community relations and migration

In examinations of community relations, a focus on localities has been linked to housing markets that reflect distributions of economic and political power. The tendency for minority groups to be clustered in particular areas as a result is well documented in the community cohesion literature.

As well as highlighting the allocation of housing and other resources, analysis has drawn attention to racial incidents. The new immigrant is often denied a legitimate place, whether to live or work, and the importance of locality in defining these relations is therefore crucial (Bowling, 1998).

In the case of asylum, questions about the dispersal of asylum seekers gave impetus to this concern with localities. A report to the Economic and Social Research Council by Hewitt (2002) discussed local issues affecting the victimisation of refugees and asylum seekers. It noted the extent to which negative press coverage created a climate of secrecy, doubt and inertia among community relations networks. As well as indicting media coverage as a possible factor in weakening community defences against harassment, the report asserted that, while much content analysis of media coverage on refugee issues had been undertaken, there had been too little work on audience reception. In particular, there was a need to differentiate the reception by particular groups, to examine conversation and rumour, and to understand the role of communication networks in the localities, including refugee groups themselves.

Exploring media impacts

In our case study, the assessment of local media impacts explored the public forums and decision-making layers within the state and civil society by conducting local interviews not only with key actors and local representatives but also with members of communities in two boroughs with concentrations of refugees and asylum seekers.

Interviews with key actors make it possible to explore the process of communication as perceived by local representatives. Interviews were conducted with each local authority, and with the police, local refugee community organisations, plus other relevant actors in the two boroughs. In addition, the views of other interested parties such as the Commission for Racial Equality were sought.

The use of focus groups was intended to elicit responses to samples of media representations of asylum seekers and to carry out an exploration of the extent to which the media influences attitudes towards asylum seekers and refugees and, more generally, community tension. In order to reflect as far as possible the views of different community segments, focus groups were conducted in the two boroughs with four groups:

- one adult group (predominantly White British), drawn from settled communities;
- an adult group drawn from Black and minority ethnic communities;
- one youth group comprising mainly Black and minority ethnic teenagers; and
- one youth group comprising mainly White teenagers.

We cannot claim that the focus groups give a fully representative account of local views, but they do reveal the frankly aired perceptions of a range of local residents.

The sessions were divided into

- a discussion of responses to a press headline simply containing the word 'asylum';
- an assessment of the group's previous exposure to the media;
- discussion of media sample material; and
- discussion of community relations.

The newspaper sample materials included a photograph of a large group of asylum seekers, a report following results of an opinion poll on asylum, a report of a statement by a political advisor that Black and minority ethnic communities are most affected by asylum seekers and a report accusing asylum seekers of stealing donkeys from a local park. A short film giving accounts by refugees of their difficulties in the UK, including the impact of newspaper reports, was included to assess reactions to information direct from refugees.[3]

Perceptions

Community leaders articulated a range of views that exemplified the complexity of both local attitudes and local experiences: a sense of diversity as a strength; an awareness of stress and of resource inadequacy; and an assessment of how harassment related to this local social formation. The quotations below illustrate this complexity:

"A large degree of diversity exists in this borough and because of this diversity, people celebrate the culture. The degree of diversity also gives people a voice and the police are more sensitive. There is a lot of support available and a lot of advocacy. People like coming here because it feels safer, despite overcrowding. But this doesn't mean that harassment doesn't happen."

"It is important to place harassment within the context of a crowded, stressed city. There are a high number of people put into multiple occupancy. Many people come from other London boroughs and there is huge tension about over placement. The mobility and transience of the population affects service provision and the ability to improve."

"People like to feel that we are tolerant and liberal, but there is a perception in the borough that this is just too much, or why aren't the government providing enough resources without taking away from the host community. Then there is the question of how to have this debate without being racist."

The focus groups showed a high degree of reliance on the news media for information on asylum seekers and refugees. National and local newspapers, television and radio accounted for more than half of sources of information received on asylum seekers and refugees. However, newspapers were also held in low regard: "It looks like a tabloid – so I expect that it is going to tell me something fantastic, unbelievable, untrue".

The impact of media representation was perceived to be exacerbated by right-wing campaigns that were believed by a proportion of residents:

"The right wing can go door to door and say: 'This is what the *Sun* says and this is what we say', and that will have an effect on people. Maybe not many take them seriously, but some do and that's the worry."

A range of viewpoints was found in the focus groups, with interviewees from a Black and minority ethnic organisation most supportive and aware of the international forces influencing asylum flows. A group that was drawn from the general population was critical of the numbers of new arrivals, and of the impact on local services, and particularly the effect of so many people who could not speak English, but was sympathetic to individual asylum seekers and refugees and wished for them to be integrated.

There was evidence of misinformed views, noticeably in the young persons' groups:

> "If they had come over here legally and done it properly in the first place, there would be no problem. Why don't they claim asylum the legal way instead of sneaking in – that's what I don't like about asylum seekers."

> "They are all fighting to get to this one country and when they get here all opportunities that are here for us get straight to them. All housing and jobs goes to them and we are left with nothing."

There was also evidence of hostility. In particular, views among young people tended to display hostility towards individual asylum seekers and refugees:

> "It's disgusting."

> "Send them somewhere else in the UK or send them back."

Analysis of similarities in the language used by the media and by community groups suggests that a message has travelled from press to popular audience, and we found a good example of how that message can return back to the press again, once a journalist interviews a citizen with concerns about migration:

> In the village shop, Mrs Ainsworth fears the refugees because: 'I don't think they'll be satisfied with what they are given'.
> As evidence she quotes one of the more dubious tabloid scare stories of recent months, which claimed that the asylum seekers had been killing swans for food: 'They're given money for food, but they're still stealing swans'. (Vasagar, 2003)

Modelling

Our interpretation of the evidence from the local sources led to the development of a model of 'filtering' in which certain factors reduced the impact of negative messages while other factors exacerbated them (see Figure 6.2). These factors were linked to assumptions and perceptions in the segments of the local audience, and were connected not just to access to information but also to degrees of insecurity and concern over the distribution of resources and services. Hence, the analysis of communication must descend below the dominant communications domain to examine the level of ordinary public forums where talk is influenced by social preoccupations and anxieties.

Figure 6.2: A diagrammatic model of the influence of unbalanced and inaccurate reporting

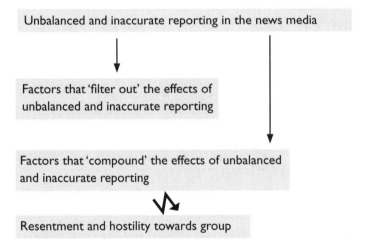

Unbalanced and inaccurate reporting in the news media

Factors that 'filter out' the effects of unbalanced and inaccurate reporting

Factors that 'compound' the effects of unbalanced and inaccurate reporting

Resentment and hostility towards group

Ø   **Factors that 'filter out' the effects of unbalanced and inaccurate reporting**
Ø   Exposure to wide and diverse information from media and other sources
     Critical attitudes to press
     Diversity awareness – sense of diverse histories and situations in a context of racism
     Aware of local press coverage which is limited and restrained
     Understanding extent of access of migrant group to basic resources and services

> Examples
> "My response to this article – just throw it in the bin!" (Focus group)
> "The impact of such media reporting may be less on this borough than it would be elsewhere. It could not be exploded by such reporting in way that other communities could because it is a very multicultural borough." (Local interview)

↔ **Factors that 'compound' the effects of unbalanced and inaccurate reporting**
↔ Exposure to narrow and sparse information from media and other sources
Uncritical attitudes to press
Lack of diversity awareness – little sense of diverse histories and situations in a context of racism
Aware of local rumour
Concerns about 'injustice' when basic resources and services not readily available to all are obtained 'free' by migrant group

> Examples
> "They are just over here to get money and start their own business and things or to take back home." (Focus group)
> "The strongest effect is where national and local papers give information which is similar to information circulating by word of mouth about local experiences." (Local interview)

As readers of the press, therefore, audiences do not simply accept what they are told. Audiences interpret national and local events through their own focal concerns. Assessing communications' impacts among representative segments of local communities is something that social cohesion strategies should acknowledge as a priority. A theoretical model of cohesion should be developed by analysts and strategists, in which the connectedness of groups is mediated and rendered meaningful by communications.

Conclusion

This chapter has sought to demonstrate that communication in many forms matters to evaluators, whether considering the press, civil society forums or ordinary talk in everyday contexts. However, communication also matters to strategists who wish to effect changes that will promote cohesion. Social cohesion in a new media age will not be simply a question of equalising access to resources such as housing, employment or social services; it will also be concerned with access to influence and participation in the development and distribution of the key information resources that lie in social communication systems. Any understanding of communication about social cohesion issues should recognise that any particular message may enter a complex and multifaceted communications field, in which everyday talk should be explored in the same careful way that media production and content are given attention.

It is clear that a significant power to define and articulate social cohesion lies with a policy establishment that enjoys access to media organisations with a substantial reach across the UK population. Those media organisations are able to represent the actors almost theatrically in 'dramas' that project vivid pictures of moral and political significance, whether the topics are asylum, 'extremism' or the impact of the recession on communities.

In this context, balance and accuracy will be the subjects of contested opinions, and evaluators will be challenged to establish what such terms mean for media analysis.

They must also face up to the issues of determining how target groups process information and how 'filters' operate to influence the reception of dominant and subordinate messages. As we have seen in our case study, media messages interact with assumptions and perceptions based on particular experiences.

These questions have to be related to a robust analytical framework and to evaluation designs that are multi-method in approach, capable of analysing content across all the communications matrices, carrying out interviews with civil society and officials, and eliciting the impressions and beliefs of a range of carefully selected and sampled target groups.

A theoretically cogent strategy for effective communication should itself be part of the social cohesion agenda. It is not clear, for example, that countering negative messages with rebuttals or positive messages is sufficient without an investment in broad, continuous communication and firm political leadership (Amas, 2008; Kitchin et al, 2009).

The scale and scope of the desired changes must be faced. Again, can face-to-face communications deliver messages that are more directly helpful to the cause of social and community cohesion than media communication? How should these be supported? How can the local communications media be engaged? Could particularly biased media be actually 'cleansed' or 'reclaimed' by political action, in order to promote the cause of social cohesion and progress? Or is it much more a question of increasing coherence and balance across the matrices of communication systems, and ensuring that all community members can participate in the forums and media, not simply to read or listen, but to question, exchange information or express positions? Profound questions about ownership and editorial control of media need to be posed. A strategy for advancing social cohesion must accept that in an information age, cohesive societies will distribute their communication potentials and capacity so that all their members benefit and take part. Unless strategists begin to acknowledge the communication dimension, evaluators reporting on such initiatives are likely to be bearers of unwelcome, if well-founded, news.

Notes

[1] The idea of conversation as a means of progressing social dialogue is significant in new media and networking, for example conversation cafés (see www.conversationcafe.org/).

[2] Statham (2003) comments on the role of politicians in defining asylum in the press.

[3] The interview schedules and the script giving further details of the content of the focus groups are in the report's appendix (ICAR, 2004).

References

Amas, N. (2008) *Housing, new migration and community relations: A review of the evidence base*, London: Information Centre about Asylum and Refugees.

Barrow Cadbury Trust (2008) *Beyond pancakes and popadoms: A report by the Barrow Cadbury Trust on integration and diversity*, London: Barrow Cadbury Trust, www.bctrust.org.uk/pdf/Beyond_Pancakes_and_Popadoms.pdf

Bowling, B. (1998) *Violent racism: Victimisation, policing and social context* (revised edition), Oxford: Oxford University Press.

Cohen, S. (2001) *Immigration controls, the family and the welfare state*, London: Jessica Kingsley Publishers.

Dustmann, C., Fabbri, F., Preston, I. and Wadsworth, J. (2003) *The local labour market effects of immigration in the UK*, Home Office Online Report 06/03, London: Home Office, http://rds.homeoffice.gov.uk/rds/pdfs2/rdsolr0603.pdf

Hewitt, T.L. (2002) *Asylum seeker dispersal and community relations: An analysis of development strategies*, London: Centre for Urban and Community Research, Goldsmith College, www.regard.ac.uk/ research_findings/R000223417/report.pdf

ICAR (Information Centre about Asylum and Refugees) (2004) *Media image, community impact: Assessing the impact of media and political images of refugees and asylum seekers on community relations in London: Report of a pilot research study, commissioned by the Mayor of London*, London: King's College London.

Ipsos MORI (2007) *Young people and British identity*, London: Ipsos MORI/Camelot Foundation.

Kitchin, H., Phillimore, J., Goodson, L., Mayblin, L., Jones, A., Pickstock, A., Weir, S. and Blick, A. (2009) *Communicating cohesion: Evaluating local authority communication strategies: Research summary*, Birmingham: Institute of Local Government Studies, University of Birmingham.

Smart, K., Grimshaw, R., McDowell, C. and Crosland, B. (2007) *Reporting asylum: The UK press and the effectiveness of PCC guidelines*, ICAR public images partnership for the National Refugee Integration Forum, Community and Media Subgroup, funded by the Immigration and Nationality Directorate, UK Home Office (London), London: City University.

Statham, P. (2003) 'Understanding anti-asylum rhetoric: restrictive politics or racist publics?', in S. Spencer (ed) *The politics of migration: Managing opportunity, conflict and change*, London: Blackwell.

The Daily Telegraph (2010) 'What is Islam4UK?', 4 January, www. telegraph.co.uk/news/newstopics/politics/defence/6931212/What-is-Islam4UK.html

Vasagar, J. (2003) 'Young guys won't sit behind fences all day long', *The Guardian*, 20 August, www.guardian.co.uk/politics/2003/aug/20/ immigrationpolicy.immigration

Vertovec, S. (2002) 'Transnational networks and skilled labour migration', WPTC-02-02, Paper given at the conference: 'Ladenburger Diskurs "Migration" Gottlieb Daimler- und Karl Benz-Stiftung, Ladenburg, 14-15 February, www.transcomm.ox.ac.uk/working%20papers/ WPTC-02-02%20Vertovec.pdf

Social cohesion in the local delivery context: understanding equality and the importance of local knowledge

Rose Doran and Michael Keating

Introduction

This chapter aims to set out how a developed understanding of social cohesion provides a broader moral and long-term context for decisions about community leadership and public service delivery in local government. It argues the importance of grounding broad philosophical concepts and policies of community/social cohesion in the reality of understanding and addressing local inequality and disadvantage, and the importance not just of local measurement, but also of local authorities' qualitative knowledge of the communities in which they work.

The chapter acknowledges the stark economic reality currently faced by both national and local government, and the challenges this presents in terms of striking a balance between equality and aspiration; rights and responsibilities. We argue that there will always be a moral dimension to local service delivery, and that efficiency and morality are not mutually exclusive but, in fact, both necessary considerations in designing and delivering services that meet the needs of local communities, enable councils and communities to cope with change, and strengthen social cohesion.

Community cohesion

As the community cohesion discourse has developed, so has the role of local public service delivery within it. As noted in other chapters, the term 'community cohesion' is strongly associated with the report of the Independent Review Team, chaired by Ted Cantle (Cantle, 2001), which followed the disturbances in towns in Northern England in

2001, and the 2007 report from the Labour government's Commission on Integration and Cohesion *Our shared future* (COIC, 2007), arguably precipitated by the London bombings in July 2005 and the impacts of the sharp, and unforeseen, rise in European Union (EU) accession migration after 2004. It is inevitable, given this genesis, that the terminology is perceived as having a basis in issues of race, religion and conflict, with a focus on poor White and Muslim communities in particular.

The Cantle Report, in fact, makes numerous references to the need to address underlying and systemic inequality – the role of socioeconomic disadvantage, poor educational attainment and the impact of housing policy all make an appearance in its recommendations. Although explicitly rooted in the particular demography of Oldham, Burnley and Bradford, what many took away from it, and the Home Office in particular which commissioned the report, was the emphasis on the need for all local authorities to actively promote 'contact and understanding' between people from different racial or religious backgrounds. The Home Office cohesion indicators (Home Office, 2003), developed partly in response to Cantle, perpetuated the focus on race and faith at a national level with the following indicators: 'the diversity of people's different backgrounds and circumstances are appreciated and positively valued'; 'the percentage of people who feel that local ethnic differences are respected' and 'the number of racial incidents recorded by police authorities per 100,000'.

Local government responded to this by, in many cases, arguing for a broader definition of 'community cohesion'. We agree with the conclusion of other authors within this publication, that 'social cohesion' is a more useful and appropriate term, allowing as it does for a more complex understanding of the dynamics *within* communities, as well as between them, and for a more natural fit with the equalities agenda. However, we would also argue that many local authorities had already started to use 'community cohesion' to describe this anyway. After all, local service providers are in the business of taking national policy and rhetoric and making it work locally.

Our shared future (COIC, 2007) reflected the widened emphasis and explicitly argued for a more broad-based definition of integration and cohesion. It was largely successful in doing this, and in making the link with equality in its focus on the importance of 'similar life opportunities' and 'visible social justice'. Local government and its partners in the voluntary and community sector (VCS) largely welcomed the report. Some of the recommendations, though, were hotly contested and it is worth reflecting on what these were, and what it tells us about how local government was positioning itself in relation to community cohesion.

Many of the councils that the Improvement and Development Agency (IDeA)[1] consulted with at the time of the report's publication felt far more comfortable with the concept of 'cohesion' than they did with the concept of 'integration'. There was by no means a wholesale acceptance within the local government sector that integration as conceptualised by the government at the time, or the Commission, was a good thing. Many felt that the government's language (DCLG, 2008a) sounded more like assimilation than integration, with a focus on 'helping migrant communities to fit in with the way we do things here'. A focus on 'integration' rather than 'inclusion' implicitly placed the emphasis on the few (to integrate) rather than the many (to include) and led to concerns among councils and VCS partners that community cohesion was largely being conceptualised as the responsibility of poorer more marginalised communities, rather than society as a whole. Councils also expressed a challenge to the perceived idea that community cohesion was primarily about local authorities actively intervening to promote mixing between people from different backgrounds, at the expense of tailored or specialist services to specific communities, and felt that the recommendation overlooked the ability of both initially specialist – for example for a new migrant community – and other services to develop over time and respond naturally to change.

The rhetoric of *Our shared future* also reflected the popular rejection of 'multiculturalism', epitomised in Trevor Phillips' (2005) famous claim that Britain was 'sleepwalking into segregation'. The argument, essentially, was that the focus on respecting difference that had gained currency within the race relations discourse of the 1970s had made government and society as a whole afraid to promote integration, and had resulted in policies THAT encouraged separateness and 'ghettoisation'. Cantle (*The Guardian*, 2005; 2008) has also voiced qualified support for this view. The Commission's clearest attack on multiculturalism was expressed in a recommendation on Single Group Funding, which argued that groups working with a specific community, and not actively seeking to promote or build cohesion with others, should only be funded in exceptional circumstances, and that 'becoming more outward facing' should be a condition of continued funding. Many in local government and the VCS felt that this recommendation clearly privileged integration over equality and overlooked the importance of strength and confidence *within* communities as a key factor in effective social cohesion. The recommendation was ultimately 'officially' rejected in the government's response to the Commission's report (DCLG, 2008b).

What is the role of local government in relation to social cohesion?

It is useful to reflect on this chain of events because it tells us a great deal about the way that local government and its partners have mediated national policy and the ongoing discourse on community cohesion in the effective delivery of services to local people. Councils did take on board the more directly interventionist aspirations of the community cohesion agenda and indeed many do deliver specific projects to bring people together, for example at sporting and cultural events. But they are also increasingly focusing on the equalities they feel underpin good social cohesion. In part this has been informed by a persistent strand within the research, which shows that deprivation, not diversity, is the key determinant for poor community cohesion (Hickman et al, 2008; Laurence and Heath, 2008; IPPR, 2010).

It is also important to mention here two other key related policy terms that have helped local areas to make sense of social cohesion within their locality – 'community engagement' and 'wellbeing'. Engagement makes explicit the importance of the relationship between citizens and the state/service providers, while wellbeing in particular enables policy decisions to transcend discussions of 'difference' to focus on factors that impact on happiness, health and satisfaction in all communities (Bacon et al, 2010). This has perhaps been particularly helpful when considering equalities and social cohesion in more affluent and less racially and religiously diverse communities.

Councils' work on equalities and community cohesion has therefore, in many places, become primarily focused on tackling physical barriers to equality and barriers to social mobility, improving the relationship with local people and developing a positive narrative to change attitudes through effective communication. There is a broader pragmatic acceptance that you cannot always bring people into direct contact with one another, but you can still dispel myths and create a less constrained physical and social geography.

This 'hearts and minds' dimension of local cohesion policy can perhaps be most clearly seen in its spread to councils with low levels of racial or religious diversity. While some of this is down to a broadening of our understanding of the relationship between equality and cohesion, for example into concerns around age and intergenerational relations, it is also down to a shift in focus from holding minority communities responsible for the creation of unrest, to an acknowledgement that the prejudices of people in areas of low ethnic and religious diversity can be exacerbated by social and geographic factors that reinforce separateness and difference (Wood et al, 2006).

Social cohesion and the equalities agenda in local government

In parallel with the developing discourse on cohesion, the understanding of equality in a diverse and dynamic society has also developed and strengthened, culminating in the Equality Act 2010.

In 2007, the Equality and Human Rights Commission (EHRC) brought together the Equal Opportunities Commission, the Commission for Racial Equality and the Disability Rights Commission. One of the EHRC's primary tasks has been to work towards a 'good relations' framework (Johnson and Tatam, 2009). In many ways, 'good relations' terminology is interchangeable with 'community cohesion'. However, by situating good relations alongside other aspects of equality, the EHRC has placed it in a conceptual space that sees positive relationships and treatment of difference and diversity as a necessary factor for equality, rather than just a consequence.

As well as allowing for a more multifaceted concept of identity, this definition therefore recognises both the impact of relationships on equality outcomes and also the desirability of 'good relations' as an end in itself. Arguably, unlike community cohesion, which at its most didactic places an emphasis on the need for interaction and integration, the equalities discourse, and good relations in particular, is rooted in human rights, which gives it a more powerful moral logic than simple aspirations for people to get along.

The Equality Act 2010

Included in the parliamentary wash-up just before the 2010 General Election, the new Equality Act sets out to strengthen protection, advance equality and simplify the law through a range of specific actions. One of its most significant provisions is, a new integrated Equality Duty on public bodies that extends the public duties for race, gender and disability to age, sexual orientation, religion or belief, gender reassignment and also includes pregnancy and maternity. Other provisions, such as using public procurement to improve equality and banning age discrimination outside the workplace, if implemented effectively, could have a great impact. The drive to develop a more sophisticated understanding of how individuals actually experience life is seen in the provision for protecting people from dual discrimination, that is, direct discrimination because of a combination of two protected characteristics.

The coalition's 'programme for government' has a specific section on equalities (HM Government, 2010a) and the Conservatives' pre-election statements included mention of 'background' alongside the equality strands (Conservative Party, 2010). Interestingly the first government announcement that was made was *Working for lesbian, gay, bisexual and transgender equality* (HM Government, 2010b), which includes explicit mention of relationships within communities, for instance tackling homophobic hate crime and increasing civic participation.

The main provisions of the Equality Act came in in October 2010 and the Public Sector Equality Duty (general and specific duties), comes into effect in April 2011.

The Equality Framework for Local Government

IDeA has long had a dedicated resource for work on equalities, more recently joined by community cohesion. The linking of equalities and community cohesion, and the priority it is given, reflects the concerns of local government. Councils have been using the Equality Standard for Local Government since 2001 but in 2009 the Equality Framework for Local Government (IDeA, 2009) was launched as a simpler and smarter improvement tool to strengthen the confidence of councils to understand how everyday service delivery is influenced by equality and how they can be seen to be providing services fairly. The Framework was developed in consultation with English local authorities.

Based on three levels of achievement ('developing', 'achieving' and 'excellent'), the Framework is designed to:

- aid compliance with the equality public duties;
- provide a way of carrying out self-assessment and thereby evidence for external assessment;[2]
- help meet customer care standards; and
- foster a partnership approach and efficient use of resources through the adoption of the model by other public authorities.

It is underpinned by the wider definition of equality that demonstrates how a mix of gender, age, ethnicity, disability, sexual orientation and religion/belief describes each one of us and thereby helps us understand how we experience life chances (including physical security, health, education, family life, participation and legal security) (Equalities Review, 2007).

The Framework is focused on five performance areas:

* knowing your community and equality mapping;
* place shaping, leadership, partnership and organisational commitment;
* community engagement and satisfaction;
* responsive services and customer care; and
* a modern and diverse workforce.

Self-assessment and peer challenge by members and officers are used to test its effectiveness. The Framework strives to exemplify a local government sector-led approach to support since it is agreed and owned by local government rather than being dictated by central government or an inspectorate. It helps councils articulate why they have decided to provide certain services, based on a real understanding of the area, and what they aspire to do next. The focus is on 'what makes a difference', and sustainability and minimising bureaucracy are major features.

It is therefore not a didactic measurement tool but is designed to foster self-awareness and continuous improvement. The aim is to encourage reflection on existing practice and vital space for debate of how best to approach decision making and service delivery that strengthen opportunity and outcomes for all. It is right to say that every area is unique and must develop its own responses to community need, but the Framework is supported by a commitment to identify and share good practice.

The Framework is grounded in the realities of local service delivery. Figure 7.1 illustrates this. It may seem obvious, but in fact much of the rhetoric – both political and academic – situates equality outside or alongside the mainstream business of working in partnership to deliver efficient, effective services to complex, fluid local communities. 'Excellence' as conceptualised by the Framework depends on equalities and social cohesion fundamentally informing the way a council and its partners work, and the way they understand and relate to the local community. The importance of these structural and strategic factors – good leadership, good partnership and the ability to plan and respond effectively to change – can be clearly seen in the examples below from the two 'excellent' authorities. Councils and partnerships that manage to deliver real improved outcomes are those that have an overarching approach and a clear, shared narrative, as well as individual examples of good practice.

Figure 7.1: How the Equality Framework improves performance

In early 2010, an online survey was sent to every local authority in England to assess how many were using the Framework and how useful it was to delivering services. With a response rate of 65% across all types of authorities and regions, 98% of respondents were either using the Framework or had plans to. This percentage was consistent across Conservative, Labour, Liberal Democrat and 'No Overall Control' councils. Only two councils were currently assessed as 'excellent' but 68% currently intended to move from 'developing' to 'achieving' and on to 'excellent'. The survey confirms the feedback gained from councils through peer challenge and the Local Government Improvement and Development Equality Community of Practice.[3] This qualitative evidence highlights a range of work including strong partnerships between the county councils and their districts, inventive methods for strengthening the community leadership of elected members and developing understanding of how equality delivers long-term efficiency.

However, when asked about further areas for support and guidance, 'knowing your community' was the most common at 48%, followed by 'improving representation of under-represented groups' at 32%. Given the tenor of much national discussion, this highlights a perhaps unsurprising local anxiety about the nature of communities. This anxiety is manifested in a desire to have an accurate picture of what is happening in a place – and indeed this search for accuracy can sometimes act as a brake on actual policy and service development. Much of the discussion of equalities and social cohesion therefore focuses on measurement. But measurement is nothing without the broader contextual knowledge of what might be driving certain outcomes, and how that might be addressed. This is where the richness in local government's day-to-day approach can become evident.

The importance of this local understanding is ever present in the policy literature but the vital and informal role of local councillors, staff and partners in delivering this through an overarching equality ethos is perhaps less well explored. It is this ethos that the Framework, at its heart, seeks to advocate.

This can be a challenging space for public sector organisations to operate in. They are frequently the subject of hostile media coverage at both a national and local level, which rarely seems interested in a sophisticated analysis of the complexities and controversies that can surround relationships within and between communities. This spotlight has often undermined the reputation of individual councils and the sector as a whole. The 'whole systems' approach[4] to equality and social cohesion therefore that the Framework seeks to foster and support is also designed to build confidence and capacity. It allows space to recognise persistent social realities such as crime and poverty, while enabling councils to recognise their ability to handle problems constructively and sensitively. This can again be seen in the two councils that have so far achieved 'excellent' status – The London Borough of Tower Hamlets and Rotherham Metropolitan Borough Council.

London Borough of Tower Hamlets

The population of Tower Hamlets is diverse, with 33% of its population of Bangladeshi origin. It is a young place and over 79% of residents aged under 19 are from minority ethnic communities. In contrast, 60% of the population aged over 30 are from White ethnic groups. Faith is a strong feature, with 78% of residents saying they have a religion or belief: approximately half of this number is Muslim. The borough borders the City of London and includes Canary Wharf; immense wealth and economic opportunity sit alongside some of the country's most deprived wards – 18% of households live on less than £15,000 while the average salary for those who work in the borough is £64,000.

In the history of this part of London there are many points where a narrative about equality and cohesion could start. While the language may have changed, the area now known as Tower Hamlets has been the place of settlement for migrant communities for centuries, whose arrival into an area already overcrowded, and with a poor population and a shortage of housing, has often met a hostile reception. In 1993, the first British National Party (BNP) councillor in Britain was elected locally. During the campaign, housing allocation was a major debate, often posed as a contest between settled 'indigenous' communities and the 'new' Bangladeshi community. In the months after the election there was a lot of racial tension. Although the BNP councillor lost his seat in the local elections the following year, the council was forced to reflect on what these divisions, usually seen as racial, meant. In particular, it considered how to create a place that could appreciate its diversity, tackle the inequality that often results and shape a cohesive community. Anchored in this anti-racist work, the council has developed its equalities practice so that, in January 2010, it was the second authority to achieve 'excellent' against the Equality Framework.

Leadership on equalities and cohesion are at the highest level within the borough's local strategic partnership. With a strong executive, this is supported by a series of community plan delivery groups (co-chaired by elected members, these involve officers from all public agencies and the VCS) and resident engagement based in eight local area partnerships. The focus on, and commitment to, equality is therefore at the heart of the place.

Following extensive consultation with local residents, the themes of the Community Plan attempt to embrace the life experiences of all local people – 'A Great Place to Live', 'A Prosperous Community', 'A Safe and Supportive Community' and 'A Healthy Community'. Overarching these is 'One Tower Hamlets', capturing the shared aim to make the borough a place in which people live together harmoniously and are treated with respect and fairness, regardless of their differences. One Tower Hamlets goes beyond an aspiration; it drives strategic and operational interventions to tackling poverty and inequality, strengthening community cohesion and building community leadership and personal responsibility. This is evident in the strong equalities and community cohesion focus of the local area agreement and in specific partnership strategies between the council and the health service and the police for example.

In 2009, in developing new Equality Schemes for Age, Sexual Orientation and Religion/Belief, as well as a refreshed Race Scheme, the council analysed evidence of inequality (across all strands) between individuals and groups locally. Drawing on the Equality Measurement Framework categories (EHRC, 2009), the Equality Schemes aimed to provide a description that distinguishes between inequality of *access* and inequality of *outcome*. For example, it is clear that many new communities are less able to access public services, as they may not be aware of the services that exist, may not be eligible and may experience language barriers. To respond to this inequality of access, the council and its partners recognised that they have a duty to engage with these communities to identify and minimise barriers and improve access. However, they also recognised that for some groups and individuals, tackling inequality of outcome is not a case of simply improving access to services but requires a more holistic response to a range of factors. Mapping inequality across the equality strands in this way has helped to identify areas of persistent and systemic inequality that arise from a complex interplay of factors and require a holistic and long-term response.

While the borough's diversity arguably makes it a more likely candidate for putting equality and cohesion at the centre of its practice, the same degree of commitment is not always seen in other equally diverse places. Tower Hamlets' approach drives outcomes in key areas such as educational attainment that buck outside expectations of diverse and deprived communities: over the last four years, Black Caribbean pupils have improved on their General Certificate in Secondary Education (GCSE) performance by 18 percentage points, Bangladeshi pupils by eight percentage points and Black African pupils by five percentage points. Home to a large Muslim population and the East London Mosque alongside an established White working-class community, the borough has seen none of the disturbances and unrest that have characterised more segregated communities. It is notoriously difficult to measure any of this, but it does seem that we can cautiously say that a strong and embedded approach to equalities seems to have noticeable benefits in terms of social cohesion. This is demonstrated in ways that other areas would find difficult to contemplate. For instance, with the highest number of Muslim councillors of any local authority, the council has also been seventh in the Stonewall Workplace Equality Index (see www.stonewall.org.uk) for the last two years.

Another noteworthy aspect of the Tower Hamlets approach is its focus on managing change. The borough experiences high levels of population churn, and has done for centuries. The 'One Tower Hamlets' story therefore focuses on the nature of diversity in its broadest sense, rather than exclusively on the relationships between specific sections of the population. This enables the council to foster a proactive approach that benefits all communities, rather than a reactive one that falls into a cycle of responding to specific issues.

Rotherham

In contrast, Rotherham is a semi-rural borough and is, in many ways, a 'typical White working-class' community. This typicality led the philosopher Julian Baggini (2007) to choose Rotherham for his exploration of the English national psyche *Welcome to Everytown* and Jamie Oliver to choose it for his *ministry of food* series on challenging 'typical' British eating habits (*Jamie's ministry of food*, Fresh One Productions, shown on Channel 4, 2007). Simon Charlesworth (2000) used his native Rotherham to reflect on the working-class experience of entrenched marginalisation and lack of voice. It would be disingenuous to argue that the last 10 years have effectively addressed the impacts of alienation and socioeconomic disadvantage, but now there is perhaps a renewed recognition that income inequality and the national narrative about 'working-class' communities matters greatly. It is also worth bearing in mind what this tells us about the need for an overarching understanding of inequality and cohesion, which goes beyond local authority boundaries, and which we argue for elsewhere in this chapter as part of the business of national government.

Of course, such generalisations rarely seem as straightforward on closer inspection, and that is as true of Rotherham as it is of anywhere, but it does show that the 'Tower Hamlets' argument – 'it's all very well for them to put equalities at the heart of what they do, but we don't have that kind of ethnic diversity, pace of change or contrast between wealth and poverty' – simply does not stand up if somewhere like Rotherham can demonstrate real improvements to outcomes for local people through its approach to equalities and cohesion. What Rotherham has, in common with many former industrial towns, is inequality in relation to the rest of the country, which impacts on perceptions and experiences at a local level.

Rotherham's population has been increasing steadily over recent years. Like the rest of the United Kingdom (UK), Rotherham has an ageing population, with the number of people aged over 70 expected to grow by around 70% over the next 25 years. The borough's minority ethnic population is also changing, making up 6.6% of the total population in 2007 compared to 4.2% in 2001. The largest group is of Pakistani origin (2.2%) and recently more people have come from Eastern Europe and Africa. In 2009, 16.2% of the population was entitled to disability-related benefits, well above the English average of 11.6%, and indicating a high rate of long-term sickness. This in turn means that the percentage of carers is higher than average – 30,284 people (12.2%) provided unpaid care according to the 2001 Census, compared to 9.9% for England.

Effective partnership, equality as a core value and the ability to cope with change are at the heart of Rotherham's approach. For example, under the auspices of its local strategic partnership, the Rotherham Women's Strategy was produced, in conjunction with the police and the VCS and in 2008 a wider range of partners agreed the Rotherham Joint Carers' Strategy. These strategies have ensured that promoting equality of opportunity, tackling unlawful discrimination and promoting good community relations are all at the heart of the council's role as community leader, service provider, commissioner and employer.

A robust approach to 'knowing the community' is illustrated by supplementing good local data with more qualitative approaches such as 'community profiles' that create a richer description of local communities, informed by all local service providers and consultation with local people. The council works closely with its partners on numerous fora to engage with local people, including the Adult Services Consortium, Rotherham Ethnic Minority Alliance, Rotherham Women's Network, the Older People's Forum, Rotherham Inter-Faith Forum, Mosque Liaison Group and LGBT Rotherham Ltd.

Considerable work has been undertaken to promote the positive aspects of a changing demography, and to ensure that more long-established communities feel consistently listened to and involved. Much of this work is dependent on the council's focus on all aspects of equality, for example key issues such as age and disability.

The 'Hot Spots' project (2009–2010) created a partnership approach to addressing affordable warmth, finance, safety and health by providing households with a single point of contact for energy saving and grants advice, home fire safety checks, a benefit entitlement check and stop smoking advice and support. Local residents made an average saving on energy bills of £125 per year and one in four referrals resulted in people accessing additional benefits. As a direct result of Hot Spots referrals, £82,316 per year in additional welfare benefits was awarded.

'Fairs Fayre' was an event that raised awareness about the services available for disabled people, with over 70 organisations participating and 4,000 individuals accessing information about employment, benefits, education, equipment, universal services and support and leisure activities. Older people were concerned about access and mobility and a number of physical improvements have been made as a result. These practical points about access therefore become drivers for improving the daily experience for disabled people and in turn their interaction with those who are not.

In common with Tower Hamlets, Rotherham has a strong and consistently publicised narrative in the form of 'One Town, One Community'. This message has been crucial in countering local support for the Far Right, which is a persistent issue for the borough. The council also approached the *Prevent*[5] agenda sensitively in order not to fuel anti-Muslim sentiment, and Councillor Mahroof Hussain, the council's lead member for community development and engagement, is nationally recognised for his work on both *Prevent* and community cohesion.

The business and moral case for equalities and cohesion

The evidence from councils who have been assessed against the Framework so far shows a willingness to engage with both the business and moral case for equality. This has been true across all types of political control, with highly business-oriented and efficiency-focused county councils such as Kent (Kent County Council, 2010) recognising the benefits to the whole community of considering the needs of society's most marginalised. This has important implications for social cohesion in a time of cuts to public service funding. Councils are not seeing equalities as an 'add-on' but, as in the case of Tower Hamlets, as the key way of prioritising and focusing both their community leadership role and their delivery of services.

Linking equalities with the human rights agenda provides a strong and necessary basis for arguing for the importance of services that may be considered expensive or even unpopular in purely business terms. The social cohesion discourse allows councils to consider the implications of decisions that may seem trivial or unpopular without recourse to an understanding of perceptions and dynamics within and between communities. One of the work programmes supported by the equalities and cohesion team within Local Government Improvement and Development has been a programme in partnership with the Homes and Communities Agency focused on meeting the needs of Gypsy and Traveller communities (IDeA, 2008). This is not just about interaction, or about measurement, but about councillors overcoming their own prejudices and having the confidence to challenge vocal opposition to Gypsy and Traveller sites within local communities. Following the training, which explores the equalities and human rights dimensions of the issue, a ward councillor from North Wiltshire was moved to stand up at a packed and hostile public meeting and state: "Tonight is the night to do what is right and not what is popular", leading to the council approving a Gypsy planning application for the first time. Other councils have taken a similar stance on these small (but diverse) and often misrepresented communities, with results that have ultimately been to the benefit of the community as a whole.[6] It illustrates the central role that a qualitative and lived understanding of equalities and local perceptions has on informed and successful local decision making.

One of the key moral debates facing equalities and social cohesion practice today is, of course, socioeconomic inequality. The evidence for a direct causal link between deprivation and poor social cohesion is strong, and yet the gap continues to widen. The arguments for the benefits to society as a whole of greater wealth equality have been well made, albeit largely by those on the political left (Wilkinson and Pickett, 2009; Dorling, 2010). It remains to be seen whether the new administration's drive for 'localism' will enable councils to address systemic disadvantage fundamentally, and whether careful prioritisation and decision making by local councils and their partners can ensure that the harsh fiscal regime currently being implemented on the public sector does not disproportionately affect the poorest in society (Institute for Fiscal Studies, 2010; McCarvill, 2010). A moral dimension to decision making and targeting of resources at a local level, supported by a move towards more local control and determination could, arguably, be a good thing. With the removal of national and regional inspection and performance management, a more fully developed social cohesion rhetoric, linked to a strong foundation in equalities and human rights, will be an important reference and driver for local government decision making.

Conclusion

As society has become more complex and mobile, we have an increasing need to understand the way that public spending decisions impact and interact with increasingly diverse and dynamic communities. Local government makes decisions, lots of them, about how and where to concentrate public resources to maximise the benefit to local people. Getting the balance wrong can lead to a sense of injustice and, at worst, civic unrest or severely impaired outcomes for particular sections of the community. Getting the balance right depends on good empirical knowledge of who lives in a local area, how the area is changing, and where inequality exists. But it also depends on a nuanced and practical knowledge of community dynamics, gained through a council's day-to-day interactions with the community it serves.

The concept and ideal of social cohesion is necessary to local government in framing the wider objectives of reduced inequality, good relations and a strong local narrative. It also enables us to address issues of multiple identity, perceptions and relationships that are not addressed by equalities alone. But the broadened concept of equalities is the scaffolding that supports this, and provides a more tangible and practical focus for organisations that are, ultimately, in the business of delivering services.

In straitened times we are likely to see more emphasis on the business case of efficiency and productivity than we are on the moral case for public services, and yet all decisions have a moral dimension. Social cohesion is not just about mitigating the 'cost' of conflict, but also about allowing space for the moral debates about what our society should be, and how our government and public services both facilitate and lead those values. The coalition government's emphasis on 'localism' may, at its best, provide an opportunity for councils and their communities to mediate universal aspirations of tolerance, fairness and equality in a way that makes genuine sense within their local area, and is tailored to the needs, aspirations and views of local communities. Although there has been some concern expressed about the risks associated with localism, the Equality Act and the Equality Framework provide vital points of reference for councils and their partners to inform and support their local approach. We would also argue that a national rhetoric on social cohesion is important for the same reason. Local government has a key role to play in making informed and objective decisions with a professional judgement that retains the impetus to do 'what is right and not what is popular'.

Considering the interface between the national viewpoint and local knowledge provides the opportunity to challenge perceptions and allow local experience to shape decisions. Tower Hamlets' refusal to accept poor educational attainment as an immutable consequence of deprivation and diversity, for example, shows that by addressing inequality head-on we do not have to accept a situation as an inevitable consequence of entrenched social structures beyond our immediate control (and therefore not worth trying to change).

Evidence gathered through the use of the Equality Framework for Local Government demonstrates that, when councils understand their local diversity and work to tackle the inequality that can arise, this fosters more cohesive communities. By linking equalities to a wider discussion of social cohesion – and what is in the interests of society as a whole – councils are able to make sophisticated, complex and difficult decisions about how and where to target local services to address disadvantage for the benefit of society as a whole.

Notes

[1] Created in 1998 to support sector-led improvement and innovation in local government, IDeA receives a top-slice of Revenue Support Grant to work with local authorities and their partners to develop and share good practice through networks, online resources and support from councillor and officer peers. It also delivers commissioned work for local and central government. In July 2010, IDeA's name was changed to Local Government Improvement and Development.

[2] The coalition government has abolished the Comprehensive Area Assessment but councils will remain subject to external inspections, particularly of services for vulnerable residents.

[3] 'Communities of Practice' provide an online policy sharing and discussion platform, hosted by Local Government Improvement and Development: www.communities.idea.gov.uk

[4] Where equality is incorporated into service planning and delivery at all levels and within all service areas – for example within directorate and team plans, Equality Impact Assessments and human resources practices – and the equality objectives of the council and its partners are clearly understood and inform activity and decision making for all staff, councillors and stakeholders.

[5] *Prevent* – the previous government's national strategy to prevent people becoming or supporting violent extremists.

[6] For example, see Fenland District Council's 2010 Local Government Chronicle Equalities and Diversity Award.

References

Bacon, N., Brophy, M., Mguni, N., Mulgan, G. and Shandro, A. (2010) *The state of happiness: Can public policy shape people's wellbeing and resilience?*, London: The Young Foundation.

Baggini, J. (2007) *Welcome to Everytown: A journey into the English mind*, London: Granta.

Cantle, T. (chair) (2001) *Community cohesion: A report of the Independent Review Team*, London: Home Office.

Cantle, T. (2008) *Community cohesion: A new framework for race and diversity* (2nd edition), London: Palgrave Macmillan.

Charlesworth, S. (2000) *A phenomenology of working class experience*, Cambridge: Cambridge University Press.

COIC (Commission on Integration and Cohesion) (2007) *Our shared future*, London: COIC.

Conservative Party (2010) *A contract for equalities*, London: Conservative Party.

DCLG (Department for Communities and Local Government) (2008a) *Review of migrant integration policy in the UK*, London: DCLG.

DCLG (2008b) *The government's response to the Commission on Integration and Cohesion*, London: DCLG.

Dorling, D. (2010) *Injustice: Why social inequality persists*, Bristol: The Policy Press.

EHRC (Equality and Human Rights Commission) (2009) *The Equality Measurement Framework*, Manchester: EHRC.

Equalities Review (2007) *Fairness and freedom: The final report of the Equalities Review*, London: Cabinet Office.

Finance Markets (2010) 'IFS comments on spending cuts', 24 June, www.financemarkets.co.uk/2010/06/24/ifs-comments-on-spending-cuts/

Hickman, M., Crowley, H. and Mai, N. (2008) *Immigration and social cohesion in the UK*, York: Joseph Rowntree Foundation.

HM Government (2010a) *The coalition: Our programme for government*, London: Cabinet Office.

HM Government (2010b) *Working for lesbian, gay, bisexual and transgender equality*, London: Government Equalities Office.

Home Office (2003) *Building a picture of community cohesion: A guide for local authorities and their partners*, London: Home Office.

IDeA (Improvement and Development Agency) (2008) *Providing Gypsy and Traveller sites*, London: IDeA Local Leadership Academy.

IDeA (2009) *The Equality Framework for Local Government*, London: Improvement and Development Agency, www.idea.gov.uk/idk/core/page.do?pageId=9491107

IPPR (Institute for Public Policy Research) (2010) *Exploring the roots of BNP support*, London: IPPR.

Johnson, N. and Tatam, J. (2009) *Good relations: A conceptual analysis*, Manchester: EHRC.

Kent County Council (2010) *Equality and diversity policy statement*, Maidstone: Kent County Council, www.kent.gov.uk/your_council/priorities,_policies_and_plans/policies/equality_and_diversity/equality_and_diversity_policy.aspx

Laurence, J. and Heath, A. (2008) *Predictors of community cohesion: Multi-level modelling of the 2005 Citizenship Survey*, London: DCLG.

McCarvill, P. (2010) *Equality, entitlements and localism*, London: Institute for Public Policy Research.

OPSI (Office of Public Sector Information) (2010) *The Equality Act 2010*, London: OPSI.

Phillips, T. (2005) 'After 7/7: sleepwalking to segregation', Speech given to Manchester Council for Community Relations, 22 September.

The Guardian (2005) 'Harmony's herald', 21 September 2005, www.guardian.co.uk/society/2005/sep/21/communities. guardiansocietysupplement2

Wilkinson, R. and Pickett, K. (2009) *The spirit level: Why more equal societies almost always do better*, London: Penguin.

Wood, P., Landry, C. and Bloomfield, J. (2006) *Cultural diversity in Britain: A toolkit for cross-cultural co-operation*, York: Joseph Rowntree Foundation.

Part Three
Policy areas

EIGHT

Housing, spatial patterns and social cohesion

Peter Ratcliffe

Introduction

In certain key senses, housing remains a Cinderella issue in both research and policy terms. Indicative of this is the fact that in the, otherwise excellent, report of the Runnymede Trust Commission into the future of multi-ethnic Britain (Parekh, 2000), housing was alone among the major institutional arenas in not being seen as important enough to merit a chapter. It was occasionally mentioned as a sub-theme in the context of debates about residential patterns but it nevertheless failed to assume a real material presence. This is misguided. Both spatial patterns and the built environment are crucial to an effective understanding of the nature of social relations within neighbourhoods, and of 'quality of life' and material wellbeing. They are therefore at the very core of debates about 'inclusive and cohesive' societies.

Chapter One in the current volume traced the development of New Labour thinking from the late 1990s. Core themes were the need to tackle 'social exclusion' and thereby promote 'inclusion'. As with the more recent policy paradigm labelled 'community cohesion', these contained a multitude of quite distinct sub-themes. Arguably, the effect was that the policy agenda became fragmented and confused. The New Labour discourse surrounding the 'exclusion/inclusion' dualism was notable in its refusal to engage directly with all-pervasive material concerns such as poverty, inequality, racism and so on.

The 'community cohesion' agenda places major emphasis on what Flint (2008) terms 'political communitarianism'. Problems evident in particular areas were to be tackled by people taking more responsibility for their lives and for the future of their neighbourhoods: a contemporary social variant of the adage 'patient heal thyself'. Responsiblisation thus prioritises responsibilities over rights, and delegates a vital community renewal function to those who are often least likely to be able to fulfil it. Arguably, this represents an abrogation of duties on the part of central government, a form of reasoning countered by the latter's claim that this enhances local empowerment. Whatever view one takes on this matter, it is clear that a 'political communitarianism' approach sees cohesion policy and communitarianism (a) as having the potential to solve perceived social problems in particular localities and (b) as holding the key to fix the 'broken society'.

The idea of the 'broken society', which is especially popular in contemporary political debates, simply rehashes earlier characterisations of 'the excluded' (or underclass) by suggesting that there are people who reject the normative culture and in so doing threaten the coherence of the nation. At the core (once again), however, are material inequalities. It is no coincidence that those accused of undermining the body politic are both predominantly poor and living in some of the worst housing the nation has to offer.

This brings us to the crux of the issues addressed by this chapter, which looks at how housing policy should be evaluated in relation to the cohesion debate. We need to ask how housing, the built environment and spatial patterns impact on social stability and cohesiveness. In doing so, we also need to assess the relative significance of the local, regional, national and global dimensions of the problematic. By their very nature, cohesion policies are targeted principally at the local level. They see the main problems as stemming from ethnic, cultural and religious difference. In the same way that multiculturalism posited that these differences could be 'negotiated' without reference to material and power-based inequality, cohesion strategies tend to rely on (local) inter-cultural communication. A brief exploration of these issues forms the first element of the analysis that follows.

Second, it is self-evident that (ethnic) segregation and spatial patterns have, since 2001, been central to national debates on cohesion and integration. At the risk of oversimplifying highly complex arguments, the coverage of the issues can be divided roughly into four dominant, interlinked policy areas:

- the quality of housing and the built environment (including, in the former context, occupancy levels);
- the salience of contemporary population shifts to social cohesion;
- policies geared towards a reduction in segregation levels (including debates about increasing access to a wider range of housing options and proposals to create balanced/sustainable/mixed communities); and

- the viability of using renewal and regeneration policy to fulfil social goals.

It is not the function of the current chapter to review the voluminous literature in these areas: that would be a monumental task. A number of publications are especially worthy of note, however. The book by Harrison and Phillips (2005), for example, has the distinction of being one the very few major publications to focus specifically on the linkage between housing issues and those more pertinent to the debates around community cohesion. Also of significance in the current context are articles by Robinson (2005, 2007) and, more recently, the works from Flint and Robinson (2008) and Finney and Simpson (2009). These will nevertheless provide an important backdrop to many of the arguments that follow.

The key function of this chapter is to reorientate housing policy debates around the core theme of social, as distinct from 'community', cohesion. This inevitably invokes both a very different policy agenda and, crucially, a new context for evaluation.

Social cohesion: the relative significance of the local, regional, national and global

As noted above, policies aiming to engender a more stable social formation tend to begin by targeting the local: communities, neighbourhoods and towns/cities. At one level this is perfectly defensible. Local tensions tend to be codified within historical trajectories and, as such, have an obvious uniqueness. They may or may not have ethnic or cultural difference at the fulcrum, but they clearly have the potential to impact on social stability. Population shifts of the sort discussed below may then exacerbate these tensions. In these circumstances, local governance has a crucial role to play.

The limits of local policy action, however, are revealed by a critical realist analysis, in other words the search for real underlying forces that lie beneath the world of epiphenomena. Much of what *appears* to be 'local' has much deeper and more extensive roots. As demonstrated effectively in a planning policy statement from the Department for Communities and Local Government (DCLG, 2006b), conflict between groups identified as of different ethnic/cultural heritage may easily be misinterpreted. This racialisation of conflict can blind the unwary observer to struggles over scarce resources between poor communities. Such material factors hint at the roots that are, to varying degrees local, regional, national and even global.

In so far as racism is historically entrenched or endemic, this is also not amenable to local forms of governance: it requires a broader national strategy. Community cohesion policy and practice, for all Cantle's (2009) claims to the contrary, fail to fulfil that role. Forthright civic leadership to curb political agitation from extreme right groups and parties such as the British National Party (BNP) may mitigate some of the immediate effects but, on its own, is unlikely to achieve a lasting drop in tensions (DCLG, 2006b). The same applies to local agencies represented by the media, community organisations and the police (see Grimshaw and Smart in Chapter Six of this volume).

The problem has therefore to be viewed in a holistic manner. There are certain things that are amenable to local and/or regional solutions, for example community development and housing supply/renewal; others that can only be addressed nationally (for example economic and urban policy); and yet others that are outwith the *immediate* (national) policy realm either because they are global in nature (geopolitical tensions and global economic inequalities) or because they are deeply entrenched historically (racism, Islamophobia, xenophobia and ethnocentrism).

To say that the last of these are beyond the 'immediate' remit of policy does not, however, mean that they are not ultimately amenable to such action. The problem is that the current cohesion policy agenda merely exacerbates the underlying tensions and conflicts. To argue, for example, that United Kingdom (UK) policy in the Middle East does not impact in any way on multi-ethnic communities in Britain is patently false. It is similarly erroneous to argue that community tensions can be lessened without addressing the problems associated with endemic racism (*especially in poor communities*). As will be discussed below, the latter issues are ever-more acute where these deprived areas are also subject to rapid population churn (Finney and Simpson, 2009).

The significance of housing quality and the built environment

Successive editions of *Improving opportunity, strengthening society* (DCLG, 2005, 2006a, 2007, 2009a) rightly draw attention to ongoing problems of overcrowding especially within poorer sections of the, predominantly, Muslim, Pakistani and Bangladeshi communities (see also Platt, 2005, 2007; Owen et al, 2006). What makes the plight of these households much worse, however, is the fact that this overcrowding is invariably accompanied by both deteriorating housing quality (even unfitness) and poor external environment (Owen et al, 2006; Ratcliffe, 2009).

The literature demonstrates clearly that heavy concentrations of these communities and their segregation from local White communities (and indeed from other migrant groups) have a long history (for a detailed summary of these debates, see Ratcliffe, 2009).

Not surprisingly given their significance to urban Britain, their formation from the 1950s onwards is well documented (Dahya, 1974; Smith, 1989; Lewis, 1994). But many writers focusing on the determinants of settlement patterns come to very different conclusions as to what these are. Expressed most simply, they place the dominant emphasis on either the forces that *constrain* choice or the expression of social agency in the sense of exercising (*unfettered*) choice (Ratcliffe, 2009). The dominant view was that, although the latter factors clearly played a part in household decision making,[1] 'choice' was rarely – if ever – unfettered, given a panoply of constraints ranging from racism and discrimination (both individual and institutional) and fear of harassment and attack to poverty (leading to a weak housing market position). In this context, spatial concentration was inevitable.

What this tells us is that the debate about 'self-segregation' is by no means a new phenomenon. It has, however, been reactivated in the past few years by the 'cohesion debate'. A process that was once seen as a predominantly positive phenomenon has now been seen in precisely the opposite light. The question is whether this new emphasis is driven by a concern for the future wellbeing of the segregated communities themselves or rather a concern for social order. We would argue that the latter is the case. In other words, it represents a return to the victim-blaming culture of earlier decades.

The Liverpool 'riots' of 1919 were viewed by the then government as the result of high concentrations of Black residents in the dock areas; segregation of this kind being seen as increasing the prospects of sedition. The truth of the matter was that these groups had little choice but to cluster, on account of a relatively weak position in the housing market and fears for their personal safety (May and Cohen, 1974). Many decades later, in the 1960s, parallel arguments were often applied to the Black community in Birmingham (Rex and Moore, 1967). Then, following the Brixton 'riots' in 1981, the then Home Secretary, William Whitelaw, blamed lax immigration control for the events – presumably on the grounds that the events would not have occurred had the residents not been permitted to enter the country (Solomos, 1987, 2003; Rowe, 1998).

The contemporary relevance of the spatial to social cohesion

As we have seen, however, the dominant social policy focus on ethnic segregation, infused with the suggestion that communities have begun to exhibit 'parallel lives', is a relatively recent phenomenon. The reason is self-evident: it stems from wider geopolitical forces and the 'othering' of Muslim communities (McGhee, 2005). The attendant rise in Islamophobia, both from state and civil society, has resulted in a disproportionate focus on apparently dissident sections of the Muslim population, especially among the young (Kundnani, 2007a; Fekete, 2009). Given this demonisation of Islam, however, it is not surprising that young people reflect on their material position and interpret their treatment in the UK (past and present) within this wider, geopolitical context.

What we effectively have is a 'racialisation of space', evidenced for example by conflicts over planning applications for mosques (McLoughlin, 2005). The areas that contain significant concentrations of Muslim communities are seen, *a priori*, as prone to actual or potential sedition. Combined with the allegation/assumption that these communities are closed to outside, that is, non-Muslim, observers, all residents are presumed to represent a potential risk to wider society: in short, they are effectively portrayed as 'suspect communities' (McGhee, 2008, p 52). The responsibilisation agenda seems, therefore, to have been extended to mainstream (that is, 'peaceable', probably 'Westernised') Muslims to monitor fellow Muslims. *Preventing Violent Extremism* (known simply as *Prevent*), a policy initiative introduced by the New Labour government in its latter years, institutionalised this process and cemented the racialisation process discussed earlier.

Funding levels for particular areas were determined by the size of the potential 'problem' allegedly stemming from a particular locality: in other words, the density of Muslim settlement. Among a host of local interventions, seminars were held with constituent groups on how to spot the tell-tale signs of radicalisation. Evidence of this came from the recent screening on national television of a workshop for Muslim women in which participants were expected, as part of a role-play exercise, to assume the identity of local police officers. This was clearly intended to achieve two results: to hone their monitoring and investigative skills and to increase the level of empathy with the police (by demonstrating how difficult their job is without the assistance of local residents).

A recently published report from the Institute of Race Relations (Kundnani, 2009) describes this policy as one of 'the most elaborate systems of surveillance ever seen in Britain'.[2] Echoing the words of Derek McGhee quoted above, it:

> in effect constructs the Muslim population as a 'suspect community', fosters social divisions among Muslims themselves and between Muslims and others, encourages tokenism, facilitates violations of privacy and professional norms of confidentiality, discourages local democracy and is counter-productive in reducing the risk of political violence. (Kundnani, 2009, p 8).

In other words, it appears to run counter to the whole idea of creating 'cohesive communities': it drives wedges between people. The same could be said about the introduction of CCTV surveillance in certain Muslim neighbourhoods in Birmingham, a practice first exposed by *The Guardian* newspaper in the summer of 2010.[3]

In terms of explaining exactly where, how and why urban tensions develop and flourish, we arguably need a much more nuanced analysis than one that relies on simplistic mantras based on the idea of an archetypal 'enemy within' or the perceived dangers of ethnic segregation.

It is generally recognised that continued immigration from the expanded EU and beyond generates significant challenges for both national and local policy makers. This was indeed one of the key drivers behind the setting up of the Commission on Integration and Cohesion (COIC, 2007).[4] The key point that is often not fully recognised, however, is that the impact of immigration is never uniform. Already-poor neighbourhoods are far more prone to population 'churn' (see Simpson in Chapter Four of this volume) than more affluent ones. In particular, net immigration into these localities within the past decade has tended to be both rapid and diverse (in ethnic terms). This 'geodemographic profile' (Burrows, 2008) is inevitable given that migrants, for example from recent EU accession countries, come to the UK looking for work and tend by definition to be relatively young and of modest means. The effect on local schools, housing and medical resources is predictable. And with the settled population already struggling to access adequate services, inter-communal resentment and tensions are almost inevitable. More affluent areas, in contrast, are relatively immune. This once again points to the need for an analysis grounded in an appreciation of the significance of material inequalities.

We now turn to perhaps the key question for this section of the chapter: is segregation on the basis of ethnic, cultural or faith background a problem *per se*? We defer until later the question of whether 'mixed communities' are a 'good idea' and, if so, whether they are likely to lead to more 'cohesive' neighbourhoods. Then there is the thorny, and indeed more fundamental, issue of whether 'social mix' is a *legitimate* target for policy intervention, whatever the likely prognosis (that is, success or failure in terms of generating 'mix').

The argument, that 'segregation' is, by definition, detrimental to the prospects of social inclusivity and the generation and maintenance of a stable society, is all pervasive. In explicit and less explicit forms this runs through the entire 'cohesion agenda' and much of the academic literature associated with it. In the United States (US) it is considered heretical to challenge or even question this prevailing orthodoxy. In this case, however, the legacy of enslavement and 'Jim Crow' has been (consistently) much higher levels of segregation between African and White Americans than experienced among comparable groups in the UK (Peach and Rossiter, 1996).[5] These US 'ghettos' are also far more historically entrenched and stubbornly intransigent (Ratcliffe, 2004).

Ludi Simpson has, throughout the past decade, been one of the relatively few dissenting academic voices (see Finney and Simpson, 2009, p 13; and Simpson in Chapter Four of this volume). With policy development over the past few years focusing more and more not just on segregation but also on *certain kinds* of segregation, however, these voices are becoming louder. Even *Our shared future* (COIC, 2007) argued that the problems associated with segregation had been overstated. The key point, however, is that most concern among government and policy circles has been reserved not for multi-ethnic areas in general but multi-ethnic areas *with high concentrations of Muslims* (Kundnani, 2007b; Burnett, 2008). In comparison, other forms of segregation, most notably the (increasingly popular) phenomenon of gated communities, has been accorded relatively little attention (Blandy, 2008).[6] The same is true for the 'routine segregation' of middle-class communities from other sectors of the population.

From the government's perspective, social order is necessarily accorded prime importance and other aspects of a 'cohesive' society are regarded as more peripheral. The problem is that this *de facto* interpretation of cohesion is fatally flawed. Quite apart from the problems arising from the obsession with Muslim communities, it is evident that talking about relations between people of 'different backgrounds' (see Chapter One of this volume) is also interpreted by most as a coded reference to ethnicity. But many of the contemporary conflicts and tensions in Britain are grounded primarily in differences of age/generational position, class and poverty (even if they may appear on the surface to have a significant ethnic dimension). We therefore need a more sophisticated interpretation of 'segregation'.

The key questions for the remainder of the current chapter are: how do we both improve access to good-quality housing and promote more stable and cohesive neighbourhoods? *Segregation is interpreted in this, much wider, sense, and we eschew simplistic and misleading concepts such as 'self-segregation'.*

Access to housing (and the widening of housing options)

Our arguments thus far have suggested that 'segregation' as deployed in the contemporary policy agenda has a highly particularistic character. Few have raised serious concerns about the 'self-segregation' of the White middle class or for that matter the longstanding 'self-segregation' of Hasidic Jewish communities.[7] However, the emphasis on spatial patterns does create the space within public discourse to focus on one compelling reason for addressing the *concentration* issue,[8] namely the link between concentrations of poverty, overcrowding and disrepair and the spatial patterning of poorer sections of certain minority groups.

What is being suggested here is that, irrespective of the view one takes on the wider merits/demerits of *ethnic* segregation (in terms of social cohesion), it is possible to defend certain policy strategies that will have the *effect* of thinning concentrations. These are:

- increasing access to social housing (Ratcliffe et al, 2001);
- addressing the problem of 'racial steering' (in all housing sectors);
- deploying regeneration policy so as to promote greater 'social mix'.

We now consider each of these in turn.

Increasing access to social housing

Some communities have a low degree of penetration into the social housing sector. This applies to many of those currently in the worst-quality housing, acquired by buying into the low-income owner-occupier market. The reasons for this are hotly debated; the crux being whether the core reasons are cultural, material or structural. Research in Bradford (Ratcliffe et al, 2001) concluded that there was a host of diverse factors conspiring to produce this result; ranging from the image of mainstream housing associations as 'White institutions for White people', the siting of main offices, the complexity of applications procedures and staff attitudes towards minority groups, to a mismatch between the needs of minority applicants and the types/sizes of properties available. To improve access to the sector would have the effect of both improving the living conditions of those at the poorest end of the private housing stock and gradually lowering levels of ethnic concentration. A variety of recommendations were proposed to achieve this end, including shared vacancy lists with the council and 'one-stop shops' sited in the busiest shopping areas of the city centre. To counter the resistance of those concerned about the potential threat to their personal safety (resulting from moving into an area outside a 'traditional' minority settlement area), 'group lettings' were encouraged. The latter were seen as a crucial element of a relocation scheme incorporating 'on the ground' support mechanisms.

A similar idea was then enshrined within the policy approach known as 'choice-based lettings': this simplified the allocation process by dispensing with the points-based system (Hills, 2007). It also had the twin advantages of increasing choice and of bringing the social housing applications process more in line with that traditionally associated with the private sector. The general consensus among social housing analysts, however, is that results have been mixed. In other words, in some cases it has 'failed' in the sense of not leading to a fall in segregation levels, while in others the results are, in this respect at least, more positive.

Extra pressure on the (already saturated) social housing stock resulting from continuing migration flows meant that allocation systems came under ever-increasing scrutiny. There were certain allegations, ill-advisedly repeated by one housing minister, that migrants were gaining preferential treatment. Then, addressing a well-publicised meeting of the Local Government Association, the chair of the Equality and Human Rights Commission gave further credence to the allegations by calling for an investigation into possible 'bias against Whites' in allocations policy (Phillips, 2007). Conceding that there was no concrete evidence beyond the purely anecdotal (and that even this was questionable), he nevertheless suggested that an investigation was in the public interest (and duly set up such a study). The results, reported in spring 2009, showed that there was no evidence that 'social housing allocation favours foreign migrants over UK citizens' (Rutter and Latorre, 2009, p ix).[9]

The prominence Phillips accorded to the initial allegation, however, meant that it is still given credence by those predisposed to believe it. The myth was aired once again in a BBC *Panorama* programme in the run-up to the 2010 General Election (on 19 April 2010). The programme, provocatively titled *Is Britain full?*, featured a young (White) mother living in appalling squalor on a social housing estate in Barking, Essex. While eschewing the label of racist, she argued that migrants were effectively jumping the queue for decent social housing (ahead of her).

Addressing the problem of 'racial steering' (in all housing sectors)

Despite being illegal under the provisions of the Race Relations Act 1976 as amended by the Race Relations (Amendment) Act 2000, there is evidence that 'racial steering' (often of an extremely subtle kind) may still be responsible for increasing levels of segregation (Ratcliffe et al, 2001). The phenomenon occurs when a housing professional (or institution, via its organisational culture) reduces the options offered to housing applicants (on the basis of their ethnic origin – majority or minority). Recent evidence has revealed that this form of discrimination has even had an effect with regard to new ('White') migrants from Eastern Europe (Lynn, 2009). Here, estate agents were seen to collude with landlords in reducing the housing options open to certain applicants. Responding to the results of the research, one discrimination lawyer was quoted as saying: 'It feels like we may as well, in some cases, be going back to the days of "no blacks, no dogs, no Irish"....' (Lynn, 2009).

There is evidence that this process transcends housing market sectors but it is important to remember that it can occur even in the absence of conscious intent on the part of individuals: such processes may be part of an institutional ethos/culture. Thus, for example, a White family may not be offered properties in an area known to contain minority groups, and a South Asian applicant may only be offered properties in 'Asian areas'. In both cases, the motive may be the belief that there is a desire on the part of these groups to live in a mono–ethnic environment, that is, that the *applicant* seeks 'self-segregation'.[10]

Research in Bradford and Leeds suggests that this and other forms of 'exclusionary' behaviour on the part of (mainstream) estate agents are leading to novel housing search and property exchange strategies. These feature (most notably) advertisements in community centres and places of worship and home-made posters in the front windows of properties for sale. The latter complement the rising number of micro-businesses in the form of minority-run agencies (Phillips and Ratcliffe, 2002; Phillips et al, 2007). The combined effect of these factors (whether unintended or not) is a maintenance of, or even intensification of, levels of minority concentration.

Once again, though, it casts doubt on the 'self-segregation' thesis and, in so far as the end result is an entrenchment of housing inequality, there is an argument for direct intervention in the realm of institution behaviour to ensure that housing market professionals understand the need to treat all customers equally. Under current legislation they could, and arguably should, deploy more proactive, positive-action strategies to encourage customers to consider the widest range of possible housing options.

Deploying regeneration policy so as to ensure greater social mix

Regeneration has often been seen as a source of conflict between communities. This is especially the case where schemes appear to benefit residents of a particular minority ethnic heritage. On occasions they have been seen as indicating discrimination against White households on the part of local authorities, and the political Right has exploited such interpretations for its own ends. If we look at the evidence of a history of regeneration policies and practices over the past 40 years or so, however, precisely the opposite is shown to be the case. It is Black and minority ethnic groups who have historically lost out in the allocation of renewal/regeneration funds (Rex and Moore, 1967; WMCC, 1986; Ratcliffe, 1992). This was due to the fact that, although these early schemes were explicitly *designed* as 'colour blind', prioritisation in terms of targeting spend was often not so. This is because decisions were often swayed by strong local political interests. To put it simply, poor White areas tended to be accorded priority over similarly poor Black and minority ethnic areas.

Funding streams in the 1990s such as Single Regeneration Budget, City Challenge and then the National Lottery produced little change. Considerable experience and expertise were required to succeed in the competition for funds and these tended to be concentrated in the hands of established (White) residents and residents' organisations. With growing political strength at the local level, however, the balance of power began to shift through the 1990s and into the next decade. But with success, as we have now witnessed, came problems of a different kind. Under area-based initiatives, poor areas with large concentrations of households from minority groups began to see inward investment (DCLG, 2006b). This, as we have seen in towns like Burnley and Oldham, fuelled resentment on the part of poor White people and these feelings were intensified by the intervention of extremist groups such as the BNP (Kalra, 2003).

There are a number of ways that regeneration can be used to tackle segregation and create more socially mixed neighbourhoods. Indeed, there were hopes that the housing renewal elements of the *Community Cohesion Pathfinder Programme 2003* would have this effect. Unfortunately, this appears not to have been the case. In the schemes scrutinised in research undertaken for the major report noted above (DCLG, 2006b), community cohesion and indeed the whole issue of ethnicity appeared to be highly marginal to the stated aims and objectives. Robinson and Pearce (2009, p 26), in an evaluation of nine Pathfinder areas, suggests that this is unsurprising given the lack of both compulsion to address 'community cohesion' issues and guidance as to what the latter might entail. Phillips et al (2008, p 83), on the other hand, suggest that Oldham and Rochdale represent major exceptions in that they sought 'to widen housing options and provide greater equality of opportunity in order to enable residential mobility and present better prospects for building more sustainable multi-ethnic neighbourhoods'.[11]

Some private housing developments, for example a major housing project close to the centre of Blackburn, have consciously attempted to match location and internal design/decor to the tastes and preferences of both White and South Asian groups. In this specific case, though, it simply did not work – there being little interest from White families. More research is needed to determine why this was the case. Was it, for example, due to White households being led to believe that house values would be compromised by the presence of Asian families, rather than any direct antipathy towards Asians as potential neighbours? If so, it would be a further example of 'racial steering', if rather more subtle than the forms seen earlier. This sort of misconception and its underlying sources can, and should, be challenged by appropriate interventions by both housing professionals and local authority leaders (as part of a civic values agenda). In doing so, it is important also to take on board the possible salience of local factors in decision-making processes.

The Department for Communities and Local Government (DCLG, 2009b, pp 5-6) argued that the Housing and Regeneration Bill will empower the Homes and Communities Agency 'to drive forward regeneration and the delivery of new social and affordable housing in sustainable, mixed tenure estates'. This leads directly to the final area of debate in relation to spatial integration strategies: the idea of generating more mixed, balanced and sustainable neighbourhoods.

Balanced and sustainable communities

The problem is that government thinking to date seems to be extremely muddled. A process of elision at times suggests that they are thought to be 'the same thing'; on other occasions they are used to refer to entirely different entities (DCLG, 2006c). And whereas the key thrust of policy is clearly towards greater 'social mix', many of the developments given planning approval are anything but 'mixed', *however* the latter is defined. Obvious cases here are 'gated communities', retirement villages, low-cost housing schemes and so on. Furthermore, initial commitments by developers to incorporate an agreed proportion of 'affordable homes' in new housing schemes rarely come to fruition as developers seek only marginally to widen access and avoid socially rented housing allocated to those in need. Put simply, it is not in developers' interests to build low-cost homes (on relatively high-cost land) and therefore if they are able to bend an agreement they are likely to do so.

This suggests two things: first, that central government needs to tighten up its overall thinking in this area;[12] and second, it needs to toughen up auditing and inspection regimes. This still leaves one thorny issue: will this form of social engineering 'work'? Here, we return to the earlier question as to the link between spatial integration and social integration (and 'cohesion').

One of the most prominent scholars in this area, David Robinson (2005, p 1425), has this to say on the matter of whether these strategies will lead to greater interethnic interaction and 'cohesion':

> It is ... questionable whether housing policy can effect change in residential settlement patterns and promote increasing interethnic mix at the neighbourhood level ... even if interethnic residential integration can be actively promoted, it cannot be assumed that interethnic interaction will inevitably follow.

We also do not know whether this 'ethnic interaction' would be harmonious, despite the fact that the latest analysis based on the 2005 Citizenship Survey concludes that 'ethnic diversity is, in most cases, associated with community cohesion' (Laurence and Heath, 2008, p 47). Putnam (2007) has argued, with considerable evidence from the US, that in the short to medium term, immigration and ethnic diversity tend to reduce social solidarity and social capital.

Significantly, the latest research from the Joseph Rowntree Foundation (Jayaweera and Choudhury, 2008) concludes that the ethnic/religious mix of neighbourhoods did not have an impact on residents' involvement in organisations, and challenges the assumption that the residential clustering of people from particular ethnic or religious backgrounds is necessarily a barrier to social interaction across those boundaries. A final highly pertinent point, or 'reality check', might be: even if housing policy does lead to a change in the composition of some neighbourhoods, the impact of this is likely to be highly marginal in terms of the national picture, given that the maximum annual change achievable in the housing stock is around a few percentage points.

Finally, it might be worth noting the work of Morrissey and Gaffikin (2006) around planning in contested space in Belfast where there is a high degree of residential segregation.[13] Belfast is an area with (in Putnam's terms) significant bonding social capital but very little bridging social capital. In a Protestant area of the city, new social housing was strongly opposed because it was thought that it would bring Catholics into the area. The Protestant residents preferred private housing, which would anonymise religious affiliation. This type of sectarianism presents difficulties for policy makers. Morrissey and Gaffikin advocate what they call 'smart pluralism' where a shared moral baseline does not need to be achieved (except for agreement to engage and negotiate with respect) but areas are identified where one side needs to convince the other side of the merits of their case in order to get the outcome they desire. Alliances are therefore built around planning and place shaping that provide secure and welcoming shared spaces.[14] Thus, wider planning policy needs to be looked at alongside housing policy.

Conclusion

This chapter has argued that the overriding focus of cohesion policy on (ethnic) segregation is misguided, and that the alleged tendency of certain communities to 'self-segregate' is simply wrong. In this we endorse the point made by Simpson (in Chapter Four of this volume) that much of what appears on the surface to support the latter thesis is in reality simply the product of a relatively youthful population growing *in situ*. It is undeniable that the arrival of significant numbers of new migrants in deprived areas (for example from the expanded EU) almost inevitably leads to increased local tensions. But in essence there is nothing specifically 'ethnic' about either the drivers of this 'population churn' or the end result: it essentially reflects the settlement of those with few housing (and labour market) options.

There is some evidence from recent research (Bailey and Manzi, 2008) that mixed tenure developments may enhance interaction between residents from different backgrounds (in class and ethnic terms). It is partly for this reason that they are a central plank of current policy on 'sustainable communities'. We have argued, however, that the main reason one might wish to defend such policies is not that they may lead to lower (ethnic) segregation levels but that there are potential gains in terms of increasing housing options and of raising the overall living standards of minority groups (and also, importantly, less affluent White people). This reorientation of the policy framework has inevitable implications for evaluation strategies. The central focus would need to shift towards an assessment of the gains in living standards and housing quality for all those whose options are currently constrained/compromised (that is, irrespective of ethnic origin or faith group).

It should perhaps be emphasised once again that, although relations between those from putatively different groups in ethnic terms appear at times strained, the root causes are invariably far more complex. Compounding ever-present factors such as racism and right-wing agitation, there may be locally specific historical dimensions to tensions. However, the enhanced strains of living in relatively impoverished and (emotionally and economically) stressful circumstances may well be more significant catalysts.

In conclusion, it is worth reiterating three key strands of the above arguments. First, major doubt has been cast on the merit of focus policy so heavily on physical concentrations of minority communities (see also Flint, 2009). Second, it is important to remember that the principal drivers of housing position and spatial patterns are income and social class (and not ethnicity). Finally, the chapter has stressed the rather limited power of the state in effecting change in housing market processes.

Notes

[1] Factors here include family and friendship networks, employment prospects and cultural amenities.

[2] www.irr.org.uk/spooked/

[3] The fierce controversy continued into the autumn: on 19 October 2010 it was reported that 'West Midlands Police face legal action from human rights group *Liberty* if they do not commit to removing controversial CCTV cameras. *Project Champion* received complaints from residents and civil liberty campaigners for placing "intrusive" CCTV cameras into Birmingham's

predominately Muslim areas of Sparkbrook and Washwood Heath' (www.
publicservice.co.uk/news_story.asp?id=14470).

[4] It could be argued with some justification, however, that the main subtext
was to do with concerns about the perceived security risk posed by Islamic
radicalism.

[5] This holds for any minority group when compared to the 'White' population
– except in a small number of highly localised cases.

[6] Steele (2009, unpaginated) extends this point by arguing that 'young
professionals living in "hotel style" apartments, and older middle-class white
people in USA-style retirement villages are cut off from wider society'.

[7] This is not, of course, to deny the continued presence of anti-Semitism; all
too frequent incidents being monitored by the Community Security Trust
(CST). Also, see Flint (2009).

[8] See Ratcliffe (1996) for debates about the relationship between concentration
and segregation.

[9] See also the important article by Robinson (2010) on EU migration and
social housing.

[10] This suggests that 'self-segregation' may take on the mantle of a self-fulfilling
prophecy.

[11] It is worth noting here the positive results achieved by the Rochdale
Inclusion Project (Robinson et al, 2004; DCLG, 2006b).

[12] It needs, for example, to ask the obvious questions such as: is a more socially
'mixed' area necessarily a more 'cohesive' and 'sustainable' one? Does 'balance'
mean the same as 'mix', or does it imply fixed targets/quotas(?) in terms of
constituent groups of residents?

[13] It is important to note that, as elsewhere in Northern Ireland, segregation on
ethno-religious grounds is more pronounced in working-class communities
than in relatively affluent areas (Shirlow and Murtagh, 2006).

[14] The research cited in the previous footnote also rightly points to the
challenges faced by state agencies seeking to promote positive social change

given deeply entrenched historical and cultural identities, housing market dynamics in interface areas and the activities of paramilitary organisations.

References

Bailey, N. and Manzi, T. (2008) *Developing and sustaining mixed tenure housing developments*, York: Joseph Rowntree Foundation.

Blandy, S. (2008) 'Secession or cohesion? Exploring the impact of gated communities', in J. Flint and D. Robinson (eds) *Community cohesion in crisis? New dimensions of diversity and difference* (pp 239-57), Bristol: The Policy Press.

Burnett, J. (2008) 'Community cohesion in Bradford: neoliberal integrationism', in J. Flint and D. Robinson (eds) *Community cohesion in crisis? New dimensions of diversity and difference* (pp 35-56), Bristol: The Policy Press.

Burrows, R. (2008) 'Geodemographics and the construction of differentiated neighbourhoods', in J. Flint and D. Robinson (eds) *Community cohesion in crisis? New dimensions of diversity and difference* (pp 219-37), Bristol: The Policy Press.

Cantle, T. (2009) *Community cohesion: A new framework for race and diversity* (2nd edition), Basingstoke: Palgrave Macmillan.

COIC (Commission on Integration and Cohesion) (2007) *Our shared future*, London: COIC.

Dahya, B. (1974) 'The nature of Pakistani ethnicity in industrial cities in Britain', in A. Cohen (ed) *Urban ethnicity* (pp 77-118), London: Tavistock.

DCLG (Department for Communities and Local Government) (2005) *Improving opportunity, strengthening society*, London: DCLG.

DCLG (2006a) *Improving opportunity, strengthening society: One year on, a progress report*, London: DCLG.

DCLG (2006b) *Managing for diversity: A case study of four local authorities*, London: DCLG.

DCLG (2006c) *Planning policy statement 3: Housing*, London: DCLG.

DCLG (2007) *Improving opportunity, strengthening society: Two years on, a progress report*, London: DCLG.

DCLG (2009a) *Improving opportunity, strengthening society: A third report on the government's strategy for race equality and community cohesion*, London: DCLG.

DCLG (2009b) *Housing and Regeneration Bill*, London: DCLG.

Fekete, L. (2009) *A suitable enemy: Racism, migration and Islamophobia in Europe*, London: Pluto.

Finney, N. and Simpson, L. (2009) *'Sleepwalking to segregation'? Challenging myths about race and migration*, Bristol: The Policy Press.

Flint, J. (2008) 'Welfare state institutions and secessionary neighbourhood spaces', in J. Flint and D. Robinson (eds) (2008) *Community cohesion in crisis? New dimensions of diversity and difference* (pp 159-76), Bristol: The Policy Press.

Flint, J. (2009) 'Cultures, ghettos and camps: sites of exception and antagonism in the city', *Housing Studies*, vol 24, no 4, pp 417-31.

Flint, J. and Robinson, D. (eds) (2008) *Community cohesion in crisis? New dimensions of diversity and difference*, Bristol: Policy Press.

Harrison, M. and Phillips, D. (2005) *Housing, 'race' and community cohesion*, Coventry: Chartered Institute of Housing.

Hills, J. (2007) *Ends and means: The future roles of social housing in England*, CASE Report 34, London: Centre for Analysis of Social Exclusion, London School of Economics.

Jayaweera, H. and Choudhury, T. (2008) *Immigration, faith and cohesion: An exploration of the factors that affect community cohesion in urban areas in England with significant Muslim populations*, York: Joseph Rowntree Foundation, www.jrf.org.uk/knowledge/findings/socialpolicy/2190.asp

Kalra, V. (2003) 'Police lore and community disorder: diversity in the criminal justice system', in D. Mason (ed) *Explaining ethnic differences: Changing patterns of disadvantage in Britain* (pp 139-52), Bristol: The Policy Press.

Kundnani, A. (2007a) *The end of tolerance: Racism in 21st century Britain*, London: Pluto Press.

Kundnani, A. (2007b) 'Integrationism: the politics of anti-Muslim racism', *Race and Class*, vol 43, no 4, pp 67-72.

Kundnani, A. (2009) *Spooked! How not to prevent violent extremism*, London: Institute of Race Relations.

Laurence, J. and Heath, A. (2008) *Predictors of community cohesion: Multi-level modelling of the 2005 Citizenship Survey*, London: DCLG.

Lewis, P. (1994) *Islamic Britain*, Oxford: I.B. Taurus.

Lynn, G. (2009) 'Migrant workers face rental block', BBC News Channel, 4 August, http://news.bbc.co.uk/1/hi/business/8181486.stm

McGhee, D. (2005) *Intolerant Britain? Hate, citizenship and difference*, Buckingham: Open University Press.

McGhee, D. (2008) *The end of multiculturalism? Terrorism, integration and human rights*, Maidenhead: Open University Press/McGraw-Hill.

McLoughlin, S. (2005) 'Mosques and the public space: conflict and cooperation in Bradford', *Journal of Ethnic and Migration Studies*, vol 31, no 6, pp 1045-66.

May, R. and Cohen, R. (1974) 'The interaction between race and colonialism: the Liverpool race riots of 1919', *Race and Class*, vol 16, no 2, p 111-26.

Morrissey, M. and Gaffikin, F. (2006) 'Planning for peace in contested space', *International Journal of Urban and Regional Research*, vol 30, no 4, pp 873-93.

Owen, D.W., Beckford, J., Peach, C. and Weller, P. (2006) *(Review of) the evidence base on faith communities*, London: DCLG.

Parekh, B. (Commission on the Future of Multi-Ethnic Britain) (2000) *The future of multi-ethnic Britain: The Parekh Report*, London: Profile Books.

Peach, G.C.K. and Rossiter, D. (1996) 'Level and nature of spatial concentration and segregation of minority ethnic groups in Britain, 1991', in P. Ratcliffe (ed) *Social geography and ethnicity in Britain: Geographical spread, spatial concentration and internal migration: Ethnicity in the 1991 Census, Volume 3*, London: HMSO.

Phillips, D. and Ratcliffe, P. (2002) *Movement to opportunity? South Asian relocation in northern cities*, Economic and Social Research Council (ESRC) End of Award Report, Swindon: ESRC.

Phillips, D., Davis, C. and Ratcliffe, P. (2007) 'British Asian narratives of urban space', *Transactions of the Institute of British Geographers*, vol 32, no 2, pp 217-34.

Phillips, D., Simpson, L. and Ahmed, S. (2008) 'Shifting geographies of minority ethnic settlement: remaking communities in Oldham and Rochdale', in J. Flint and D. Robinson (eds) (2008) *Community cohesion in crisis? New dimensions of diversity and difference* (pp 81-97), Bristol: The Policy Press.

Phillips, T. (2007) 'LGA European Year speech' to the Local Government Association, London, 1 November.

Platt, L. (2005) *Migration and social mobility: The life chances of Britain's minority ethnic communities*, York: Joseph Rowntree Foundation.

Platt, L. (2007) *Poverty and ethnicity in the UK*, Bristol: The Policy Press.

Putnam, R.D. (2007) 'E Pluribus Unum: diversity and community in the twenty-first century' [The 2006 Johan Skytte Prize Lecture], *Scandinavian Political Studies*, vol 30, no 2, pp 137-74.

Ratcliffe, P. (1992) 'Renewal, regeneration and "race": issues in urban policy', *New Community*, vol 18, no 3, pp 387-400.

Ratcliffe, P. (ed) (1996) *Social geography and ethnicity in Britain: Geographical spread, spatial concentration and internal migration: Ethnicity in the 1991 Census, Volume 3*, London: HMSO.

Ratcliffe, P. (2004) *'Race', ethnicity and difference: Imagining the inclusive society*, Maidenhead: Open University Press/McGraw-Hill.

Ratcliffe, P. (2009) 'Re-evaluating the links between "race" and residence', *Housing Studies*, vol 24, no 4, pp 433-50.

Ratcliffe, P. with Harrison, M., Hogg, R., Line, B., Phillips, D. and Tomlins, R. (2001) *Breaking down the barriers: Improving Asian access to social rented housing*, Coventry: Chartered Institute of Housing.

Rex, J. and Moore, R. (1967) *Race, community and conflict: A study of Sparkbrook*, London and Oxford: Oxford University Press.

Robinson, D. (2005) 'The search for community cohesion: key themes and dominant concepts of the public policy agenda', *Urban Studies*, vol 42, no 8, pp 1411-27.

Robinson, D. (2007) 'Living parallel lives? Housing, residential segregation and community cohesion in England', in H. Beider (ed) *Neighbourhood renewal & housing markets: Community engagement in the US & UK* (pp 163-85), Oxford: Blackwell.

Robinson, D. (2010) 'New immigrants and migrants in social housing in Britain: discursive themes and lived realities', *Policy & Politics*, vol 38, no 1, pp 57-77.

Robinson, D. and Pearce, S. (2009) *Housing market renewal and community cohesion*, London: DCLG.

Robinson, D., Coward, S., Fordham, T., Green, S. and Reeve, K. (2004) *How housing management can contribute to community cohesion*, Coventry: Chartered Institute of Housing.

Rowe, M. (1998) *The racialisation of disorder in twentieth century Britain*, Aldershot: Ashgate.

Rutter, J. and Latorre, M. (2009) *Social housing allocation and immigrant communities*, London: EHRC.

Shirlow, P. and Murtagh, B. (2006) *Belfast: Segregation, violence and the city*, London: Pluto Press.

Smith, S.J. (1989) *The politics of 'race' and residence: Citizenship, segregation and White supremacy in Britain*, Cambridge: Polity Press.

Solomos, J. (1987) *Riots, urban protest and social policy*, Policy Papers in Ethnic Relations, no 7, Swindon: CRER/ESRC.

Solomos, J. (2003) *Race and racism in Britain*, Basingstoke: Palgrave Macmillan.

Steele, A. (2009) *Segregated housing 'undermines' community*, Salford: University of Salford, www.salford.ac.uk/news/details/822

WMCC (West Midlands County Council) (1986) *A different reality: An account of Black people's experiences and their grievances before and after the Handsworth rebellions of September 1985*, Birmingham: WMCC.

NINE

Education policy, social cohesion and citizenship

Audrey Osler

Introduction

Across the globe there has been, since the early 1990s, increased interest in the role of citizenship education in creating cohesive societies, by both national policy makers and international organisations. This chapter focuses on the role of education generally and citizenship education in particular within the United Kingdom (UK) government's goal of fostering cohesion, examining both the policy framework for schooling in England and those policies that address the education of adult migrants. These policies are situated within a historical context, since much of what is advocated in schooling today appears to reflect a longstanding goal of promoting a hegemonic national identity or 'national cohesion', dating from the late 19th century.

The chapter examines the dynamic between citizenship and cohesion agendas, and reflects on tensions and contradictions between official policies, intended outcomes and differentials in student attainment. The aim is to make explicit some assumptions about learners that underpin policies, and to explore the meanings of terms such as 'diversity', 'citizenship' and 'community cohesion' within education policy. In considering ways of evaluating the effectiveness of education for social cohesion, a key assumption is that education policy and practice and the wider social policy agenda need to be underpinned by a commitment to universal human rights.

Civic values, education and cohesion: historical context

Twenty-first-century advocates of citizenship education were not the first to see such learning as important in enabling societal stability, if not cohesion. As early as 1651, political theorist Thomas Hobbes's *Leviathan* was arguing for specific provision of a conservative form of (adult) civic instruction, with time set aside from labour, in which people be taught their duties and the rights of the sovereign, so as to avoid violence and civil unrest. On the curriculum were patriotism, resistance to demagogues, respect for government, responsible parenthood and law and order. Hobbes argued that alongside knowledge there should be a focus on attitudes (Heater, 1990).

From the introduction of mass schooling in the late 19th century, European governments saw education as a means to promote national identity and pride. In this sense, traditional civic education, taught in Britain largely through national history and celebrations such as Empire Day, might be said to have been about national cohesion.

The British experience and role of education for citizenship in schools from this period to the present day differs from other European nation states. For example, from the late 19th century, citizenship education in France has tended to remain high on the political agenda, having its roots in the need to consolidate national support for the Third Republic when democracy was restored in 1871 (Osler and Starkey, 2001).

The philosopher, John Dewey, observed how nationalism, mediated through state education, replaced the earlier cosmopolitan traditions of the Enlightenment:

> So far as Europe was concerned, the historic situation identified the movement for a state-supported education with the nationalist movement in political life … education became a civic function and the civic function was identified with the realization of the ideal of the national state. The 'state' was substituted for humanity; cosmopolitanism gave way to nationalism. (Dewey, [1916] 2002, p 108)

According to Dewey, publicly funded mass education, introduced when nationalism was at its zenith, not only replaced an earlier tradition of education as a charitable function (often run by religious interests), but also contributed to the demise of an earlier cosmopolitan tradition of loyalty to fellow humanity. Schooling became a central element of the nationalist project.

From 1918, following the First World War, pacifist interests had a direct impact on education where, in France, they were prioritised by many primary school teachers, and contrasted strongly with the militaristic messages of textbooks (Siegel, 2005). Pacifist beliefs encouraged a return to cosmopolitan values; loyalty to fellow humanity was promoted as part of the French republican tradition of patriotism, rather than in opposition to it. Education was fundamental, since teacher-activists were convinced that the prevention of war required more than international diplomacy and economic cooperation; sustainable peace required attitudinal change, whereby people 'abandoned their chauvinistic impulses and embraced cross-national understanding as the keystone of global stability' (Siegel, 2005, p 3).

UK political and educational policies differ considerably between the countries of England, Wales, Scotland and Northern Ireland both historically and currently, so that different approaches and meanings are given to citizenship and social cohesion in and through education in these different contexts. The analysis that follows largely addresses developments in England and Wales, where until the establishment of devolved government through the Welsh Assembly in 1998, education policy was broadly similar. In Scotland and Northern Ireland, policies and legal frameworks differ and religious affiliation has been a significant factor influencing educational opportunity, social status, mobility and employment (Gallagher et al, 1994; Paterson and Iannelli, 2006).

In England, debates about the role of education in promoting either nationalist or alternative cosmopolitan visions of society were played out in debates among professional historians and teachers about the role of history in schools. On one side were those who wished to promote pride in the military and the Empire. On the other were those who believed that nationalism was the major cause of war and who argued for a programme of world history, emphasising international cooperation and social progress. This latter viewpoint was upheld by the League of Nations, which argued that 'history syllabuses must also be purged of war if they were to become an effective instrument of peace' (Elliott, 1980, p 40). A small group of progressive educationists and liberal thinkers founded what was to become the UNESCO-affiliated World Education Fellowship, committed to democracy, world citizenship, international understanding and world peace.

In the second half of the 20th century, what was remarkable was the absence of education for democratic participation. National history and pride continued to be promoted, but such civic education as existed was rarely explicit. In any case, history, seen as the main means of promoting civic attitudes, failed in the post-war period to secure a strong place in the curriculum (Elliott, 1980). An elitist, knowledge-based civic education, known as 'British Constitution', was available to privately educated and/or academically able students, but Conservative thinkers remained suspicious of any form of political education, equating it with indoctrination. A Conservative education minister, Rhodes Boyson, was quoted as saying: '[p]olitics, like sex education, is something that should be left to the family' (Heater, 1990, p 221). Conservatives were equally suspicious of local authorities, which from the 1970s began promoting multicultural education, generally understood as reflecting elements of Caribbean, Indian and Pakistani cultures in the curriculum, and occasionally including explicit anti-racist messages.

Interest in young people's political education developed in the wake of the 1968 student revolutions. The lowering of the voting age to 18 years also contributed to a growing interest in political education. Pressure for change came from the Politics Association's Programme for Political Education (PPE), led by Bernard Crick, which emphasised the concept of 'political literacy' (Crick and Lister, 1978). An independent committee of inquiry, chaired by Lord Swann and responding to Black community concerns about schools' failure to support Black students' academic performance, made direct reference to the PPE in its report, *Education for all* (DES, 1985). It highlighted racism in schools and society, concluding that all schools, regardless of ethnic make-up, should develop political education that can 'play a part in countering racism at both institutional and individual levels' (1985, p 336). In response, some local authorities switched from an exclusive focus on minority ethnic communities as problems to one in which structural inequalities and racism were discussed. Others, including some with low-density minority ethnic populations, began to develop curricula designed to address racism within White populations. These trends co-existed with a belief that differentials in student outcomes might be bridged if school curricula addressed minority students' cultures and experiences.

There was never a uniform country-wide policy of multiculturalism in education. Local authorities that began, post-Swann, to develop policies challenging racism as a barrier to participation were stopped in their tracks by the pressures of the Conservative government's national education reforms. The Education Reform Act 1988 introduced a highly prescriptive national curriculum into England, Wales and Northern Ireland, ensuring that students in publicly funded schools experienced a traditionally focused common curriculum. The new curriculum not only curtailed efforts to implement the Swann Report, but by removing locally led responsibility for curriculum development and limiting teacher autonomy, also undermined policies and practices in multicultural education in areas where these were already established (Tomlinson, 2009).

The Speaker's Commission on Citizenship (SCC) (1990) recommended that *active citizenship* be promoted, in schools and society. This focus on active citizenship complemented the Conservative government's neoliberal agenda, which identified social services not primarily as a state responsibility but as one that citizens could fulfil through voluntary associations. Although citizenship became a cross-curricular theme, guidance on citizenship education had minimal impact on schools, which were preoccupied with implementing the heavily subject-focused curriculum. Although the SCC failed to achieve concrete outcomes, it served to 'prompt discussion of what should be of value in a democracy, and whether, in any case, we value democracy' (Murdoch, 1991, p 441).

Citizenship and citizenship education

Despite the work of work of T.H. Marshall (1950), who importantly extended the concept of citizenship beyond political and civic matters to encompass social rights, and the work of later scholars, citizenship did not become part of political discourse until the late 1980s. 'Citizenship' was then proposed as a solution for a diverse set of societal problems, although the term remained unclear and unfamiliar to a wider public. Journalist Hugo Young (1988, quoted in Heater, 2009, p 18) observed: '[s]omething is rotten in the state of Britain, and all the parties know it…. The buzz word emerging as the salve for this distress is something called citizenship…. [T]here is an immense unsatisfied demand for it to mean something.'

The regular usage of the term 'citizenship' in the context of immigration control, throughout the 20th century, largely eclipsed meanings associated with active citizenship and citizen participation. Immigration laws were applied to specific migrants identified as undesirable and/or seen as posing a threat of violence and undermining social cohesion (Finney and Simpson, 2009). It is hardly surprising that the term 'citizenship', used in the context of a racialised debate about desirable and undesirable immigration, became associated with exclusion.

During the 1990s, a number of teachers and other commentators expressed the view that citizenship studies were inappropriate since learners were not citizens but subjects. This reflects a peculiarly British antipathy for studying politics at school. Fogelman (1991) observed how school principals, questioned about the citizenship education in their schools, suggested that the area of study contained little or no political matter. Among possible causes of depoliticised citizenship education are: no widely agreed narrative of the distribution of political power; an uncodified constitution coupled with a political culture 'with only the vaguest ideas about constitutionality'; hostility to Europe, often expressed in simplistic constitutional terms; and right-wing anxiety about left-wing propaganda (Frazer, 1999, pp 17-18). Additionally, teachers may lack confidence in addressing political matters in a political climate in which a less clearly articulated set of agreed democratic and human rights principles exists than in other international contexts (Hahn, 1999; Osler and Starkey, 1999).

It was not until the introduction of citizenship as a national curriculum subject in 2002 that any form of explicit civic education was widely practised in English schools. This successful initiative was achieved by Education Secretary David Blunkett, who appointed Bernard Crick to chair an advisory group on citizenship and democracy in schools. The resulting Crick Report (QCA, 1998) achieved cross-party consensus and was the foundational document of the new curriculum. Political literacy, social and moral responsibility and community involvement were identified as the three main elements. The report acknowledged the longstanding diversity of the UK and its constituent nations, but avoided debate about other forms of diversity, with only a passing reference to the multicultural nature of Britain. It failed to recognise gender differences or discuss unity and diversity in a multicultural democracy. Instead, Crick stressed unity or cohesion (Osler, 2005). Citizenship, in the civic republican tradition, was presented as a complete project, with no recognition of barriers to participation or ongoing struggles to claim equal citizenship rights or, indeed, human rights (Osler, 2000b). Following lobbying from the Education in Human Rights Network (Crick, 2000; Osler, 2000a), the final report, while not placing human rights at the heart of the project, acknowledged that students should learn about key international human rights documents.

Pykett (2007), who interviewed members of the Crick advisory group, noted how many played down the political significance of citizenship education and the controversial nature of their work. Two areas of tension were the degree to which learners should exercise autonomy in decision making and the question of multiculturalism. In referring to 'the homelands of our minority communities' (QCA, 1998, p 17), the Crick Report adopted 'a colonial flavour' and implied that minority groups must change their behaviour to become more British and law abiding (Osler, 2000b). The report's discourse of tolerance masks 'an erasure of difference' (Pykett, 2007, p 306).

It was only after the 2005 London bombings that there was significant political interest in favour of teaching about diversity within citizenship education. 'Diversity', which had previously only been used in education policy discourse with reference to market forces and 'parental choice', was from this point associated with visible minorities. In 2006, the Ajegbo Report (DfES, 2007) was commissioned, in direct response to official concerns about terrorism and a desire to promote Britishness, shared values and patriotism, through both citizenship and history (Osler, 2008, 2009b). Ajegbo's recommendation of a new strand on 'identity and diversity; living together in the UK' was adopted in the revised citizenship curriculum. Following long-established patterns, minorities were linked to social instability, to separation and, in the case of British Muslims, to the new threat of international terrorism.

The Ajegbo Report, while advocating critical thinking on race, did not achieve this. It offered no explanation of why significant numbers of schools were half-hearted or worse in complying with race relations legislation, nor did it acknowledge the structural disadvantage, expressed in differential examination outcomes and exclusion rates (Tikly et al, 2006) that students from particular ethnic groups encounter. Relatively weak messages about an inclusive British identity, promoted through the citizenship curriculum, contrasted with negative portrayals of migrants from both media and government relating to immigration, naturalisation and asylum (Finney and Simpson, 2009) and with an equally negative portrayal of British Muslim populations.

Following Ajegbo, the second version of the citizenship curriculum, enacted from 2009, reasserts the role of history in promoting national identity and national cohesion and making learners familiar with British values and culture. In this respect, it draws directly from Crick, assuming that minorities need to learn how 'we' behave and understand 'our' way of doing things. Integration is presented as a one-way process, similar to that advocated by the Department for Communities and Local Government (DCLG, 2008).

The 2009 curriculum builds on an approach advocated by former Prime Minister Gordon Brown, emphasising Britishness and British history. Brown (2006) referred to a loss of national confidence, coinciding with the end of the Empire, and argued for a re-emphasis on patriotism:

> [T]o address almost every one of the major challenges facing our country – [including], of course, our community relations and multiculturalism and, since July 7th, the balance between diversity and integration; even the shape of our public services – you must have a clear view of what being British means, what you value about being British and what gives us purpose as a nation.

Although Brown did not present cosmopolitanism and patriotism as mutually incompatible, he echoed concerns about 'diversity and integration', linking these directly to terrorism. The local and global dimensions of his vision disappeared once he focused on schools. He argued that British history, presented as a grand narrative of progress towards liberty and democracy, should be central to citizenship education. The political rhetoric overlooked the realities of 21st-century history education with its emphasis on critical thinking and advocated a model of school history similar to that of the early 20th century, emphasising national cohesion and unquestioning loyalty.

Educational legal and policy frameworks

The Stephen Lawrence Inquiry highlighted institutional racism not only in the police force, but also across a range of public services, including education (Macpherson, 1999). It proposed the school curriculum be reformed to promote racial justice and diversity. The government response (Home Office, 1999) highlighted citizenship education as the main vehicle by which young people in England should learn to value diversity and challenge racism. This expectation was something of an afterthought, since the Crick Report made only passing reference to multiculturalism and none to racism.

The initial positive government response to the Stephen Lawrence Inquiry was not matched by any commitment by education ministers to ensure that schools address racism as a barrier to full citizenship. Indeed, ministers avoided any use of the word 'racism', even when discussing significant differentials in educational outcomes (Osler, 2002). Nevertheless, the subsequent Race Relations (Amendment) Act 2000 required schools to develop race equality policies, and Ofsted to monitor their progress. Ofsted's leadership had shown itself reluctant to address racial justice (Osler and Morrison, 2000) and the organisation was singularly ill-equipped to take on this role. Despite this, Ofsted (2005, p 26) found that more than one in four education authorities were failing to comply with race relations legislation.

Following the 9/11 attacks, education has come under greater public scrutiny, particularly concerning ways in which policies and practices enable or undermine 'community cohesion'. Immediately prior to 9/11, Ouseley (2001) identified a 'virtual apartheid' in Bradford and the failure of city schools to address living together in a multicultural society. The Cantle (2001) review, which examined violent disturbances in a number of towns in Northern England, claimed that distinct religious and ethnic communities were living in geographical proximity without developing cultural or social bonds, suggesting that schools have a key role in challenging apparent 'parallel lives'.

Under the Education and Inspections Act 2006, schools have a legal duty to promote community cohesion. Specific guidance issued to schools by the Department of Education (DCSF, 2007) defines community cohesion as 'working towards a society in which there is a common vision and sense of belonging among all communities' (p 3) in which 'the diversity of people's backgrounds and circumstances is appreciated and valued' (p 3), 'similar life opportunities are available to all' (p 3) and where 'strong and positive relationships exist and continue to be developed in the workplace, in schools and the wider community' (p 3). Curriculum guidance advocates school-linking, locally, nationally and internationally, and enabling students through the curriculum to develop a better understanding of other cultures (QCDA, 2010). The curriculum guidance focuses largely on the celebration of diversity, but does encourage an exploration of political issues relating to realising 'similar life opportunities' for all. The Equality Act 2010 extends schools' legal duties, but at the time of writing specific guidance to schools was not available.

Faith schools, which from 2001 were given official encouragement to play a larger part in public education, have been subject to particular scrutiny. A number of minority faith schools have moved from the private to the public sector, while maintaining control over student admissions and the content of religious education. Research by the Runnymede Trust on schooling and community cohesion (Osler, 2007) revealed how many schools (both faith and non-faith) were struggling to fulfil their legal duty to promote community cohesion. Some schools with a relatively homogeneous student population considered it sufficient to establish linking or twinning arrangements with schools with a different student population, in order to fulfil their statutory obligations, without necessarily developing clear aims. In response to the Runnymede project, Education Secretary Ed Balls suggested a possible change in emphasis in the Labour government's support for faith schools, stating: '[i]t is up to the local community to decide what it wants ... we are not leading a drive for more faith schools' (quoted in Berkeley, 2008, p 4).

Demand for minority faith school places depends, in part, on the responses of those schools without any faith affiliation to the religious beliefs and identities of students. A decision by the House of Lords (R [on the application of S.B.] v. Governors of Denbigh High School [2006] U.K.H.L 15) that a school's refusal to adapt its school uniform rules to accommodate the beliefs of one of its students who wished to wear the *jilbab* (a full-length loose gown regarded by a minority of strict Muslims as the only form of appropriate public dress for an adult woman) generated considerable media discourse about religious dress in publicly funded schools and other public areas. Yet, schools in England have for a long time accommodated other moderate adaptations of school uniform in order to respond to students' religious beliefs. The *hijab*, which was banned from French schools in 2004, has long been accommodated in schools in England as well as into the uniforms of the UK police and military. The focus within cohesion discourses on women's Islamic religious dress suggests that Islam is seen as a limiting case for inclusion, with Muslims, particularly Muslim women, presented as the Other, who need to adapt to society's prevailing norms (Osler, 2009b).

Since the 2005 London bombings, education policy agendas on community cohesion and citizenship have become more closely intertwined. Yet, neither agenda seems to be closely linked to parallel educational policy goals, namely improving the educational outcomes of students in general and those ethnic groups that schools have failed. Gillborn (2006) argues that citizenship education has served as a placebo; in presenting citizenship as the sole means by which race equality in schools might be promoted, the government avoided introducing concrete measures to address racial justice. While this analysis underplays the role of teacher agency in policy implementation, it is the case that political leaders identify racism in education as an interpersonal issue, avoiding discussion of its institutional nature (Blair, 2006; Osler, 2009b).

Any analysis of citizenship education policy needs also to take into account the ways in which learners also exercise agency in responding to their local contexts, media discourses and citizenship education programmes (Pykett, 2009; Hollingworth and Archer, 2010). While policy makers have been slow to assure children and young people of their right to express their views on matters affecting them in educational policy making and in schooling more generally, research confirms that they are not simply passive receivers of educational initiatives relating to citizenship and cohesion, but attach meanings of their own to initiatives designed to increase their participation and strengthen social justice (Osler, 2010).

Institutional racism, defined in terms the government accepted as 'collective failure of an organisation to provide an appropriate and professional service to people because of their colour, culture, or ethnic origin' (Macpherson, 1999, p 28) is reflected in the continuing attainment gap between Black and White students, as recorded in the Youth Cohort Study (YCS).[1] The 'standards' agenda, adopted as a central plank of New Labour education policy, and implemented through target setting to raise the proportion of young people leaving school with higher-grade General Certificate in Secondary Education (GCSE) results, has resulted in an overall improvement in academic attainment, but not closed the gap between the highest-attaining ethnic group and the lowest. Examining the period 1989-2004, and drawing on YCS data, the number of White students attaining higher-grade GCSE results rose from 30 to 55%, or 25 percentage points. In the same period, Black students in this sample saw an improvement of 16 points, from 18 to 34%. By these measures, despite overall improvements, the gap widened from 12 to 21 percentage points over the 15-year period (DfES, 2005, adapted in Gillborn, 2008, p 58).

Community cohesion policies in education exist without reference to ongoing inequalities in educational outcomes. Although, under the Education and Inspections Act 2006, all schools have a statutory duty to promote community cohesion, the little research that is available (Osler, 2007; Berkeley, 2008) suggests that schools' goals are often unclear and not evaluated. Neglect of academic outcomes in government statements on community cohesion and schooling mean that cohesion is seen by school leaders as an additional legal requirement, separate from the central focus of government policy, namely to raise academic standards. Material differences in outcomes between ethnic groups are often glossed over in official statements that aim to demonstrate that academic standards are improving.

Citizenship education and testing of adult migrants

The introduction of citizenship education into schools was part of a wider New Labour social project, including 'civil renewal' and policy developments relating to immigration and asylum. David Blunkett (2003, pp 4-5) working as Home Secretary between 2001 and 2004, extended the agenda he began as Education Secretary, claiming that, in addition to citizenship education, civil renewal also addressed 'freedom, duty and obligation', 'participation' and 'self-government' within 'communities'.

Concerns with crime, security, civility and decency are echoed in the 2008 Green Paper *The path to citizenship*, which contains government proposals for reforming the processes by which migrants meet the requirements for naturalisation. The stated reasoning for change is not only to streamline immigration, thereby 'reducing the possibilities for abuse' and maximising the benefits of migration, but also 'putting British values at the heart of the system' (Home Office, 2008, p 9). Migrants are thus subject to civilising offensives, which are then extended to other populations who are said to lack values, such as 'antisocial' young people, the unemployed and 'inadequate' parents, in the Conservative 'Broken Britain' discourse.

In the Green Paper, immigrants, far from being portrayed as aspirant citizens capable of making positive contributions, are repeatedly associated with crime (Osler, 2009a), with the words 'crime', 'criminal', 'prison' and 'detention' frequently used. There is also mention of murder, rape and crimes against children, with such crimes implicitly, but never explicitly, linked to migrants. Negative messages about newcomers are contrasted with 'British values', alternatively expressed as 'shared values' and 'our values'. The document gives the impression that Britain is a country under siege by certain unspecified newcomers unlikely to subscribe fully to such values.

Yet, as Parekh (quoted in DfES, 2007, p 91) has observed, 'we can refer to British shared values only in so far as we can say that the UK has decided to commit to those values and in this sense take ownership of them.' The values to which the UK has formally committed are, in fact, human rights values, as expressed in the Universal Declaration of Human Rights 1948 and subsequent ratification of international human rights instruments, including the European Convention on Human Rights 1950, incorporated into domestic law through the Human Rights Act 1998.

As well as making reference to active citizenship, the Green Paper introduces the concepts of 'earned citizenship' and 'probationary citizenship', suggesting that community cohesion requires that 'all migrants "earn" the right to citizenship and ... demonstrate their commitment to the UK by playing an active part in the community' (Home Office, 2008, p 12). A volunteering programme is proposed, in which aspirant citizens are required to engage with others beyond their cultural groups. Since cohesion is understood to be about inter-group relations, aspirant citizens are required to engage in inter-group volunteering. Valid volunteering implies inter-group activity. In this model, for example, those who volunteer to teach Arabic in a supplementary school, supporting children in developing mother-tongue skills, cannot earn their citizenship through this means, since it is perceived as an intra-group activity. An alternative, valid activity would be volunteering at a primary school, with children drawn from different cultural groups to one's own.

Along the 'path' to citizenship, aspirant citizens are eventually accorded the status of 'probationary' citizen. The right to residence can be revoked or full citizenship status postponed if individuals fail further tests, such as continuous employment. Although no evidence is provided to support such a case, the assumption is that migrants are undeserving, less likely to obey the law, and must therefore earn their rights. They are placed in a similar category to the settled minority communities in the Crick Report, needing greater guidance than others in the processes of learning 'our' values. Those who drafted the Green Paper appear to believe that the realisation of societal cohesion rests not on equality of opportunity, or shared human rights, but on passing a series of tests, not applied to those who are citizens from birth.

The notion of earning rights is problematic for a number of reasons. First, everyone in the UK is protected by the European Convention on Human Rights 1950, which applies regardless of citizenship status. Entitlement to human rights is not earned; it derives from our humanity. While certain qualifications may apply in the process of naturalisation, such as a fixed period of residence, it does not follow that the right is earned. Earning rights is presented as a test of a newcomer's loyalty or allegiance. Citizenship cannot depend (or be tested by) a sense of belonging or feeling of citizenship. Minimally, the loyalty that can be expected is political loyalty, not a commitment to any political party but to the polity. A feeling of belonging or love of country may follow from citizenship status, but it cannot be demanded or proven. Some migrants may well have an instrumental approach to citizenship; citizenship as belonging may follow if rights are accessed on the basis of equality. Commitment is not assured through tests, but from equality of opportunity and inclusion in the civic community.

Requirements to speak English, take a citizenship test, attend a citizenship ceremony and take an oath or pledge are informed by the political philosophy of Bernard Crick, who chaired the Home Office advisory group that produced the *Life in the United Kingdom* handbook (Home Office, 2005). Citizenship tests 'are very often used as a tool to control the level and composition of immigration, often at a time when there are changing attitudes to immigration, particularly political or populist pressures to limit immigration in general, or specific kinds of immigration' (Etzione, 2007, p 353).

The Life in the UK (citizenship) test was introduced for adults seeking naturalisation in November 2005 and extended to cover those seeking permanent residence in April 2007. Since 2007, the test has been based on the second edition of the handbook (Home Office, 2007). White (2008, p 224) observes that the second edition adopts a less open tone than the first, with several references to tolerance and diversity removed and a 'you-will-need-to-toe-the-line-if-you-live-here' approach. The citizenship test, which is completed online and consists of a series of 24 multiple-choice questions drawn from a bank, cannot assess attitudes, only knowledge.

Those migrants required to prove their competence in English language are also expected to attend citizenship-based language classes based on a curriculum designed to introduce them to life in the UK. It is worth considering the areas of citizenship knowledge tested and whether these correspond with what Miller (2006) has referred to as cultural citizenship (the right to know and speak) rather than political (the right to reside and vote) or economic (the right to work and prosper) citizenship. Citizenship test knowledge relates to chapters 2 to 6 of the handbook (changing society; a profile of the UK today; government; everyday needs; and employment). Aspirant citizens are not tested on chapters addressing history, the law, practical sources of information or community cohesion and shared values. Significantly, the section of the handbook that addresses human rights is excluded from the test. Interestingly, areas judged significant in the school curriculum (the law, Britain as a diverse society and British history) are missing from the adult curriculum. There is some recognition of women's barriers to citizenship, something absent from the Crick Report. Sexual harassment at work is mentioned, but legal safeguards against racial discrimination and disability discrimination are not.

The handbook reflects a minimalist approach, whereby the (passive) citizen is informed about basic political rights and duties, but not encouraged to reflect on the cultural aspects of citizenship or examine history, law, struggles for justice or the means to contribute to these struggles. Adult learners faced with a complex test, juggling multiple and sometimes contradictory social and academic goals, including work, family obligations and the need to secure their future status, may adopt an instrumental approach, focusing on those elements required to pass the test. Aspirant citizens thus have little incentive to devote time to their histories, collective narratives, shared values, justice and human rights that are not reflected in the test. Potentially engaging learning processes are reduced to citizenship classes, amounting to a form of 'disciplinary citizenship' (Delanty, 2003). Rights are only guaranteed when individuals earn them by fulfilling corresponding duties.

Looking to the future: evaluating citizenship and political education

Much of what has been proposed as the community cohesion education policy agenda is about promoting a sense of national cohesion or national loyalty, using both the citizenship curriculum and history education to this end. In this respect, curriculum policy echoes concerns articulated over a century ago. The focus today differs in one significant respect: today's policies are justified by reference to concerns about terrorism, and portrayed as necessary to discipline minorities in schools, as well as adult migrants. Integration continues as a one-way process, focused on both newcomers and established visible minorities.

There is little official recognition that a sustainable and cohesive society is directly related to a sense of belonging predicated on equal access to educational goods. Efforts to promote 'community cohesion' that ignore the material disadvantages of specific groups, deep institutional inequalities between learners and a continuing attainment gap between different ethnic groups are, at best, compromised. At worst, they breed cynicism and disengagement among those they purport to include. Failure to discuss endemic racism and disadvantage within schooling compounds these problems.

Focusing on the school curriculum, this chapter concludes with a tentative set of indicators for evaluating citizenship education, which recognises young people as agents in their own learning, rather than passive receivers of educational goods. Citizenship education needs to be perceived as a dynamic and developmental process whereby students are given opportunities to create their own narratives and critically examine multiple perspectives, drawing on biographical and family experiences as well as written texts, rather than be disciplined into conformity by so-called British values and a grand narrative of British history.

Societal cohesion depends on inclusion and this inclusion implies reflexive, creative and constructive processes of learning. Learners explore multiple identities, including their own, rather than learning to categorise and essentialise others. So, for example, faith schools, which currently privilege students' (presumed) faith identities, need to recognise that young people's identities are multiple, situated and often flexible (Osler and Starkey, 2003; Mitchell and Parker, 2008), and may or may not privilege belief. Equally, schools with a secular foundation need to take concrete steps to guarantee students' freedom of thought, conscience and religion.

Education policy is not a one-way process by which government dictates to teachers and administrators. Instead, it involves the application, interpretation and sometimes subversion of the original goals. For this reason, processes of evaluation need to be built on the application of policies and analysis of outcomes, with reference to shared human rights, standards and principles. An overriding principle for effective citizenship education is that it is situated within a wider project in which equality of educational outcomes is an overriding and prioritised aim.

The learner needs to be recognised as a holder of human rights and citizenship education should be based on the learner's status as a holder of human rights, rather than a member of a particular polity. Not all learners in a school will necessarily be citizens of the nation state, but all are holders of human rights: political, social and cultural.

The following checklist is adapted from an analysis of education projects funded by the European Commission (Osler and Starkey, 1999), to ascertain ways in which they might contribute to young people's citizenship. It is informed by Delanty's (2003) study of citizenship as a learning process. Effective political education for citizenship that supports social cohesion might be expected to include:

- information about and experience of democracy and human rights in theory and practice;
- key skills for social and economic inclusion;
- a focus on equality of outcomes, addressing the specific needs of minorities, women and other groups experiencing material disadvantage;
- a specifically anti-racist focus and examination of barriers to citizenship encountered by minorities;
- opportunities to explore and reflect on various identities and cultural attributes, create personal narratives and develop processes of self-learning;
- cooperative practice, teamwork and the development of collective narratives and the study of cognitive models, which enable learners as a group to make sense of the world;
- experiential learning;
- democratic decision making, including participation in the management of learning and, where appropriate, the learning institution;
- independent reasoning and critical awareness;
- effective communication skills, including those for transnational and inter-cultural communication;
- community engagement;
- skills for negotiation and critical participation;
- development of learners' capabilities to support transformative action as citizens.

Conclusions

Although publicly funded schools in the UK are not as sharply segregated by income, social class, race and ethnicity as those in the US, it nevertheless remains the case that these elements play a significant role in determining the segregated nature of much of schooling, particularly in urban areas. Working-class and minority ethnic students remain more vulnerable to disciplinary forms of citizenship training, which aim to instil so-called 'mainstream' British values. Citizenship education, in its most narrow conceptions, forms part of a wider project to articulate and define civilising values and to stress the expectations and requirements (but not rights) of citizenship. Similar trends can be identified in a number of other European nation states, such as France, Denmark and the Netherlands, which are *de facto* multicultural societies, whether or not this is acknowledged.

The challenge is to change and develop policies of social cohesion in education for transformative ends, supporting the development of cosmopolitan citizens with a sense of solidarity to fellow human beings (in their neighbourhood, nation and globally), regardless of nationality or ethnic identity, rather than a narrow national objective of an inward-looking disciplinary citizenship training, which is effectively assimilationist and thus disrespectful of learners' dignity.

As Spencer (2000, p 22) has argued, '[h]uman rights principles are the essence of social and moral responsibility, and thus should lie at the heart of citizenship education.' Human rights principles provide a framework in which conflicting interests and moral dilemmas might be discussed and debated in the classroom and beyond. This approach implies citizenship education as political education in the Freirian sense, and a broader understanding of political literacy than that advocated by Crick. It is more than the sum of knowledge, skills and attitudes. It implies a critical understanding of the individual's experience and position in society, in structures and in processes of change. Equally, it implies collaboration between learners so as to enable genuine transformation and a realisation of human rights for all. Only when learners are equipped to transform society can it be asserted that citizenship education has the potential to support social cohesion.

Note
[1] The Youth Cohort Study (YCS) adopts the term 'Black' to include those who identify as Black Caribbean, Black African and Black Other in the Census. 'White' encompasses those who identify as White British and other White categories within the Census. The YCS allows us to compare the attainment

of students designated as Black, White, Indian, Pakistani or Bangladeshi. These broad categories do not address the migration status of students.

References

Berkeley, R. (2008) *Right to divide?*, London: Runnymede Trust.

Blair, T. (2006) *Our nation's future: Multiculturalism and integration*, Speech given at 10 Downing Street, 8 December.

Blunkett, D. (2003) *Civil renewal: A new agenda*, London: Home Office, www.communities.gov.uk/documents/communities/pdf/151927.pdf

Brown, G. (2006) *Who do we want to be? The future of Britishness* Speech give at the Fabian Society, 16 January, www.fabians.org.uk/events/speeches/the-future-of-britishness

Cantle, T. (2001) *Community cohesion: A report of the Independent Review Team*, London: Home Office.

Crick, B. (2000) 'Friendly arguments (1998)', in B. Crick (ed) *Essays on citizenship* (pp 123-45), London: Continuum.

Crick, B. and Lister, I. (1978) 'Political literacy', in B. Crick and A. Porter (eds) *Political education and political literacy* (pp 37-47), London: Longman.

Delanty, G. (2003) 'Citizenship as a learning process: disciplinary citizenship versus cultural citizenship', *International Journal of Lifelong Education*, vol 22, no 5, pp 597-605.

DCLG (Department for Communities and Local Government) (2008) *The government's response to the Commission on Integration and Cohesion*, London: DCLG, www.communities.gov.uk/documents/communities/pdf/681624.pdf

DES (Department of Education and Science) (1985) *Education for all: Report of the Committee of Inquiry into the Education of Children from Ethnic Minority Groups* (Swann Report), London: HMSO.

Dewey, J. ([1916] 2002) 'Democracy and education: an introduction to the philosophy of education', in S.J. Maxcy (ed) *John Dewey and American education* (Volume 3), Bristol: Thoemmes.

DfES (Department for Education and Skills) (2005) *Youth Cohort Study: The activities and experiences of 16 year olds: England and Wales 2004*, SFR04/2005, London: DfES.

DfES (2007) *Curriculum review: Diversity and citizenship* (Ajegbo Report), London: DfES.

DSFC (Department of Children, Schools and Families) (2007) *Guidance on the duty to promote community cohesion*, London: the Stationery Office.

Elliott, B.J. (1980) 'An early failure of curriculum reform: history teaching in England 1918-1940', *Journal of Educational Administration and History*, vol 12, no 2, pp 39-46.

Etzione, A. (2007) 'Citizenship tests: a comparative, communitarian perspective', *Political Quarterly*, vol 78, no 3, pp 353-63.

Finney, N. and Simpson, L. (2009) *'Sleepwalking to segregation'? Challenging myths about race and migration*, Bristol: The Policy Press.

Fogelman, K. (1991) *Citizenship in schools*, London: David Fulton.

Frazer, E. (1999) 'Introduction: the idea of political education', *Oxford Review of Education*, vol 25, nos 1 & 2, pp 5-22.

Gallagher, A.M., Cormack, R.J. and Osborne, R.D. (1994) 'Religion, equity and education in Northern Ireland', *British Educational Research Journal*, vol 20, no 5, pp 507-18.

Gillborn, D. (2006) 'Citizenship education as placebo: "standards", institutional racism and education policy', *Education, Citizenship and Social Justice*, vol 1, no 1, pp 83-104.

Gillborn, D. (2008) *Racism and education*, London: Routledge.

Hahn, C.L. (1999) 'Citizenship education: an empirical study of policy, practices and outcomes', *Oxford Review of Education*, vol 25, nos 1 & 2, pp 231-50.

Heater, D. (1990) *Citizenship: The civic ideal in world history, politics and education*, London and New York, NY: Longman.

Hollingworth, S. and Archer, L. (2010) 'Urban schools as urban places: school reputation, children's identities and engagement with education in London', *Urban Studies*, vol 47, pp 584-603.

Home Office (1999) *Stephen Lawrence Inquiry: Home Secretary's action plan*, London: Home Office.

Home Office (2005) *Life in the United Kingdom: A journey to citizenship*, London: The Stationery Office.

Home Office (2007) *Life in the United Kingdom: A journey to citizenship* (2nd edition), London: The Stationery Office.

Home Office (2008) *The path to citizenship: Next steps in reforming the immigration system*, London: Border and Immigration Agency.

Macpherson, W. (1999) *Stephen Lawrence Inquiry*, London: The Stationery Office.

Marshall, T.H. (1950) *Citizenship and social class and other essays*, Cambridge: Cambridge University Press.

Miller, T. (2006) *Cultural citizenship: Cosmopolitanism, consumerism, and television in a neoliberal age*, Philadelphia, PA: Temple University Press.

Mitchell, K. and Parker, W.C. (2008) 'I pledge allegiance to … flexible citizenship and shifting scales of belonging', *Teachers College Record*, vol 110, no 4, pp 775-804.

Murdoch, J.L. (1991) 'Encouraging citizenship: report of the Commission on Citizenship', *The Modern Law Review*, vol 54, no 3, pp 439-41.

Ofsted (Office for Standards in Education) (2005) *Race equality in education: Good practice in schools and local education authorities*, HMI 589, London: Ofsted.

Osler, A. (2000a) 'Introduction', in A. Osler (ed) *Citizenship and democracy in schools* (pp ix-xii), Stoke: Trentham.

Osler, A. (2000b) 'The Crick report: difference, equality and racial justice', *The Curriculum Journal*, vol 11, no 1, pp 25-37.

Osler, A. (2002) 'Citizenship education and the strengthening of democracy: is race on the agenda?', in D. Scott and H. Lawson (eds) *Citizenship, education and the curriculum* (pp 63-80), Westport, CT: Greenwood.

Osler, A. (ed) (2005) *Teachers, human rights and diversity*, Stoke-on-Trent: Trentham.

Osler, A. (2007) *Faith schools and community cohesion*, London: Runnymede Trust.

Osler, A. (2008) 'Citizenship education and the Ajegbo Report: re-imagining a cosmopolitan nation', *London Review of Education*, vol 6, no 1, pp 9-23.

Osler, A. (2009a) 'Testing citizenship and allegiance: policy, politics and the education of adult migrants in the United Kingdom', *Education, Citizenship and Social Justice*, vol 4, no 1, pp 63-79.

Osler, A. (2009b) 'Patriotism, multiculturalism and belonging: political discourse and the teaching of history', *Educational Review*, vol 61, no 1, pp 85-100.

Osler, A. (2010) *Students' perceptions on schooling*, Maidenhead: Open University Press.

Osler, A. and Morrison, M. (2000) *School inspection and race equality: Ofsted's strengths and weaknesses*, Stoke: Trentham.

Osler, A. and Starkey, H. (1999) 'Rights, identities and inclusion: European action programmes as political education', *Oxford Review of Education*, vol 25, nos 1 & 2, pp 199-215.

Osler, A. and Starkey, H. (2001) 'Citizenship education and national identities in France and England: inclusive or exclusive?', *Oxford Review of Education*, vol 27, no 2, pp 287-305.

Osler, A. and Starkey, H. (2003) 'Learning for cosmopolitan citizenship: theoretical debates and young people's experiences', *Cambridge Journal of Education*, vol 55, no 3, pp 243-54.

Ouseley, H. (2001) *Community pride not prejudice: Making diversity work in Bradford*, Bradford: Bradford Council.

Paterson, L. and Iannelli, C. (2006) 'Religion, social mobility and education in Scotland', *British Journal of Sociology*, vol 57, no 3, pp 353-77.

Pykett, J. (2007) 'Making citizens governable? The Crick Report as governmental technology', *Journal of Education Policy*, vol 22, no 3, pp 301-19.

Pykett, J. (2009) 'Making citizens in the classroom: an urban geography of citizenship education?', *Urban Studies*, vol 46, pp 803-23.

QCA (Qualifications and Curriculum Authority) (1998) *Citizenship and democracy in schools: The Crick Report*, London: QCA.

QDCA (Qualifications and Curriculum Development Agency) (2010) *Community cohesion in action: A curriculum planning guide for schools*, Coventry: QDCA, http://curriculum.qcda.gov.uk/uploads/Community_cohesion_in_action_tcm8-16069.pdf

Siegel, M.L. (2005) *The moral disarmament of France: Education, pacifism and patriotism 1914-1940*, New York, NY: Cambridge University Press.

Speaker's Commission on Citizenship (1990) *Encouraging citizenship*, London: HMSO.

Spencer, S. (2000) 'The implications of the human rights act for citizenship education', in A. Osler (ed) *Citizenship and democracy in schools* (pp 19-32), Stoke: Trentham.

Tikly, L., Osler, A. and Hill, J. (2006) 'The ethnic minority achievement grant: a critical analysis', *Journal of Education Policy*, vol 20, no 3, pp 283-312.

Tomlinson, S. (2009) 'Multicultural education in the United Kingdom', in J.A. Banks (ed) *The Routledge international companion to multicultural education*, New York, NY and London: Routledge.

White, P. (2008) 'Immigrants into citizens', *The Political Quarterly*, vol 79, no 2, pp 221-31.

TEN

Addressing worklessness post the financial crisis

Ines Newman

Introduction

Peter Ratcliffe, in the opening chapter of this book, argued that any attempt to achieve good relations between people from different backgrounds in the absence of a serious push on equality is destined to fail. Access to employment and an income above the poverty level are arguably the most important aspects of social cohesion. The risk of poverty is five times greater among adults in workless households than among those in working households (Palmer et al, 2008). There is evidence that being in work is a key component of mental and physical wellbeing (Freud, 2008, p 5; The Prince's Trust, 2010). It has also been argued that lack of achievement in the labour market feeds social exclusion, damaging relations between ethnic groups in Britain and putting social cohesion at risk (SEU, 2004, p 6).

This chapter raises issues about welfare-to-work policies and how they are currently evaluated. It starts by looking at the impact of the 2008/09 recession in terms of different groups in the labour market and social cohesion. It then questions the conditional welfare and the 'work first' policy. Success is being measured by reducing the number on out-of-work benefits and it is argued that this should not be the sole desired outcome and that, on its own, it provides a poor measure of equality or cohesion. Finally, it addresses wider outcomes and how a more holistic approach to evaluation could be developed.

Differential access to jobs before the 2008/09 recession

Since 1977, many changes have occurred in employment patterns within the United Kingdom (UK). The political parties have been driven by a belief in the free market and the need for limited regulation and employment protection in order to create jobs. A key change has been a rapid decline in manufacturing and in unskilled and skilled manual jobs. This has been partially offset by a growth in the service sector: both in professional and managerial jobs and in part-time, casualised employment in sectors such as personal services, retail and the leisure and hospitality industries.

The result has been a growing divide between rich and poor working households[1] and an increasing number of children in poor households. In addition, there has been a decline in male employment and an increase in female employment. At the start of 1971, the employment rate for men was 92.1% and for women it was 56.4%, a difference of 35.7 percentage points. For the three months to September 2008, the employment rate for men was 78.3% and for women 70.1%, a difference of 8.2 percentage points.

So while the numbers of people employed[2] have been generally rising over the last four decades, by 4.8 million from 1971 to 2008, the employment rate has varied but has not increased and stood at 74.4% for the three months to September 2008 compared to 74.9% in 1971 (Kent, 2009). Some women and those in minority ethnic groups have moved into the growing number of managerial and professional jobs, particularly in the public sector, but others have acted as the reserve army of labour (Bruegel, 1979), allowing capital in periods of growing employment to increase its rate of accumulation by drawing women and migrants into the labour market into low-paid, casualised employment.

New Labour came into office in 1997 promising to widen access to employment opportunities through its various 'New Deals', initially targeted at the young unemployed but then extended to lone parents, disabled people, the over fifties and the various demographic groups identified as being overrepresented among the unemployed (Dickens et al, 2000; Nunn and Johnson, 2010). The policy was supplemented by a set of policies (including the National Minimum Wage and tax credits) to 'make work pay' (HM Treasury, 2002) and area-based policies (including Employment Zones, the Neighbourhood Renewal Fund and the Working Neighourhood Fund) to reduce the employment gap between the most disadvantaged areas and the national average. Labour sought to address the issue through supply-side policies, arguing that there were plenty of vacancies for those who required jobs.

Initial attention was focused on young people, with concern about a generation lost to the labour market. There were some 490,000 unemployed people aged 16-24 and not in full-time education and a further 92,000 who were not economically active.[3] The numbers unemployed initially dropped but started to grow again from 2004/05.

As the Conservatives pointed out in their *Work for welfare* paper (Conservative Party, 2009), despite 10 years of active labour market policies, youth unemployment was higher in 2007 than in 1997 (that is, before the impact of the 2008/09 recession).[4] This was part of a trend that saw those without qualifications increasing their rate of unemployment. There was also very limited decline in the numbers claiming Incapacity Benefit, which had risen from 0.7 million in 1979 to 2.7 million by 2006 or 7% of the working population (DWP, 2006).

Some progress was made on the employment opportunities of other disadvantaged groups. Lone parents saw their employment rate rise over 10%[5] and the rate for disabled people rose by over 7%[6] from 1998 to 2008 (Kent, 2009). The employment rate for people aged 50 and over also increased by 8.6% from 1992 to 2008.

The employment position of minority ethnic groups is more complex both because the different minority groups and men and women within each group have varied outcomes within the labour market and because care must be taken when using ethnicity data as the minority ethnic groups have rather different demographics. A major study of minority ethnic groups and the labour market was completed in 2003 (PMSU, 2003). It stated that minority ethnic groups in 2003 made up 8% of the UK population but between 1999 and 2009 they would account for half the growth in the working-age population. The study showed that Indians and Chinese are, on average, doing well and often out-performing White people in schools and in the labour market. However, other groups are doing less well. Pakistanis, Bangladeshis and Black Caribbeans experience, on average, significantly higher unemployment and lower earnings than White people. Further studies have looked particularly at women's employment, showing that Black women tend to remain in full-time employment throughout family formation whereas White and Indian women are more likely to be in part-time employment. In contrast, levels of economic activity among Pakistani and Bangladeshi women fall substantially once they have a partner and fall again when they have children (Dale et al, 2004). The Prime Minister's Strategy Unit report also showed that all minority ethnic groups – even those enjoying relative success, such as the Indians and Chinese – are not doing as well as they should be, given their education and other characteristics. In fact, 'the key factors such as age, education, recency of migration, economic environment and family structure can explain just £9 of the £116 wage gap between Blacks and Whites' (PMSU, 2003, p 35). Submissions to the Business Commission on Race Equality in the Workplace suggest that up to half of the minority ethnic employment gap may result from discrimination in employment of one sort or another (National Employment Panel, 2007, p 3).

Over time, the position of minority ethnic groups has improved slightly. The Prime Minister's Strategy Unit report was able to argue that the unemployment rate of Bangladeshi, Pakistani and Black Caribbeans had decreased from 15-20 percentage points higher than that of their White counterparts in 1992 to 10-15 percentage points by 2000 (PMSU, 2003, p19). Over the next five years, until the recession, the employment rate for minority ethnic groups continued to improve. By 2008, the employment gap between the minority ethnic employment rate (59.9%) and the overall population rate (74.1%) was 14.2 percentage points compared to the high of 20% in 1994 (NAO, 2008).[7]

The government saw unemployment, particularly among young males, as a key cause of the 'disturbances' in towns in Northern England in 2001 and argued that a lack of employment opportunities affected cohesion by reducing the opportunities for contact between communities and restricting social mobility (Home Office, 2001, para 2.35). From around 2004/05, there was concern that progress on various indicators around the key target to end child poverty was starting to stall (MacInnes et al, 2009[8]) and, as will be discussed in more detail below, the response has been welfare reform and increasing conditionality in employment support.

Impact of the 2008/09 recession

So problems were already emerging before the 2008/09 recession really started to bite in terms of unemployment. There is no doubt that this recession will increase differential access to jobs although there is still a debate about the extent of this and which particular groups will be affected. Initial analysis of the claimant count showed that areas outside London were most affected by the recession and, since a large proportion (45%) of Britain's minority ethnic groups live in London, the claimant count has seen a greater rise in the White population (a 78% rise between August 2008 and July 2009) compared to that experienced by Black and minority ethnic groups (48% over the same period) (Kozdras, 2009).

But these statistics only give part of the story. First, they deal with the claimant count but do not capture those who are reluctant to claim, unable to claim or under-employed in part-time work. Second, the figures reflect the situation before the public sector cuts, which will really start to bite from April 2011. This is a key reason why men have, so far, been affected more than women, with the claimant count for men rising at twice the rate for women.[9] There is a high proportion of women and other groups disadvantaged in the labour market employed in the public sector. The numbers employed in the public sector had reached 6.09 million in September 2009 from 5.2 million in 1998 (Kent, 2009). So the public sector has been providing a cushion, reducing any increase in differential employment rates in the labour market. The Spending Review in October 2010 brought in public expenditure cuts that have been predicted to reduce public sector jobs by around 600,000.

A study, based on the General Household Survey, analysing the experience of two past recessions in order to predict the probable impact of the current downturn on individuals, provides a better guide to the future (Berthoud, 2009). It concludes that 'Pakistanis and Bangladeshis, already among the most disadvantaged groups in the country, are also shown to be highly sensitive to a potential recession, with an estimated increase in non-employment of nearly 7 percentage points. All the minorities, though less disadvantaged in normal times, also exhibit the hypercyclical pattern' (2009, p 18). Berthoud concludes that: 'The groups most affected are men, younger adults, not disabled, with poor educational records, members of ethnic minorities, living in the West Midlands' (2009, p 21). This study is confirmed by Stafford and Duffy (2009).

A study of the impact of the recession on deprived neighbourhoods (Tunstall, 2009) showed that despite narrowing from 1993 to 2008, the gap between the most deprived communities and the national average remains. Claimant unemployment in the current recession has increased most in the communities with high proportions of manufacturing workers and rented homes, and which already had highest unemployment, particularly in the West Midlands and the North of England. These communities now face the 'double whammy' of further public sector redundancies and service cuts as local authority income declines and demand for services increases. Competition for resources in deprived neighbourhoods could raise tensions between existing residents (including settled migrants) and those who have moved to the area more recently (including new asylum seekers, European Union [EU] migrants and British-born Black and minority ethnic communities accessing owner occupation in areas with lower property prices). These tensions could potentially be exploited by far-right groups.

Government response to the challenge

There has been a long debate about the role of the state and the individual in relation to work. In the post-war welfare settlement, citizenship required equal treatment and a set of civil, political and social rights (Kymlicka and Norman, 1994, p 354). In this context it was seen as the state's role to ensure full male employment and the possibility of work for all men and an adequate wage (Brown, 1990, pp 21, 32). A contribution-based insurance scheme for unemployment was considered necessary for those men and single women who temporarily or permanently lost their job. There was a debate about making this insurance scheme time limited and whether an indefinite benefit would take away the 'reciprocal obligation' on the unemployed to restore their earning power. In the event, however, the 30-week limit was not based on the likelihood of abuse (Brown, 1990, p 32) but on the belief that full employment made a longer-term benefit unnecessary.

This rights-based concept of citizenship came under attack from the New Right in the UK in the early 1980s who argued that it created a culture of dependency. The New Right emphasised obligations, including the obligation to work, as a precondition of citizenship (Kymlicka and Norman, 1994, p 356) and focused on the 'responsibility' of the unemployed to seek to earn a living. This shift towards labour market activity becoming a defining element of citizenship was to have a major impact on social cohesion as those without a job were increasingly marginalised.

At the same time, the commitment to full employment was dropped since the new theory of change (ToC) was based on a belief in competitiveness and the market. The goal became to support sustained economic growth through the market, which, it was argued, would then generate the jobs to tackle unemployment (Brown, 1990, p 204). Subsequently, all the major political parties have seen the issues of unemployment and the quality of jobs as being solved by increased flexibility in the labour market, (with limited employment protection against redundancy) and a focus on supply-side measures (active labour market policies to support those who are unemployed to find a job). Governments argued that this approach creates more growth and jobs, reduces uncompetitive, low-quality jobs and assists the unemployed in accessing the new opportunities (Nunn and Johnson, 2010). Those who have lost their jobs or are without work are given conditional support to access job opportunities. It is assumed, in this model, that those who do not take the vacancies on offer are benefit 'scroungers' who do not want to work and they must be encouraged to engage and accept 'reasonable' job offers through a sanctions regime. Ultimately, if they fail to get jobs they will be asked to work for their benefit: for the Conservatives (Conservative Party, 2009) this means 'Work for Welfare' schemes for all those unemployed for more than two years.

The Labour governments up to the 2010 General Election evaluated their ToC through a set of national indicators: a growth in Gross Domestic Product (GDP) (the key indicator for the regional development agencies); a decline in the claimant rate; a relative decline in the claimant rate in the worst-performing neighbourhoods (national indicators 152 and 153); a growth in the employment rate (national indicator 151); and a decline in 16- to 18-year-olds who are not in education, employment or training (NEET) (national indicator 117). Higher employment was assumed to increase economic and social wellbeing and reduce disaffection and tensions within neighbourhoods.

Problems with this approach

The focus on the supply side is increasingly problematic. Prior to the 2008/09 recession it was justified by the government on the grounds that there were many more vacancies than people looking for work. However, studies (eg Gordon and Turok, 2005; Webster, 2006) of the demand side of the labour market have evidenced the impact of deindustrialisation, residential sorting and discrimination. They have demonstrated that the vacancies on offer in areas with concentrations of the unemployed did not match the skills of the unemployed, that many were part time, low quality and casualised.

It was these trends that were driving up youth unemployment from 2001. Repeated claims that there is a 'culture of worklessness' have not been evidenced. In 2004, the Social Exclusion Unit was tasked by the government to carry out an extensive research study on barriers to jobs and enterprise in deprived areas (SEU, 2004). It concluded: 'The Social Exclusion Unit has not found consistent evidence for the existence of a "culture of worklessness" in these neighbourhoods, in the sense that people have completely different values and do not want to work at all' (2004, p 90). It evidenced concerns about low pay, discrimination and losing benefits.

During the 2008/09 recession, it became more difficult to justify the lack of focus on the demand side. Labour responded by creating the Future Jobs Fund and work placement schemes that offer six months' work experience. But this was a short-term way of plugging the gap until, it hoped, the market recovered and started creating new jobs. Part of the Conservative response was to argue for restricted migration to open up job opportunities for the unemployed, arguing that 'a simple, devastating fact is now clear from all the official statistics: as many as 80% of new jobs created in the past ten years have gone to migrant workers' (Conservative Party, 2009, p 10).

This misleading use of statistics is worth addressing here because it has been used by the BBC among others.[10] The source on which the Conservative Party based its statistics (Statistics Commission, 2007) makes it clear that the 80% figure includes all those born abroad (a third of whom were UK nationals). As stated earlier (PMSU, 2003), it was already evident that, because of demographic trends, minority ethnic groups would account for half the growth in the working-age population. Of a total increase in employment between 1997 and 2007 of about 2.1 million (counting all those aged over 16), around 50% were accounted for by foreign nationals but around half of these had been in the UK for more than 10 years. Many of the others reflected very high initial immigration from the new Eastern Europe accession states, particularly Poland. But the number of migrant workers has now dropped as a result of the fall in value of the pound and the rise in unemployment and emigration also rose in 2008.[11] There were 25% fewer National Insurance numbers issued to foreign workers in the first half of 2008 compared to 2007 (LGA, 2009, pp 3-4) and furthermore 14% fewer in the year to September 2009 compared to the year to September 2008.[12] The Local Government Association (LGA, 2009) document argues that many of the entry-level jobs taken by migrants are seasonal and low paid, particularly in social care (average wage £6.25 per hour) and in the agricultural sector: they do not offer routes out of poverty for the unemployed. It appears likely that the major impact of the Conservative Party's pledge to cap immigration from outside the EU may be a crisis in the farming and social care sectors or lead to a rise in the number of non-migrant workers in poverty employment rather than a rapid growth of sustainable jobs for the unemployed.

The reality for deprived neighbourhoods is highlighted in a recent study by the Joseph Rowntree Foundation (Crisp et al, 2009), which looked at how workless residents perceive the availability of work in a recession and their experiences of work. This showed that the recession has reduced the number of employment opportunities and exacerbated difficulties in finding work. Many of those interviewed saw the value in working, in terms of increased self-esteem and reducing isolation, but they gained little financially. Researchers found that poverty-level pay can force those in employment to work excessive hours, harming the quality of their family life. For those out of work, this can act as a disincentive to leave benefits. Other studies have documented how moving in and out of work can lead to debt as Housing and Council Tax Benefits are withdrawn and then take time to re-establish if the job does not prove permanent and mistakes are made with tax credits (see Kenway and Palmer, 2005; Finn et al, 2008; Hirsch, 2008, p 10; Strelitz, 2008). The coalition government's consultation paper *21st century welfare* (DWP, 2010) shows clearly that the loss of benefits and marginal tax rate for those entering work on low wages is so punitive that work often does not pay. So most people want to work but in so far as people choose a life on benefits it is often a rational decision to avoid debt and harming the quality of their family life.

This means that evaluating the success of policy by the numbers placed in work or in terms of the claimant count is overly simplistic. It is known that 70% of those placed in work through employment schemes are back as claimants within a year (Simmonds, 2009). Yet there are increasing 'punishments' if claimants refuse a 'reasonable' job or if they leave their job voluntarily. A detailed study of Swiss unemployment policies, where the unemployed lose their benefit if they refuse to enhance their employability or refuse a 'reasonable' job (defined as within two hours each way commuting distance, above 70% of the previous salary and not necessarily requiring the qualifications held by the jobseeker [Maeder and Nadai, 2009, p 69]), argues that such policies are based on the fictitious worker who 'is implicitly male … free from the marks of class or ethnicity'. In contrast, the long-term unemployed are often young, unqualified and with other disadvantages in the labour market. Maeder and Nadai (2009, pp 79–80) show clearly how painful and damaging the continuous pressure of activation towards the labour market can be – merely aggravating the social vulnerability of the unemployed instead of empowering them. They conclude that the strategy of activation individualises structural economic causes of workforce demand and conceptualises them as the problem of the unemployed person (2009, p 80). No wonder the unemployed often have low self-esteem and are disaffected. The Social Exclusion Unit report (SEU, 2004) already argued that the side effect of compulsion and sanctions is to push those who are already marginalised further from the reach of employment organisations – into the grey labour market or even criminality.

Giugni (2009, p 8) picks up these themes, arguing that the conditionality places the responsibility of getting a job on the individual rather than the state: 'This new view of dealing with unemployment profoundly modifies the relationship between citizens (in particular, unemployed) and the state … [it has] the advantage of making the individual responsible for their own situation and less dependent on the state.' This then influences how the whole society sees the welfare-to-work debate: 'The individual's responsibility not only to find work but to have life shaped by work – become embedded and ultimately "assumed". Over time, assumptions are institutionalised and so become part of a new consensus about work and welfare' (Dwyer and Ellison, 2009, p 65).

While this may bring advantages to the state and business interests in terms of reducing the power of the unemployed, maintaining them as a docile reserve army of labour and reducing the costs of welfare support, it undermines social cohesion. The April 2010 level of Jobseeker's Allowance was £65.45 a week for an adult aged 25 or over, £65.45 being equivalent to just 41% of the Minimum Income Standard for a single working-age adult (Kenway, 2009, 2010). In addition, the unemployed get Housing Benefit (although the June 2010 Budget announced that this will be cut for those unemployed more than 12 months) and Council Tax Benefit, but trying to survive on this low level of income is a real struggle and will impact on self-esteem and confidence. Increasingly, the unemployed are choosing not to claim benefits. The International Labour Organization's measure of unemployed in 2010 was 70% higher than the claimant count. In 1992, these two counts were almost the same. There are multiple reasons (Machin, 2004) why the two counts diverge but in previous recessions the gap narrowed and this time it does not appear that the gap is closing. Forcing claimants to work for their benefits is likely to increase the gap and increase social tensions and the number of disaffected young men and women who are not engaging with the system.

An alternative approach to policy and frameworks for evaluation

Helen Sullivan, in her chapter in this volume about evaluation, argued that stakeholders need to be able to access evidence in relation to the need for the interventions, the pertinence of the chosen interventions above others and the intended consequences of the interventions in terms of short-, medium- and long-term goals.

In terms of the need for intervention it has been argued that worklessness creates poverty, reduces mental and physical wellbeing and that differential access to job opportunities and wages will fuel resentment and inter-group conflict. But it has also been argued that pushing the unemployed into jobs and compulsory work schemes will not improve mental and physical wellbeing. In addition, there are an increasing number of households with one person in work that remain in poverty. Among working-age adults on low incomes, the rising number in working families now exceeds the falling number in workless ones. Over half of adults of working age who are in poverty – 3.6 million people in 2007/08 – live in households where at least one person is working (Palmer et al, 2008). So work is not always providing a route out of poverty. Low-income, insecure jobs furthermore create stress and strains on family life (Crisp et al, 2009).

So what are the desired outcomes? First, tackling unemployment requires a re-engagement with the post-war concepts of the right to a job and the role of the state in promoting full employment. Supply-side measures through active labour market policies can only go so far and without linking them to job demand and job creation they will only result in deadweight and displacement. Focusing on demand interventions underpins all the outcomes listed below and goes beyond the simple objective of employment growth. The latter can result in jobs and rising salaries for those who are already work rich. A demand-side policy that was linked to a supply-side policy would seek to create opportunities for the unemployed through both the public and the private sectors.

Second, the aim is to help people not just to gain employment but also to stay and prosper in employment. Gradually, government has moved from evaluating the success of schemes from 13 weeks in a job to 26 weeks (Simmonds, 2009) and the new coalition government is suggesting outcome payments in their Work Programme when contractors have enabled the unemployed to stay in a job for one year. But this may just push up the numbers leaving at just over a year, particularly if benefits and credits to ease transitions into work cease at a year. There is evidence that the unemployed can be trapped in low skilled, low paid jobs by policies that concentrate on 'work first' rather than opportunities to access higher skilled work (Crisp, 2009; CFE, 2009). So the emphasis should be on skills and career progression, sustaining employment rather than staying in one job and lifting the low paid out of poverty. Such policies can be implemented directly by public agencies for their own employees and within other sectors, promoted and enforced through commissioning and procurement policies. However, the evidence from a set of procurement pilots that aimed to achieve better race equality outcomes when procuring goods, works and services found that the overall impact of the procurement pilots appears to have been limited to date and most focused on Black and minority ethnic employment rather than the wider support and career progression discussed above (Tackey et al, 2009). Procurement could be a useful policy tool but outcomes need to be widened and contract compliance procedures much more rigorously enforced.

Third, there should be more emphasis on stopping people being made redundant (relating to issues such as temporary contracts and redundancy legislation). The outcomes where employment protection legislation has been combined with active labour market policies show no decrease in employment as a result of employment protection (Furåker, 2009, p 21). On the other hand, a stronger focus on employment protection could save funds and reduce insecurity. It is estimated that, in the long run, an average saving of £16,375 per employee (even before hidden costs like higher labour turnover and a fall in staff productivity are added in) can be made by preserving jobs, and keeping skilled workforces intact, rather than creating new jobs from scratch (CIPD, 2009).

Fourth, differential outcomes need to be addressed. The coalition government has pinned its hopes on a complex form of commissioning support from the private sector whereby private contractors will reap higher rewards for placing in employment for a year those categories of unemployed who face more difficulties accessing jobs. The evidence on the success of such schemes is questionable (Finn, 2008, 2009). But more fundamentally this is again a supply-side approach and it is important to also tackle the demand side and discrimination (National Employment Panel, 2007). Tackling gender, race and other forms of discrimination in the private sector still depends on individuals taking up cases at industrial tribunals. Yet the lessons learnt about good practice at these tribunals cannot be enforced on the company involved, let alone on firms or private organisations with similar employment practices. The EHRC does have powers to carry out formal investigations of a company, organisation or a whole sector but progress is slow: there is too much dependence on voluntary action and more needs to be done. Even the National Employment Panel (2007, paras 106-111) realised that public procurement, thematic reviews and focused support needed the threat of legislative backing if they were to be effective. The system for tackling discrimination needs to be toughened up so that wage and employment gaps are reduced and resentment and envy lessened.

Fifth, value needs to be placed on the contribution to society rather than just on getting a job. If suitable jobs are not available, if the unemployed person faces significant discrimination in the labour market and if they have complex problems that need to be solved if they are to retain their job, the Swiss case study showed how continuous pressure of activation towards the labour market can merely make the unemployed see themselves as deficient (Maeder and Nadai, 2009, p 79). Currently (2010) only three groups are exempt from requirements to engage in some form of work-related activity as a condition of benefit entitlement: the most severely sick and disabled Employment and Support Allowance (ESA) claimants; lone parents with babies aged under one; and full-time carers. Beyond the three exempt groups, there are numerous barriers that stop those wishing to work part time in the voluntary sector or in some unpaid capacity. Tax credits are only available if you work more than 16 hours a week; asylum seekers are not allowed to receive any remuneration; and if you are on Incapacity Benefit or Employment Support Allowance, voluntary work is often seen as proving that you are capable of doing a job (threatening your benefits).

On the positive side, the Department for Work and Pensions is piloting a Community Allowance on a very limited basis. The Community Allowance is a proposal to enable community organisations to pay local unemployed people to do part-time or seasonal work that strengthens their local community, and would also enable those people to keep their benefits and keep what they earn on top of their benefits, up to a maximum of £86 a week (which is the equivalent of 15 hours a week on the National Minimum Wage). This scheme is currently being piloted by *Create* in three pilot areas among those claiming Incapacity Benefit or ESA.[13]

The coalition government is also proposing to tackle the 16-hour rule through a 'universal' credit (DWP, 2010) and, while this is welcome, the simplification of the tax and benefits system will actually mean the end of universal benefits such as contributory National Insurance, Unemployment Benefit, Child Benefit and other benefits that are not means tested. It will signal the death knell of the post-war rights-based approach and embed a welfare structure that reinforces conditionality and the responsibility of the individual to work.

So it is important to counter this increasingly oppressive obligation to work by seeking ways to value support to the family and the wider community. It is often community activity and volunteering in deprived neighbourhoods that maintains some form of social solidarity and community infrastructure in areas where private sector investment has been withdrawn. Schemes such as the Community Allowance or time banks do allow the unemployed to improve their work skills and confidence and to contribute to the community. The London Borough of Greenwich recognised that it needed to do more to help those in disadvantaged communities raise their skill level, aspirations and employability and find work. It concentrated on lone parents, disabled people, minority ethnic groups and those with low qualification levels, in order to close the gap with the borough average. But it moved beyond evaluating its scheme through national indicators. Its evaluation

> involves the client and their case worker accessing a web-based instrument called a 'Richter Scale', which they use to communicate where they feel they are on their progression to work. They do this every time they receive an intervention. This allows a client's current situation to be assessed and, on subsequent use, the 'distance' they have travelled in terms of addressing various barriers to work. Agencies can then focus on measuring progression and the value their service has added, rather than working with those closest to attaining a job outcome. (IDeA, 2008, p 3)

This type of approach to evaluation could be used more widely and could be extended to value contributions through caring in the family or volunteering in the community rather than just in relation to progression to work.

The way in which the agency and client work together on the evaluation in Greenwich brings us to the sixth outcome. If social cohesion is going to be increased by helping people into work, the policy needs to empower the unemployed and give them a voice. Action plans agreed with Jobcentre Plus or private providers are based on an unequal relationship whereby sanctions will be imposed if the unemployed claimant is not cooperative. As Maeder and Nadai (2009, p 81) argue, the concerns of the unemployed must be taken into account in decision making or it will be impossible to integrate them in a sustainable way. Active labour market policies shaped by the unemployed themselves and their knowledge of what works can provide vital support.

Giving the unemployed a voice requires a new approach by the voluntary sector, government agencies and local government partners. It involves evaluating process as well as outcomes and providing resources to build capacity and support representation and spread learning. It also involves thinking about the voice of different groups. For example, community development approaches can help recent Black and minority ethnic migrants to a particular area to become involved, be they asylum seekers or long-term British residents, promoting solidarity and cohesion rather than competition and conflict between newer and more established communities, which may also contain settled, but possibly 'disaffected' minority groups (Blake et al, 2008).

And it is this solidarity that is the final policy objective to potentially ensure social cohesion beyond the recession. The lack of jobs has led to a nationalist call for British jobs for British workers. The unions have been active in trying to move from divisive politics to calls for a greater focus on the demand side and protection for public sector jobs.

> Inequality and the threat of poverty can act as divisive forces in the workplace and wider community, demanding collective resolve to prevent intolerance, prejudice and abuse from spreading. The outbreak of wildcat strikes and protests advocating for British Jobs for British Workers underlines the need for trade unions to unite workers around a common agenda of equality and social justice for all if we are to emerge a strengthened force from the recession. (TUC Northern Regional Council, 2009)

But there have been very limited attempts by the trades union movement or the voluntary sector to work with the unemployed and seek to give them more of a voice. As Dwyer and Ellison (2009, pp 54-5) argue, individuals are gradually induced – or *conditioned* – to 'govern themselves' through personalised work-focused interviews, guidance about job opportunities as well as targeted sanctions. This then influences how the whole society, including trades unions, sees the welfare-to-work debate. The responsibility to remain in stable employment moves from the state to the individual. Even the gravity of the financial crisis has done relatively little so far to challenge the faith in the market to solve unemployment and the belief that the failure to gain employment is primarily an individual failure. The scale of public expenditure cuts proposed may now change this and opens up the possibilities of new solidarities and challenges to conditional welfare.

Conclusion

This chapter has argued that social cohesion depends on more equal outcomes in terms of employment and wages. It has welcomed attempts to support people into work but not in the context of increased conditionality and poverty wages. It has argued that there are seven outcomes that should be sought beyond a decline in unemployment. These are:

- access to employment;
- career progression and sustainable employment;

- reductions in redundancies, particularly in the public sector;
- a reduction in employer discrimination and the wage gap between men and women and different ethnic groups;
- valuing contributions to society beyond paid work;
- giving the unemployed a voice and role in shaping their services; and
- promoting solidarity between the employed and unemployed, recent migrants and the established workforce.

It would be possible to develop a new ToC that saw the final two outcomes as a lever to move towards delivering on some of the other desirable outcomes. It would also be a relatively easy task to elaborate a new set of evaluation tools to measure progress in this area – tools that could be scrutinised and used by the unemployed themselves.

It has also been argued that, if long-term unemployment is really going to be reduced, the focus on the supply side is insufficient and must be combined with an increased focus on the demand side. It is essential to consider the impact of job cuts in the public sector; the costs of a flexible labour market that creates a casualised, low-paid reserve army of labour with limited support for progression; the reality of discrimination; and the implications of seeing paid work as the only activity that is valued for all people beyond the three groups now excluded from activation. Failure to consider these outcomes will mean a continued decline in the employment opportunities for the least skilled and those suffering discrimination and deterioration in social cohesion.

Notes

[1] See national statistics online at www.statistics.gov.uk/cci/nugget.asp?id=332 and www.poverty.org.uk/09/g.pdf. Between 1977 and 1991, the share of total disposable income received by the top fifth of households increased from 36 to 42%. The shares received by each of the lower three quintile groups fell, in the case of the bottom quintile group from 10 to 7%. The Gini coefficient rose to 2001, dipped a little until 2004/05 and is now rising sharply again.

[2] International Labour Organization (ILO) definition: people are classed as employed if they are aged 16 or over and have done at least one hour of work in the reference week or are temporarily away from a job (for example on holiday).

[3] Labour Force Survey, seasonally adjusted, updated on 09/10/2009.

[4] In 2007 unemployment of 16-24 had risen from 490,000 in 1997 to 504,000. The numbers of economically inactive had risen from 582,000 (1997) to 743,000 (2007) labour Force Survey seasonally adjusted, updated on 9 October 2009.

[5] From 46.0 to 56.3%.

[6] From 43.4 to 50.7%.

[7] See also the statistics in DCLG (2009): pp 55-7 provide a summary of some 2008 statistics.

[8] See also the annual *Opportunity for all* reports published by the Department for Work and Pensions at www.dwp.gov.uk/publications/policy-publications/opportunity-for-all/. *Opportunity for all* is the annual report on progress on the 1999 government pledge to eradicate child poverty by 2020. The reports usually appear in October.

[9] www.statistics.gov.uk/cci/nugget.asp?id=2145

[10] See Stephanie Flanders' election Reality Check report at http://news.bbc.co.uk/1/hi/uk_politics/election_2010/parties_and_issues/8634469.stm

[11] Latest data from the Office for National Statistics show that net migration was down by a third in 2008 (163,000 net immigration in 2008), driven by a rise in emigration from 341,000 in 2007 to 427,000 in 2008 (*The Guardian*, 26 November 2009).

[12] www.statistics.gov.uk/pdfdir/mignr0210.pdf

[13] http://communityallowance.wordpress.com/

References

Berthoud, R. (2009) *Patterns of non-employment, and of disadvantage, in a recession*, Colchester: Institute for Social and Economic Research, University of Essex.

Blake, G., Diamond, J., Foot, F., Gidley, B., Mayo, M., Shukra, K. and Yarnit, M. (2008) *Community engagement and community cohesion*, York: Joseph Rowntree Foundation.

Brown, J. (1990) *Victims or villains? Social security benefits in unemployment*, London: PSI, www.psi.org.uk/publications/publication.asp?publication_id=197

Bruegel, I. (1979) 'Women as a reserve army of labour: a note on recent British experience', *Feminist Review*, no 3, pp 12-23.

CFE (2009) *Staying in, moving up: Employment retention and progression in London*, London: Mayor of London.

CIPD (Chartered Institute of Personnel and Development) (2009) *Redundancy 'a false economy'*, London: CIPD, www.cipd.co.uk/pressoffice/_articles/050108Costofredundancy.htm?IsSrchRes=1

Conservative Party (2009) *Work for welfare: Real welfare reform to help make British poverty history: Policy Green Paper no 3*, London: Conservative Party.

Crisp, R., Batty, E., Cole, I. and Robinson, D. (2009) *Work and worklessness in deprived neighbourhoods: Policy assumptions and personal experiences*, York: Joseph Rowntree Foundation.

Dale, A., Dex, S. and Lindley, J.K. (2004) 'Ethnic differences in women's demographic, family characteristics and economic activity profiles, 1992-2002', *Labour Market Trends*, vol 112, no 4, pp 153-65.

DCLG (Department for Communities and Local Government) (2009) *Improving opportunity, strengthening society: A third progress report on the government's strategy for race equality and community cohesion: Volume 2*, London: DCLG, www.communities.gov.uk/publications/communities/raceequalitythirdreport

Dickens, R., Gregg, P. and Wadsworth, J. (2000) 'New Labour and the labour market', *Oxford Review of Economic Policy*, vol 16, no 1, pp 95-113.

DWP (Department for Work and Pensions) (2006) *A new deal for welfare: Empowering people to work*, Norwich: The Stationery Office.

DWP (2010) *21st century welfare*, London: The Stationery Office.

Dwyer, P. and Ellison, N. (2009) 'Work and welfare: the rights and responsibilities of unemployment in the UK', in M. Giugni (ed) *The politics of unemployment in Europe: Policy responses and collective action* (pp 53-66), Farnham, Surrey: Ashgate.

Finn, D. (2009) 'The "welfare market" and the flexible New Deal: lessons from other countries', *Local Economy*, vol 24, no 1, pp 51-8.

Finn, D., Mason, D., Rahim, N. and Casebourne, J. (2008) *Delivering benefits, tax credits and employment services: Problems for disadvantaged users and potential solutions*, York: Joseph Rowntree Foundation.

Freud, D. (2008) *Reducing dependency, increasing opportunity: Options for the future of welfare to work: An independent report to the Department for Work and Pensions*, Leeds: Corporate Document Services.

Furåker, B. (2009) 'Unemployment and social protection', in M. Giugni (ed) *The politics of unemployment in Europe: Policy responses and collective action* (pp 17-34), Farnham, Surrey: Ashgate.

Giugni, M. (2009) *The Politics of Unemployment in Europe: Policy Responses and Collective Action*, Farnham, Surrey: Ashgate.

Gordon, I. and Turok, I. (2005) 'How urban labour markets matter', in I. Buck, I. Gordon, A. Harding and I. Turok (eds) *Changing cities* (pp 242-64), London: Palgrave.

Hirsch, D. (2008) *What is needed to end child poverty in 2020? Round-up: Reviewing the evidence*, York: Joseph Rowntree Foundation.

HM Treasury (2002) *The modernisation of Britain's tax and benefit system No 10: the Child and Working Tax Credits*, London: HM Treasury, www. politiquessociales.net/IMG/pdf/new_tax_credits_2_.pdf

Home Office (2001) *Building cohesive communities: A report of the Ministerial Group on Public Order and Community Cohesion, 2001*, London: Home Office, www.communities.gov.uk/documents/ communities/pdf/buildingcohesivecommunities.pdf

IDeA (Improvement and Development Agency) (2008) *Greenwich: Tackling worklessness through the LAA*, London: IDeA, www.idea.gov. uk/idk/core/page.do?pageId=8618760&aspect=full

Kent, K. (2009) 'Employment changes over thirty years', *Economic & Labour Market Review*, vol 3, no 2, pp 30-6, www.statistics.gov.uk/ elmr/02_09/downloads/ELMR_Feb09_Kent.pdf

Kenway, P. (2009) *Should adult benefit for unemployment now be raised?*, York: Joseph Rowntree Foundation.

Kenway, P. (2010) *Working-age 'welfare': Who gets it, why, and what it costs*, York: Joseph Rowntree Foundation.

Kenway, P. and Palmer, G. (2005) *Making it fair: Council Tax Benefit and working households*, London: LGIU, https://member.lgiu.org. uk/whatwedo/Publications/Documents/Making%20It%20Fair%20 council%20tax%20benefit%20and%20working%20households.pdf

Kozdras, S. (2009) 'Ethnic groups: the impact of the recession', *Working Brief*, October, p 18.

Kymlicka, W. and Norman, W. (1994) 'Return of the citizen: a survey of recent work on citizenship theory', *Ethics*, vol 104, no 2, pp 352-81.

LGA (Local Government Association) (2009) *The impact of the recession on migrant labour*, London: LGA, www.lga.gov.uk/lga/core/page. do?pageId=1493681

Machin, A. (2004) 'Comparisons between unemployment and the claimant count', *Labour Market Trends*, vol 112, no 2, pp 59-62.

MacInnes, T., Kenway, P. and Parekh, A. (2009) *Monitoring poverty and social exclusion 2009*, York: Joseph Rowntree Foundation.

Maeder, C. and Nadai, E. (2009) 'The promises of Labour: the practices of activating unemployment policies in Switzerland', in M. Giugni (ed) *The politics of unemployment in Europe: Policy responses and collective action* (pp 67-81), Farnham, Surrey: Ashgate.

NAO (National Audit Office) (2008) *Increasing employment rates for ethnic minorities*, London: DWP.

National Employment Panel (2007) *60/76:The Business Commission on Race Equality in the Workplace*, London: National Employment Panel.

Nunn, J. and Johnson, S. (2010) 'Labouring and learning towards competitiveness; the future of local labour markets after Harker, Leitch and Freud', in I. Newman (ed) *The future of local economic development*, London: Routledge.

Palmer, G., MacInnes, T. and Kenway, P. (2008) *Monitoring poverty and social exclusion 2008*, York: Joseph Rowntree Foundation.

PMSU (Prime Minister's Strategy Unit) (2003) *Ethnic minorities and the labour market: Final report*, London: Cabinet Office, www.cabinetoffice. gov.uk/media/cabinetoffice/strategy/assets/ethnic_minorities.pdf

Simmonds, D. (2009) *Tackling worklessness: Helping people stay in work*, London: IDeA, www.idea.gov.uk/idk/aio/10114031

SEU (Social Exclusion Unit) (2004) *Jobs and enterprise in deprived areas*, London: ODPM.

Stafford, B. and Duffy, D. (2009) *Review of evidence on the impact of economic downturn on disadvantaged groups*, DWP Working Paper no 68, London: DWP, http://research.dwp.gov.uk/asd/asd5/WP68.pdf

Statistics Commission (2007) *Foreign workers in the UK: Briefing note*, Newport: Statistics Comission, www.statscom.org.uk/uploads/files/other/foreign%20workers%20briefing%20note%20Dec%202007.pdf

Strelitz, J. (2008) *Eradicating child poverty:The role of key policy areas: Ending severe child poverty*, York: Joseph Rowntree Foundation.

Tackey, N.D., Barnes, H., Fearn, H. and Pillai, R. (2009) *Ethnic Minority Employment Task Force race equality procurement pilots*, Research Report RR600, London: DWP.

The Prince's Trust (2010) *The Prince's Trust YouGov Youth Index 2010*, London:The Prince's Trust, www.princes-trust.org.uk/news/100104_youth_index_2010.aspx

TUC (Trades Union Congress) Northern Regional Council (2009) *Coping with the downturn: February 2009*.

TUC Northern, www.tuc.org.uk/economy/tuc-15933-f0.cfm?regional=3

Tunstall, R. (2009) *Communities in recession: The impact on deprived neighbourhoods: Round up: Reveiuing the evidence*, York: Joseph Rowntree Foundation.

Webster, D. (2006) 'Welfare reform: facing up to the geography of worklessness', *Local Economy*, vol 21, no 2, pp 107-16.

ELEVEN

New communities and social cohesion: third sector approaches to evaluation

Marjorie Mayo, Vaughan Jones and Juan Camilo Cock

Introduction

Given the book's overall focus on 'social cohesion' – rather than the more limited approach that has been envisaged via government initiatives to promote 'community cohesion' – this chapter starts by arguing the case for the importance of active engagement to build social solidarity across the broadest possible range of civil society organisations. Having set out the case for the importance of third sector involvement overall, the chapter moves on to focus on third sector challenges in relation to evaluation, including those involved in the evaluation of community development-based initiatives and approaches that involve participative research strategies.

Finally, the chapter concludes by exploring the development of evaluation research strategies in the third sector through a case study for illustration, that of PRAXIS, a non-governmental organisation that seeks to help new migrants (including refugees and asylum seekers) to settle; also fostering reconciliation, human rights and social justice, working with established as well as with new communities.

Why this focus on the civil society and the third sector?

Why, then, this emphasis on the involvement of civil society in general and the third sector more specifically? There is already considerable recognition that a community development approach is going to be needed, if progress is to be made, from the bottom up, challenging divisions within and between communities and building effective alliances to tackle common issues and problems across these divides. Previous research, undertaken with colleagues, exploring ways of developing strategies to promote both community engagement and community cohesion, concluded that these depended on 'the development and implementation of community development strategies' (Blake et al, 2008, p 71).

This previous research argued that community development professionals need to work with informal networks to reach new communities, while continuing to work with more established communities and structures, building sustainable relationships of understanding and trust. Third sector organisations have vital roles to play here, it was suggested, supporting outreach work; providing bridges and safe spaces for communities to meet and to negotiate differences; facilitating shared events, including festivals, sports events, community outings and welcome events; and, most importantly, supporting community advocacy and campaigns that challenge racism and other forms of discrimination (Blake et al, 2008). While it is essential for local authorities to resource community development work, it is also vitally important to safeguard the third sector's independent role, in order to build sustainable relationships of trust from the bottom up. It has emerged, for example, that local authority 'myth-busting' exercises have inherent limitations. When leaflets are circulated, to dispel popular misconceptions about newcomers – such as the misconception that newcomers are jumping the queue, to access social housing – people are not necessarily convinced at all. Indeed, they may even confine their reading to the sections that set out the myths in question, rather than reading the sections that refute the myths, thereby actually reinforcing rather than challenging their previous opinions. And this would seem to be particularly the case in the current political context, given popular distrust of formal politics in general and politicians more specifically (see Chapters One and Six in this volume for more detailed discussions of myth-busting).

There is, then, evidence to suggest that third sector organisations can play significant roles in combating social exclusion, engaging with new communities and enabling them to access services, providing safe spaces for different interests to meet and enabling them to identify and work in solidarity on issues of common concern (Blake et al, 2008; Wilson and Zipfel, 2008). Trades union and community-based organisations have also been developing joint approaches, building solidarity in defence of wages and employment conditions, as in the case of the Campaign for a Living Wage, in London, a broad third sector coalition campaigning for fair wages for migrant workers and other exploited workers.

Finally, too, there are examples of civil society organisations' contributions to challenging racism and xenophobia through community-based education for active citizenship (Grayson, 2010; Hartley, 2010). Reflecting on community-based adult learning initiatives provided by South Yorkshire Workers Education Association, in partnership with Northern College and others, these accounts provide illustrations of promising practices, working with new communities, including refugees, asylum seekers and migrant workers, as well as with established communities, addressing issues of common concern and developing understanding within an increasingly globalised context. Activities ranged from the development of practical information technology skills to facilitate communication for geographically isolated groups of refugees and asylum seekers across South Yorkshire and internationally, through to study visits including a visit to Edinburgh, to participate in the 2007 demonstration to the meeting of the G7, in support of the global campaign to Make Poverty History (Grayson, 2010; Hartley, 2010). In summary, then the role of third sector organisations can be argued to be centrally important in a variety of ways in terms of building social solidarity, both locally and indeed beyond.

Particular challenges for evaluation in the third sector

So what particular challenges does this pose for evaluation? In addition to the challenges involved in applying theories of change (ToCs) – including identifying implicit ToCs and identifying how to attribute causes and effects in complex and often rapidly changing contexts, as outlined in Chapter Two by Helen Sullivan – there would seem to be additional factors involved. Community development-based approaches to research and evaluation so often aim to generate processes that are *themselves* participatory and empowering, with evaluation being viewed as an empowering 'learning tool' for the organisations and individuals involved. The overall objective, then, is not simply to produce a report(s) based on research evidence but for the research process to be central to the development of enhanced critical understanding and more effective action to promote social solidarity, among all the community interests concerned. So the communities in question need to be actively involved in the research process at every stage.

This active engagement needs to take place throughout the processes involved, from agreeing aims and objectives, to developing research strategies and measurement tools, building evidence-based reflection into the cycle of action, reflection and further action in the light of reflection. In Freirian terminology (Freire, 1972), this action–reflection cycle has been described as 'praxis', Freire having been associated with the development of this concept as part of participative approaches to adult learning and community development more generally. This action–reflection cycle has been fundamental to participatory approaches to development and to adult learning in general. Newman's (2008) participatory evaluation of REFLECT adult community education and development programmes demonstrate this. As she explains, REFLECT 'emphasises a reflection–action cycle, noting that reflection without action can quickly become meaningless, while action without reflection can limit the potential for learning or success. In this way, reviewing or evaluating activities is in-built into the process' (2009, p 383).

But this immediately raises key questions about participatory approaches more generally, including questions about who/which communities are involved in these processes, which differing interests/ conflicts of interest and power imbalances need to be taken into account and how transparency and democratic accountability can be ensured (Cooke and Kothari, 2001; Mosse, 2001). These questions are certainly explored in the literature on evaluating community participation and community development, as well as in the literature on community participation and development more generally – issues of inclusivity and accountability featuring significantly in studies such as those by Barr and Hashagan (2000) and Burns et al (2004). As Newman concludes, assessing her experiences of developing participatory approaches in the evaluation of the REFLECT programme in Nigeria, 'no participation will be perfect' but despite inherent limitations, with honesty and balance underpinning the approaches, evaluations can still be empowering (Newman, 2008, p 393).

There are particular issues to be addressed further, then, both for evaluating community development work in general and for evaluating community-based initiatives to promote cohesion and social solidarity more specifically. The importance of positive action for a fair and just society has been recognised in the ABCD approach (Achieving Better Community Development), as developed by the Scottish Community Development Centre – a partnership between the Community Development Foundation and the University of Glasgow (Barr and Hashagan, 2000). The ABCD approach has been widely used for evaluation purposes, offering a framework for understanding, planning, evaluating and learning, emphasising 'the participation of all stakeholders, especially communities themselves' (Barr and Hashagen, 2000, p 3). While providing a much-valued tool and recognising that there can be conflicts of interest between stakeholders, within and between communities as well as between communities and professionals, resource providers and policy makers, the ABCD framework focuses, in practice, on relatively consensual approaches. This implies fundamental commonalities of interest, and gives relatively little attention to underlying conflicts of interest, especially those conflicts relating to wider structural inequalities. As it has been argued elsewhere in this book, however, it is precisely these structural inequalities that so crucially need to be addressed if social solidarity is to be advanced. So for the purposes of this chapter, the evaluation of civil society engagement in promoting social solidarity needs to take account of these factors – and to explore them with participants throughout the process, if the results are to be genuinely empowering.

Some of the factors that make participative action research inherently problematic include precisely such underlying conflicts of interest, often rooted in significant differences of power, among the different participants. There is a considerable literature already addressing questions of power imbalances between researchers and those researched, including a series of studies arising from work based at the Institute of Development Studies (Blackburn and Holland, 1998; Estrella, 2000; and others). And there is much to be learnt from studies identifying the impact of power imbalances *within* communities, including imbalances of power based on gender and age. Participative research, then, poses its own additional challenges (Mayo and Rooke, 2008; Newman, 2008).

Having pointed to some of the challenges, however, it is also important to recognise the continuing relevance of some of the dimensions of these earlier approaches to evaluation. The ABCD approach provides valuable guidance to the development of research strategies, for example, including the importance of:

- direct observations/ethnographic research;
- document analysis, together with a critical examination of other forms of written evidence, findings from official surveys and other data sources – the so-called 'hard data' that funders generally seek;
- generating knowledge via interviews;
- focus group discussions.

Community-based evaluations have, in addition, demonstrated the relevance of case study research, exploring the impact of different interventions over time (particularly crucial if the aim is to build social solidarity on a sustainable basis).

An effective strategy needs to include some combination of different methods and approaches. So the strategy may draw on official data, for example, while being mindful of the limitations of particular research tools/measurement instruments such as particular survey questions and specific 'facts' (such as patterns of the reporting of racist incidents). But these types of data will be complemented with other sources of data, based on observations, community-based surveys/group discussions and case studies, tracking impacts over time (for example via the life histories of both individuals and community organisations).

The following case study illustrates some of the opportunities and challenges in developing participative and empowering approaches to evaluation in relation to building increasing social solidarity, working with established as well as newer communities to refute negative myths and stereotypes and developing joint action over shared interests, based on mutual respect. The case study in question has been developing evaluative research in this field as a direct result of a five-year programme to support research capacity building in the third sector, supported by the Economic and Social Research Council, the Office of the Third Sector and the Barrow Cadbury Trust, launched in 2007.

Developing Praxis' evaluation strategy

Praxis describes itself as 'a busy centre in East London visited by over 10,000 people each year. It provides a wealth of advice and support services', the website continues, 'to migrants and refugees from all over the world, as well as a welcoming meeting place for displaced communities' (www.praxis.org.uk). The focus is on 'Being with displaced communities, listening and acting through our common humanity to create and nurture reconciliation, human rights and social justice'. Praxis works holistically, engaging with established as well as with newer communities, drawing on community development principles. As the mission statement explains, 'Praxis has a vision of a world where people are no longer forced to move but are able to do so for mutual enrichment'.

Praxis' choice of name refers back to the Greek for 'action', with resonances of Freirian action–reflection–action cycles. So, in addition to providing advice, mentoring, English language skills and vocational training support to individuals, it has developed what it describes as 'our own action learning approach to community development' (www.praxis.org.uk) that 'enables the leaders of refugee and migrant communities to share their experiences, build solutions to their problems together and voice their concerns to policy makers'. Participative action research has been central, then, as Praxis has developed its initiatives in Tower Hamlets and Barking and Dagenham, East London.

The Third Sector Research Capacity Building Programme opened up new opportunities to build on previous forms of collaboration with one of the universities involved – Goldsmiths, University of London. Based in South East London, Goldsmiths had already developed links with Praxis (Praxis had been providing student placements for example). As part of the Third Sector Research Capacity Building Programme, along with the University of Lincoln and Manchester Metropolitan University, Goldsmiths had been awarded resources to provide placements and vouchers for third sector organisations, offering the equivalent of some 60 days of researchers' time, in the case of the placements (and some 20 days each, in the case of the smaller voucher opportunities). The placements and vouchers were to enable third sector organisations to strengthen their own research, as well as offering wider implications for research in the third sector more generally.

This came at an opportune time for Praxis, as the organisation faced increasing challenges as a result of the activities of the Far Right, mobilising with a particular focus on Barking and Dagenham. The British National Party (BNP) had won seats on the local council in 2006 and was aiming to take a parliamentary seat in the then forthcoming (2010) General Election. Migration had become a central issue, with migrants being blamed for a range of problems, from the loss of employment opportunities (following job losses from the Ford plant in Dagenham) through to the lack of affordable social housing, leaving the sons and daughters of long-term established communities struggling to afford to set up home in the area at all.

Praxis' management committee members were asking themselves how the organisation could be most effective, in the face of these threats, proactively working to promote community cohesion and social solidarity. Evaluating the impact of the organisation's support to individual migrants was relatively straightforward, compared with the challenges of evaluating the impact of their community development work. From Goldsmiths' point of view, this research project was potentially valuable to third sector organisations more generally, as well as being so relevant for Praxis, in the pre-election context.

The report (Camilo Cock, forthcoming) that emerged from this research was produced on the basis of close collaboration, as the joint authorship of this chapter illustrates. As this report explained, the first task was to explore varying (and competing) definitions and perspectives, to clarify what, precisely, was to be evaluated and why.

The promotion of equalities as the basis for social solidarity was, however, absolutely central to Praxis' mission. This wider definition was, then, the basis for developing Praxis' evaluation strategy.

The next task was to review government interventions and government approaches to the measurement of social cohesion to identify which of these would have relevance, taking account of any inherent limitations. Public Service Agreement (PSA) 21, covering the issue of community cohesion, was clearly relevant, for example. Before getting into the detail of any particular indicators, however, it was important to identify the underlying structural issues that were strongly linked with cohesion – or the lack of cohesion – within localities, so that these could be taken into account. In particular, deprivation and inequality had been identified as centrally important, together with access/lack of access to employment and affordable housing (Hudson et al, 2007). Crime, drugs and pollution were also identified, as undermining factors, while educational attainment, on the other hand, had positive associations with higher levels of tolerance (IPPR, 2010). Praxis' evaluation strategy would clearly need to take account of trends in relation to these underlying issues, given the significance of issues such as employment and housing – or the lack of job opportunities and affordable housing in the context of East London.

The local context would also be centrally important, as the background for evaluating Praxis' interventions. Tower Hamlets has a long history of receiving newcomers, from the Huguenots settling in Spitalfields in the 17th century, the Irish in search of a livelihood, coming to dig out the docks in the 19th century, the Jews, fleeing Russian pogroms in the late 19th and early 20th centuries, to the Bangladeshis, arriving more recently, in the second half of the 20th century. Diversity *per se*, is not necessarily associated with tensions between communities, though (Creasy et al, 2008). In contrast, Barking and Dagenham has been more stable until relatively recently, in terms of the rate of population churn. The rate and novelty of these recent changes has been associated with increasing anxieties and tensions, however. Other local contextual factors to be taken into account include the patterns of relationships with local structures of governance and the strength and vitality of civil society, including third sector organisations more generally. Any changes in these types of factors may be expected to affect the impact of Praxis' work in the two East London boroughs in question. As the Commission on Integration and Cohesion pointed out, local conditions vary and one size does not fit all (COIC, 2007). Variations are to be anticipated over time as well as space.

The most comprehensive study that was identified, here, was that carried out by Laurence and Heath (2008). This study modelled the levels of community cohesion, as measured by a set of individual-level and community-level indicators, alongside the national indicators (for all their limitations, as discussed in Part Two of this book) together with a set of sociodemographic and attitudinal variables. This model has the advantage of combining both objective and more subjective data to provide a relatively comprehensive view of the characteristics of areas in relation to their likely levels of cohesion. While offering valuable insights into the contextual factors involved (including the crucial links between disadvantage and feelings of disempowerment, on the one hand, and the lack of cohesion, on the other), this approach does not, of course, provide explanations. Causality needs further consideration, as does the measurement of impact, whether it is the impact of government initiatives or the impact of third sector initiatives to promote cohesion and social solidarity – or both. The next task, then, was to explore models of indicators and impact, with a view to developing an effective strategy for Praxis.

Indicators and toolkits

Clearly, whatever their limitations, the Department for Communities and Local Government's (DCLG) three key indicators could provide potentially valuable benchmarks. Given that two of these are measured by local authorities' Place Survey, as well as by the Citizenship Survey, these benchmarks have relevant local dimensions. Local authorities can decide to use additional indicators too, providing further data on subjective perceptions – useful again, in terms of background information, without necessarily contributing to the analysis that would also be required.

The evaluation of the Local Links project provided some experience of evaluating the impact of an initiative to increase networking between community organisations and public servants – based on interviews and focus groups with project participants. The report concluded, however, that 'there is not a great deal of evidence at this stage that the programmes have had a significant impact on engagement in local affairs'. This would also seem to indicate the importance of taking more than a snapshot, if the impact of such interventions is to be evaluated effectively, over time.

These types of cross-sectoral interventions do seem to be potentially problematic, working with service providers as well as working alongside both new and established communities' organisations in the third sector.

The Community Development Foundation's evaluation of 'Connecting Communities Plus', a Home Office-sponsored programme of grants to small community organisations, found, on the basis of self-administered questionnaires, that the most impact had indeed been on empowering local communities to access services. But there was less evidence of any wider impact, the evaluation concluded, arguing that there should be further research into how 'cohesion' is measured.

In summary, then, the report to Praxis concluded that there was an overall lack of replicable outcome indicators for small voluntary sector organisations. There were more examples of evaluations based on outputs than outcomes, with more reliance on data from project deliverers than from project beneficiaries. Case studies of good practice were potentially relevant, but there was insufficient reflection on how such case studies were being selected or by what criteria they were being judged as illustrations of good practice.

There was, however, an extremely promising example of a toolkit for evaluating the impact of interventions in an area holistically, taking account of both the issues that underpin cohesion and cohesion itself. This was the Oldham council toolkit (www.oldham.gov.uk/community-cohesion-toolkit.htm).

The Oldham toolkit divides the evaluation process into three broad stages:

- *strategic evaluation:* where project leaders evaluate the extent to which a project's activities and outputs contribute to the desired outcome;
- *developing evaluation indicators:* for monitoring and ongoing feedback;
- *evaluation research:* in-depth activities to evaluate the outcomes and impact, including the use of focus groups, research interviews and self-completion questionnaires.

Each indicator in Oldham was matched to a strand within the council's approach to community cohesion:

- people sharing a sense of belonging and common identity;
- people strong in their own identities and respecting others;
- a more equal borough;
- people relate to each other;
- people play their part;
- resilience to threats and conflict.

The Oldham approach is not a prescriptive one. The toolkit is there as a guide, with a wide range of suggestions for projects to design their own evaluation strategies. This was therefore identified as the most useful approach for Praxis, in developing its own strategy. The next stage, then, was for Praxis to work directly with the researcher, to identify which aspects of the Oldham toolkit would be relevant, in order to develop an overall evaluation strategy that focused on Praxis' interventions holistically, over and above the monitoring that was already under way, for each specific project intervention.

Developing a holistic strategy for Praxis

There followed, then, discussions between Praxis and the researcher, working together to develop a holistic evaluation strategy for Praxis, taking account of the impact of its interventions, overall, as well as monitoring individual project outcomes and outputs, using both hard and soft data, including data collected via participative forms of research. They concluded, first, that because community cohesion is a goal that is complex with multiple factors influencing it, finding a single indicator or outcome to measure the impact of Praxis on cohesion would not be feasible. What was proposed, rather, was to build up a picture of the contributions of Praxis and its projects towards improving community cohesion at different levels, that is, individuals, families, specific migrant communities and the whole community.

As a starting point to developing this framework for evaluating the impact of Praxis on community cohesion, the Praxis' model and all its current projects were linked to the constitutive elements of the community cohesion definitions of the DCLG (see Tables 11.1 and 11.2).

The report then proposed three ways to build up this picture: developing indicators that monitor work done on specific factors that affect cohesion, using national indicators where relevant; developing a monitoring and evaluation programme focused on evaluating outcomes based on some of the elements of the definition of community cohesion; and undertaking research projects to look specifically at the wider impact of Praxis projects.

1. Developing indicators that monitor work done on specific factors that affect cohesion. A first step would be to carry out what the Oldham toolkit describes as a strategic evaluation. The aim here is to identify causal links between the outputs of projects, their desired outcomes and the wider impact on community cohesion.

Assessing the impact of a project on a community is, of course, a challenging task given the difficulty of demonstrating the share of contribution of the project on a phenomenon that is multiply caused.

Table 11.1: Definitions of cohesion

DCLG definition	Oldham definition
1. People from different backgrounds having similar life opportunities	1. A more equal borough
2. People knowing their rights and responsibilities	2. People play their part
3. A shared future vision and sense of belonging	3. People share a sense of belonging and a common identity
4. A focus on what new and existing communities have in common, alongside a recognition of the value of diversity	4. People are strong in their own identities and respect others
5. Strong and positive relationships between people from different backgrounds	5. People relate to each other
6. People trusting one another and trusting local institutions to act fairly	6. Resilience to threats and conflict

The report did, however, identify studies that established a correlation between community cohesion and other factors on which it seemed more feasible to demonstrate an impact. For example, a correlation between deprivation and a lack of cohesion has been identified, as has a positive correlation between being able to influence local decisions and community cohesion, at both the individual and community levels (Laurence and Heath, 2008). Praxis has projects that tackle both deprivation and empowerment. If Praxis can develop indicators that demonstrate an impact on these intermediate outcomes (deprivation and empowerment), then it can be shown, based on quantitative studies, that these interventions should have an impact on cohesion.

2. Developing a monitoring and evaluation programme focused on evaluating outcomes based on some of the elements of the definition of community cohesion. As it has already been argued, measuring cohesion becomes more feasible if it is disaggregated into its component parts. Praxis could define a series of outcomes related to the projects it carries out, derived from the definition of community cohesion it adopts and then develop a method for assessing progress on these outcomes.

Table 11.2: The relationship of definitions of cohesion to current Praxis projects

Praxis model	Praxis projects	DCLG	Oldham
Personal empowerment	Advice with undocumented migrants	2	
	Supermarket voucher exchange	1	1
	Doctors of the world	1	1
	Somali support service (advice and mental health)	1, 2	1, 2
	Generic advice	1, 2, 6	1, 2
	Stop it now! Child protection programme for new communities	1	1
	Praxis family care	1	1
	Tower Hamlets employment access	1	1
	Working neighbourhood fund (ESOL)	1	1, 2
	Migrants in supported employment	1	1, 2
	Migrants probation advice service	1, 2, 6	1
	Policy forums on NRPF	1, 6	1
	Somali health access project	1, 2	1, 2
	Your health matters	1, 2	1
	ESOL learning circles	1, 2	1
Positive action	Moving into work	1, 4	1, 2, 4
	Mother tongue classes	4	4
	Music/dance/theatre activities	4, 5?	4, 5?
	Vamos juntos prison visiting		4
Community relations	New Voices Festival	3, 4, 5	3, 4, 5
	Moslems for democracy	5	5
	Shaping services, questionnaires with Eastern Europeans	3, 6	3
	Your health matters (workshops for service providers in Westminster)	1, 6	1
	Interpreting	1, 6	1
	Praxis 3rd party reporting centre	6	6
Participation and voice	New residents and forum	2, 3, 4, 5, 6	2, 3, 4, 5
	Rayne Fellowship	3	2, 3
	Reach Out (National Vocational Qualifications for activist women and faith organisations)		2

This would involve going beyond monitoring outputs, such as number of clients seen or activities undertaken. Rather, it would have to be designed to measure change in the lives of beneficiaries and users of projects. In this sense, it would require extra resources in terms of staff time to collect and analyse data. Methods for collecting information, depending on the specific projects, could include attendance information, self-completion questionnaires and follow-up interviews. Suitable indicators and methods of collecting data would have to be designed specifically for each project.

3. *Undertaking research projects to look specifically at the wider impact of Praxis projects.* This would probably have to be a specific project in itself, rather than an ongoing process of monitoring, with considerable staffing and financial requirements. A project of this scope would aim to analyse directly the impact of Praxis on community cohesion by studying in depth the complex factors, including but going beyond project interventions, that affect community cohesion. It would potentially also involve undertaking research not just with Praxis users and beneficiaries but with others, more widely.

As the next step, Praxis and the research partners aim to identify modest resources to develop such a toolkit for community-based voluntary sector organisations working in areas vulnerable to factors that trigger breakdowns in community cohesion and social solidarity. This toolkit would be based on the research that has already been undertaken, but would aim to have wider relevance and potential applicability, beyond the specific concerns of Praxis, in its East London context. This would go beyond measuring outputs and performance, to address the challenges of measuring the overall impact over time, using a variety of research methods. Once such a prototype was developed; the subsequent step would be to undertake participative action research, to pilot this, with a view to sharing the findings across third sector organisations more generally.

Conclusions

This links the discussion back to some of the challenges inherent in evaluating community cohesion and social solidarity in the third sector, more generally. How far, given these challenges and complexities, can any one third sector organisation contribute to the promotion of social solidarity more widely, let alone measure the long-term impact of their interventions really effectively? How might third sector organisations develop collaborative approaches, building participative research strategies as part of their wider commitment to reflective action? And how might Praxis' experience contribute towards building a holistic and collaborative third sector approach, working in cooperation with public sector agencies, in local areas?

Participative approaches to research can, it has been argued, generate processes that are, themselves, empowering. Evaluation can be a learning tool for organisations as well as for individuals. The overall objective, it has been suggested, may not simply be the production of progress reports: the research process can be central to the development of enhanced critical understanding and more effective action to promote community cohesion and social solidarity. So the broadest possible range of voluntary and community organisations needs to be actively engaged with the research process on an ongoing basis, within localities. Public sector organisations have central roles to play, of course, both in terms of action and in terms of research processes. But this is in no way to diminish the importance of the engagement of voluntary and community sector organisations and groups, actively participating in the evaluation as well as in the promotion of community engagement and social solidarity.

References

Barr, A. and Hashagen, S. (2000) *ABCD handbook: A framework for evaluating community development*, London: Community Development Foundation.

Blackburn, J. and Holland, J. (eds) (1998) *Who changes?*, London: Institute of Intermediate Technology.

Blake, G., Diamond, J., Foot, J., Gidley, B., Mayo, M., Shukra, K. and Yarnit, M. (2008) *Community engagement and community cohesion*, York: Joseph Rowntree Foundation.

Camilo Cock, J. (forthcoming) 'Evaluating the impact of voluntary and community sector organisations on community cohesion', will be available at www.gold.ac.uk/cllce/

COIC (Commission on Integration and Cohesion) (2007) *Our shared future*, London: COIC.

Cooke, B. and Kothari, U. (2001) *Participation: The new tyranny?*, London: Zed Books.

Creasy, S., Gavelin, K. and Potter, D. (2008) *Everybody needs good neighbours? A study of the link between public participation and community cohesion*, London: Involve.

Estrella, M. (ed) (2000) *Learning from change: Issues and experiences of participatory monitoring*, London: Institute of Intermediate Technology.

Freire, P. (1972) *Pedagogy of the oppressed*, Harmondsworth: Penguin.

Grayson, J. (2010) 'Borders, glass floors and anti-racist popular education', in M. Mayo and J. Annette (eds) *Taking part? Active learning for active citizenship and beyond* (pp 156-68), Leicester: NIACE.

Hartley, T. (2010) 'Proving a point: effective social, political and citizenship education in South Yorkshire', in M. Mayo and J. Annette (eds) *Taking part? Active learning for active citizenship and beyond* (pp 141-55), Leicester: NIACE.

Hudson, M., Philips, J., Ray, K. and Barnes, H. (2007) *Social cohesion in diverse communities*, York: Joseph Rowntree Foundation.

Laurence, J. and Heath, A. (2008) *Predictors of community cohesion: Multi-level modelling of the 2005 Citizenship Survey*, London: DCLG.

IPPR (Institute for Public Policy Research) (2010) *Exploring the roots of BNP support*, London: IPPR.

Mayo, M. and Rooke, A. (2008) 'Active learning for active citizenship: participatory approaches to evaluating a programme to promote citizen participation in England', *Community Development Journal*, vol 43, no 3, pp 371-81.

Mosse, D. (2001) 'People's knowledge', in B. Cooke and U. Kothari (eds) *Participation: The new tyranny?* (pp 16-35), London: Zed Books.

Newman, K. (2008) 'Whose view matters? Using participatory processes to evaluate REFLECT in Nigeria', *Community Development Journal*, vol 43, no 3, pp 382-94.

Wilson, M. and Zipfel, T. (2008) *Communities R Us*, London: HACT.

Worley, C. (2005) 'It's not about race: it's about the community': New Labour and "community cohesion"', *Critical Social Policy*, vol 25, no 4, pp 483-96.

TWELVE

Evaluating the contribution of intergenerational practice to achieving social cohesion

Alan Hatton-Yeo and Clare Batty

Introduction

> Intergenerational practice aims to bring people together in
> purposeful, mutually beneficial activities which promote
> greater understanding and respect between generations
> and contributes to building more cohesive communities.
> Intergenerational practice is inclusive, building on the
> positive resources that the young and old have to offer each
> other and those around them. (Centre for Intergenerational
> Practice: www.centreforip.org.uk)

This chapter seeks to place intergenerational practice (IP) within the
context of recent social policy developments aimed to establish, or
to strengthen, social cohesion at local and national levels. To do this,
it begins by looking at the nature of IP and its place in the context
of national social policy developments, particularly those around
'community' and 'cohesion'. It goes on to outline the ways in which
interest in and support for IP have developed over the last 50 years
or so before considering the potential benefits of IP, together with
an assessment of how these may contribute to achieving greater
community and social cohesion. Finally, some of the opportunities
and challenges in evaluating IP outcomes within this context are
discussed. A wide range of practical national and international case
studies is included to illustrate and to develop some of the main points,
particularly around the engagement of IP with the 'harder conversations'
of cohesion – such as those concerning equality and poverty.

The chapter's discussion concludes that the evidence base for this level
of engagement does exist, but that IP requires closer alignment with

broader social programmes addressing some of the more intransigent socioeconomic issues.

Background

Rein (1994) has attributed intergenerational solidarity primarily to a sense of identity and belonging; the term 'solidarity' reflects a feeling of togetherness that is developed from close family ties and provides a basis for identification. This in turn leads to a willingness to provide mutual assistance. Spicker (2003) argues that Rein is mistaken. Mutual assistance is not only dependent on identification; the ties of solidarity are also the ties of mutual support.

Intergenerational relationships, and what is referred to as the intergenerational contract, are governed by rules, norms, conventions, practices and biology, with the 'contract' being implicit rather than arrived at through individual negotiation. Some people have also used the term 'social compact' to articulate the concept of intergenerational interdependence (Kingson et al, 1997; Henkin and Kingson, 1998/99).

Walker (2001) maintains that the economic relationship is but one consideration. The intergenerational contract also includes an ethical dimension that represents the social cohesion of societies, achieved by ensuring security for all citizens – not only those able to pay for it. Walker (2001) argues that while it makes sound economic sense to adjust to the demographic realities of an ageing society, a one-dimensional interpretation of the intergenerational contract or intergenerational relationships will undermine efforts to maintain intergenerational solidarity.

As a result, intergenerational solidarity needs to be broadly characterised in terms of those formal and informal systems, practices and understandings that enable the generations to engage in a collaborative fashion to provide mutual benefit. Such a model resonates with much of the current debate around the need to promote social cohesion and civic engagement. It has been suggested that cross-generational relationships can be identified as one of the key networks that can tie communities together (Hatton-Yeo, 2006b, pp 1-4).

A recent study by the Joseph Rowntree Foundation (2007) into community cohesion in ethnically diverse communities found that intergenerational tensions were at least as significant as cultural and ethnic divisions in mitigating against social cohesion. Some key informants in the study stressed the importance of recognising and addressing intergenerational fears and tensions, cultivating respect across the generations and acknowledging the need to be aware of the multiple identities of individuals for community relationships.

The meaning of social cohesion remains open to debate within the intergenerational literature. The literature broadly emphasises two principal elements to the concept: 'the reduction of disparities, inequalities and social exclusion' and 'the strengthening of social relations, interactions and ties' (Berger-Schmitt, 2000, p 28). In much of the literature the second element dominates and is closely tied to the concept of 'social capital'. Social capital is associated with 'people's sense of community, their sense of belonging to a neighbourhood, caring about the people who live there, and believing that people who live there care about them' (Portney and Berry, 2001, p 71). Putnam (2000) has argued that positive attitudes towards and beliefs in one's neighbours contribute to cohesion within the local community and thus to residents' willingness to participate in local affairs and to cooperate in everyday matters. As a result, life in communities with high levels of social capital, so-called 'civic communities', is seen to be good.

This approach has been an important strand of the previous government's thinking. All local authorities had to develop Sustainable Communities Strategies that the government stated should identify 'a sense of community identity and belonging', along with 'tolerance, respect and engagement with people from different cultures, background and beliefs' as requisites for sustainable communities (ODPM, 2005). There is a suggestion in this policy debate that a sense of community belonging is best developed at the neighbourhood level. Indeed, 'neighbourhood' and 'community' are generally assumed to coincide and are often talked about interchangeably. The Commission on Integration and Cohesion (COIC, 2007) in its report *Our shared future* also makes specific reference to the importance of programmes to build intergenerational understanding and respect in developing social cohesion. It is an approach that has been critiqued in the earlier chapters in this book, which, while recognising the importance of fostering strong relationships between citizens, has put the case for a wider, more inclusive, notion of '*social* cohesion', which seeks to address equalities issues as a foundation for achieving better relationships.

Letki (2008) and the Joseph Rowntree Foundation (2007) accord most closely with this wider concept of social cohesion and state that the economic status of a community is one of the strongest influences on social cohesion. Poverty has a more corrosive effect on cohesion than either ethnic or generational difference. Therefore, they argue, it is important in developing intergenerational activities to promote solidarity to consider activities that not only seek to build positive relationships but also seek to encourage aspiration and achievement and break intergenerational cycles of poverty (Letki, 2008).

> Therefore, the efforts to revive social cohesion through programs focused on intercommunity relations are misplaced if they under-emphasise material deprivation, intergenerational disadvantage, crime and low community socio-economic status. To maintain social solidarity and community cohesion 21st Century Britain needs more social and economic equality, rather than more cultural unity. Until the link between diversity and deprivation is alleviated, British communities are likely to continue to face a crisis of solidarity and collective identity. (Letki, 2008, p 122)

In Chapter One of this volume, Peter Ratcliffe writes: 'At the risk of overstating the case, it is infinitely easier to bring people together for social events than it is to solve the material differences that divide those same people' (p 33). This sentence is at the heart of the question of how effective intergenerational approaches are to building social cohesion. A review by the author of the *Journal for Intergenerational Relationships* in the five years since its publication reveals that the majority of articles published are relatively small-scale studies, often focusing on attitude change or challenging stereotypical views. While this 'myth-busting', as referred to in Chapter One, has an important role to play, the evidence for it generalising to build a more socially cohesive community is difficult to discover.

Pain (2005) reiterates the point made earlier about recognising the complexity of community relations and seeing intergenerational activities as only part of the mechanism to build community cohesion. She also notes that there is a rich array of contextual factors that need to be taken into account when considering, and trying to improve, intergenerational relations in any particular society. Focusing in on the United Kingdom (UK), she draws attention to various factors that have contributed to concerns about intergenerational relations in recent times. In so doing, Pain is emphasising the points made earlier by Hatton-Yeo and Watkins (2004, p 5):

> A range of other factors is also held to have worsened intergenerational relations...:

- Economic changes in the UK which have increased and entrenched poverty in marginalised places.
- The erosion of traditional family structures.
- A weakened sense of community, and young people not being prepared for citizenship.
- Increasing proportions of young men in particular growing up disaffected from society.
- Review of the welfare state and the support it is able to provide.

As previously described, it is integral to acknowledge the impact of diversity and poverty on social cohesion. The existing evidence suggests that activities that build intergenerational connectivity and solidarity can have a significant impact on improving social relationships. Intergenerational projects that successfully address wider social cohesion can also have an impact on developing the skills and confidence of participants to enable them to achieve the potential for greater success.

The development of IP

The first recorded examples of IP were in North America during the late 1960s and 1970s and developed as a result of a growing belief that social and demographic changes were contributing both to a reduction and an alteration in the interactions between older and younger people and to an increase in negative age-related stereotypes. These examples generally took the form of standalone projects, and were seen as a response to patterns of residential and social segregation of age groups and the negative consequences associated with these trends, such as a reduction in the extent and quality of the social networks of children and older adults (Kalish, 1969; Stearns, 1989; Henkin and Kingson, 1998/99).

During the 1980s, the purpose of IP began to change as it started to address the problems perceived as affecting two vulnerable populations: children/young persons and older adults. These problems were described as concerns about low self-esteem, drug and alcohol abuse, poor academic performance, isolation, a lack of appropriate support systems, unemployment and a lack of familial and social ties.

Early in the 1990s, the scope of IP broadened still further in an attempt to use it as an agent to revitalise communities through action programmes to reconnect the generations. By the end of the decade, the number of IPs had started to increase significantly around the world. Across Europe this was a response to emerging issues such as the integration of immigrants in the Netherlands, the social inclusion and the growth of active ageing in the UK and the perception of a crisis affecting traditional family solidarity models in Spain (Sanchez, 2008).

In 2001, the Beth Johnson Foundation, a national organisation that seeks to make a positive impact on the lives of older people in the UK, established the Centre for Intergenerational Practice (CIP) to provide a focal point for building a systematic knowledge base and understanding of IP in the UK. From its beginnings the Centre has worked to create a documented account of the wide array of intergenerational projects across the UK and to provide advice, support and guidance to practitioners and policy makers.

The growth of interest among practitioners has been accompanied by government in the UK increasingly promoting the importance of IP. In 2003, the Welsh Assembly identified the development of intergenerational work as a core objective in the Older People's Strategy for Wales. This was followed up in 2008 with the publication of a National Intergenerational Strategy for Wales (WAG, 2008), which integrated opportunities for IP across the whole of Wales. Similarly, in 2007, the Scottish Parliament identified intergenerational practice as a core policy concern. In *Safer ageing*, its strategy for ensuring the safety of older people, the Northern Ireland Office recognised the contribution that IP can make 'to building and sustaining vibrant, inclusive and safer communities' (NIO, 2009, pp 8-9).

While government at Westminster has moved more cautiously, the last two years have seen a significant increase in interest. In 2008, a cross-departmental ministerial group was established that brought together the Department for Works and Pensions, the Department for Children, Schools and Families (DCSF), the Department for Communities and Local Government, Health and the Office of the Third Sector. Under the leadership of the DCSF, this partnership launched the £5.5 million Generations Together Programme in 2009, which has the development of an evidence base on the efficacy of intergenerational projects as one of its core objectives.

The growth of interest in the UK has been mirrored by a global recognition of the importance of intergenerational approaches. The United Nations (UN) has established an expert group to consider the role of intergenerational solidarity in strengthening economic and social ties and a chapter was devoted in the 2003 UN youth report to the importance of intergenerational approaches to addressing poverty and economic inactivity (UN, 2003). There has been similar interest in Europe, with 29 April being designated as European Day of Intergenerational Solidarity. Consultation is nearing completion on the proposal to make 2012 the European Year of Active Ageing and Intergenerational Solidarity.

Forms of IP and the benefits they offer

The CIP currently supports over 2,000 organisations that are either delivering or developing intergenerational projects. Analysis of documented case studies, information in the CIP database and evidence gathered from network meetings, case studies and other surveys suggest that the main categories of IP currently operating include:

- intergenerational volunteering, within which mentoring, skill sharing and coaching are the main subcategories;
- programmes to promote community relationships, promote community safety and address fear of crime;
- programmes to promote active ageing and improved health and wellbeing; and
- programmes to support young people and families through older family members and volunteer support.

More broadly, Pain (2005) commented that existing work can be divided into four interconnected areas:

- issues of transfer and transmission between generations;
- a focus on the personal relationships and the amount, nature and implications of contact between the generations, in most cases who are related;
- a smaller amount of work examining issues of personal identity; and
- a burgeoning concern with the evaluation of intergenerational policy and practice.

The Generations Together programme, referred to above, identified a number of national policy drivers that are of particular relevance to intergenerational work. One such driver aimed to 'Build more cohesive, empowered and active communities', stating that 'active communities can be achieved by increasing levels of formal and informal volunteering, where members of the community work to meet local needs as well as by increasing active participation across a variety of cultural and sporting activities' (CAB 2007, para 1.4, p 3). IP can support the achievement of this through promoting meaningful interactions between people from different generations, backgrounds and by encouraging more social and civil participation.

Build more cohesive, empowered and active communities (PSA21).

Intergenerational practice can support the achievement of this through promoting meaningful interactions between people from different backgrounds and by encouraging more participation in culture and sport. Active communities can be supported by increasing levels of formal and informal volunteering by people from both ends of the age spectrum, where members of the community work to meet local needs. At the heart of this active participation are community-based third sector organizations, often bringing different groups together and providing the platform to meet the needs of individuals and communities. (Springate et al, 2008)

In 2008, Springate et al undertook a review of IP funded by the Local Government Association. One of their research questions was 'what kinds of outcomes can be achieved through intergenerational practice and for whom?' Their analysis identified outcomes from participation in intergenerational programmes for older people, for young people and for communities. See Figure 12.1.

An earlier analysis of over 120 programmes in Australia identified sets of clear benefits for participants similar to those later recorded by Springate et al. MacCallum et al (2006) found that for older people, benefits ranged from individual (ability to cope with mental disease, increased motivation, increased perceptions of self-worth) to relational (making friends with young people, escape from isolation) and benefits for the community (reintegration, skill sharing, volunteering). For young people, benefits noted included: increased sense of worth, self-esteem and confidence; access to adults at difficult times; enhanced sense of social responsibility; better school results; less involvement in offending and drug use; better health; improved school attendance; and greater personal resilience.

Evaluation evidence

This idea that intergenerational work can contribute to the development of social capital (defined as an increase in networks, trust or reciprocity) is supported by research studies such as that in Hong Kong (CIIF Evaluation Consortium, 2006). The Community Investment and Inclusion Fund (CIIF) was launched in Hong Kong in

Figure 12.1: Outcomes from IP

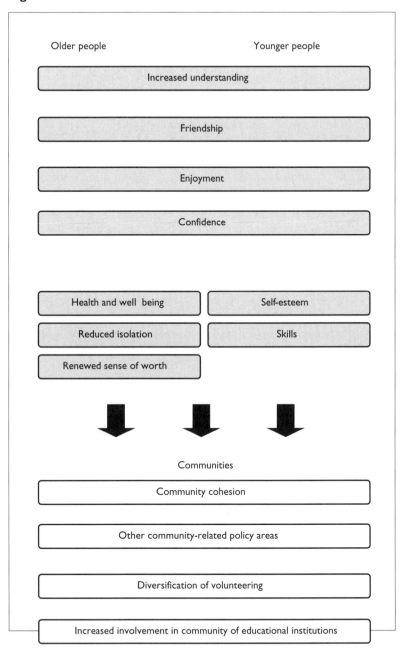

Source: Springate et al (2008, p 14)

2002 to support community-initiated projects that promoted mutual aid and concern and promoted community participation. It aimed to promote social cohesion, strengthen community networks and support family and social solidarity.

The study found that all of the selected intergenerational projects that were implemented effectively enhanced the solidarity between generations through enhancing positive images as well generating mutual help or resource exchange and assistance.

In Finland, the project 'Promoting networking among generations', was developed to promote the wellbeing of children and adolescents by providing adequate adult contacts for children and young people and by supporting the everyday life of families with children (EAGLE, 2007).The adults in the project volunteered as mentors and adult friends to the children and young people. The project's main goal was to put intergenerational relationships in place through a mentoring model supporting the development of the young people.

Perhaps of greater interest is to examine those intergenerational projects that also have a focus on addressing inequality and disadvantage. Within the UK, one of the most fully evaluated intergenerational programmes was the Year Seven mentoring project of the Beth Johnson Foundation (Ellis, 2002, 2004).This was developed in Stoke-on-Trent, an area of significant deprivation and one of the worst-performing education authorities in England, with high levels of generationally transmitted disadvantage and lack of aspiration.

The project took a mentoring approach that had three core aims:

- to raise the achievement and aspiration of pupils who were at risk of failure;
- to promote the sense of identity and value of older people;
- to connect local schools to the community and promote the understanding of the importance of education.

Evaluation of the projects demonstrated that the interrelated phases were highly effective in the first two aims. However, some of the most interesting outcomes came from the development of community generational connections as a result of the programme. Older people, who had previously been very critical of the schools and young pupils, took on a championing role together with a variety of other voluntary roles, thereby becoming very involved in linking the schools to their communities.

One major review of cohesion policy in a number of acutely divided towns in Northern England (DCLG, 2006) addressed one of the most significant divisions between generations. Much of the study focused on deprived communities with high levels of unemployment, antisocial behaviour and criminal damage, violent crime and 'turf wars' between gangs of young people. Here, it was this daily lived experience that drove the most significant wedge between the generations. One innovative project in Rochdale, however, piloted a warden scheme that employed a number of the young people identified as the most prominent repeat offenders. Evaluation of the initiative revealed that providing training and a sense of responsibility in this way led both to a remarkable change in the behaviour of the youths concerned and a marked improvement in the attitudes of other residents towards young people in general.

Similarly, one of the most successful intergenerational programmes in Germany was underpinned by both an economic and social imperative to develop a sustainable future for the community. Amtzell is situated in the western part of the Allgäu region in Germany with a population that has remained relatively stable in this region, yet the proportion of people aged above 80 is disproportionately high. An intentional intergenerational strategy has been developed to promote both the economic wellbeing of all citizens and to strengthen social cohesion (Bardey, 2006). Different age groups were intentionally mixed, and an experiment named 'the generation village' undertaken. Once the nursery school had been built close to the old people's home, a residential development named 'Young and Old' was developed, providing space for both families and senior citizens to live in and meet one another and a multigenerational sports facility was built alongside.

'Young and Old' is also the name of the network that the village has developed. Besides the kindergarten and older people's home, the network includes the school, private nursing services, clubs and even individuals. The project has begun to generate financial benefits, with Amtzell being able to reduce the number of costly acute care units as the health of its citizens improves (Bardey, 2006). Measures to foster intergenerational practice in Germany are strongly related to programmes aimed at strengthening civil engagement, active citizenship and voluntary work as many programmes, initiatives and projects are trying to engage citizens of all ages on a voluntary basis. Two good examples of projects that contribute to building civil engagement and cohesion in Germany are TANDEM and the federal model programme for Multigenerational Houses (EAGLE, 2007).

TANDEM is aimed at developing sustainable vocational qualifications for long-term unemployed young people and fostering the re-employment of long-term unemployed older workers by utilising the skills and competencies of older people to vocationally train young people in real-life settings such as car repair, carpeting, plumbing, electronics, metal work and gastronomy.

The federal model programme Multigenerational Houses is aiming to transfer the cooperation of the generations from private to public settings. Today, 250 houses are up and running, and it is envisaged that 450 houses will eventually be active in Germany. These funded houses use the expertise and potential of all the generations by being open community drop-in centres where all generations can meet. A multigenerational house is a meeting place for people of different ages in a specific city or community. It is planned as an open place, where young and old people both offer and take mutual support, and become part of a network, which brings services and the interests of people of different age groups together.

There are various accounts of intergenerational community advocacy or action projects that have taken root in the United States (US) (Kaplan and Liu, 2004; Kaplan and Lawrence-Jacobson, 2006). One such initiative is the Intergenerational Citizens Action Forum in Miami, Florida. In this model, high school-aged youth and older adult volunteers come together to learn about public policy issues of mutual concern and, in a non-partisan effort, work to effect public policy change. Older people serve as mentors to the students and help them to organise town meetings that address issues such as social security reform, crime and environmental protection. After the intergenerational teams define and prioritise critical issues to address, they receive training in how to conduct advocacy campaigns, and then initiate a community organising campaign aimed at promoting desired community changes.

The ultimate goal of this initiative is to develop concrete solutions that can be obtained through legislation or policy changes. Campaigns involve various forms of political action such as contacting legislators and policy makers, drafting legislation that is presented to relevant committees during the state legislative sessions, and writing letters to the editors of local newspapers to raise public awareness and urge action. Intergenerational teams reflect on and evaluate the success of their projects to identify what has worked well and what needs to be changed for the future.

Participating project teachers introduce legislative, intergenerational and service-learning themes into the core academic curriculum, and students receive service-learning credit for their involvement. According to project evaluation results, participating youth display an enhanced sense of civic responsibility and an increase in their competence as community change agents (Kaplan and Liu, 2004).

The Netherlands programme, Generations in Action, introduces a method for the joint participation of the young and old to empower young and older people (Mercken, 2003). The main aims of the project are to promote participation, social solidarity and citizenship; to encourage integration of the generations in the neighbourhood; to promote mutual understanding and communication between the age groups; and to gather policy information about the needs and perceptions of younger and older people. The model is an integrated approach that brings together youth work, work with older people and community development to promote mutual understanding and social cohesion in the community.

In Newport, South Wales, Charter Housing, which provides sheltered housing for older people, has developed a number of intergenerational projects particularly addressing building community connections to counter older people's concerns over the significant increase locally in the number of young migrants (Hatton-Yeo, 2006, pp 54 *et seq*). One such project was with the locally based minority ethnic women's group Ta'aleem Alnyssa. The group offers education and training for women from minority ethnic groups in a safe and friendly environment. The project's volunteers have helped members of Ta'aleem Alnyssa practice for their driving theory exam, a particularly daunting exam for those who do not have English as a first language. They have also held literacy events for women who want to improve their written and spoken English.

Conclusion and discussion

While there is a large number of IPs of different types and sizes now operating worldwide, the number of documented assessments and published evaluation studies that extend beyond providing descriptions of individual programmes is relatively small (Kuehne, 1998/99). Although there is increasing debate about how intergenerational approaches can contribute to promoting social and community cohesion (the two terms are often used interchangeably without clear definition), the body of research relating to these intergenerational approaches outside the family is limited. Notwithstanding, there remains a broader base of work exploring issues of intergenerational solidarity that needs to be highlighted.

The programmes described above have in common that they highlight a view of citizenship that involves people of all ages as active participants in local issues. Social cohesion works effectively at both community and neighbourhood levels, and the activities described reflect this as socially inclusive approaches to building community networks. The contribution of intergenerational activities towards building a more cohesive and caring society is difficult to question, although calls for 'hard evidence' continue and must be adequately addressed.

A greater challenge, however, is to locate these approaches alongside broader social programmes that also address other challenges to social cohesion such as reducing poverty, social exclusion and disadvantage. IP is a necessary participant in the 'harder conversations' that are central to community and social cohesion.

References

Bardey, A. (2006) *The city of the future: A paradise for senior citizens? The ageing society*, Goethe Institute, Munich, February, www.Goethe.de/ges/soz/dos/dos/age/woh/en1215423

Berger-Schmitt, R. (2000) *Social cohesion as an aspect of the quality of societies: Concept and measurement*, EU Reporting Working Paper no 14, Mannheim: Centre for Survey Research and Methodology, Social Indicators Department.

CAB (2007) *Public Service Agreement 21 Delivery Agreement*, London: Cabinet Office, HMSO.

COIC (Commission on Integration and Cohesion) (2007) *Our shared future*, Wetherby: Communities and Local Government Publications.

CIIF (2006) *Final report of an evaluation study on the impacts of CIIF intergenerational programmes on the development of social capital in Hong Kong*, Report for the Health, Welfare and Food Bureau, Hong Kong. Community Investment and Inclusion Fund, Hong Kong.

DCLG (Department for Communities and Local Government) (2006) *Managing for diversity: A case study of four local authorities*, London: DCLG.

EAGLE (2007) see Policies, Programmes and Initiatives at www.eagle-project.eu, Practice Showcase at www.eagle-project.eu

Ellis, S. (2002) *Changing The Lives Of Children And Older People: Final Report Of The Year Seven intergenerational project*, Stoke-on-Trent: Beth Johnson Foundation.

Ellis, S. (2004) *Identifying and supporting those children most at need: Intergenerational collaboration and action in two Stoke-on-Trent school clusters*, Stoke-on-Trent: Beth Johnson Foundation.

Hatton-Yeo, A. (2006a) *Report for volunteering in the third Age*, Stoke-on-Trent: Beth Johnson Foundation.

Hatton-Yeo, A. (ed) (2006b) *Intergenerational programmes: An introduction and examples of practice*, Stoke-on-Trent: Beth Johnson Foundation.

Hatton-Yeo, A. and Watkins, C. (2004) *Intergenerational community development:A practice guide*, Stoke-on-Trent: Beth Johnson Foundation.

Henkin, N. and Kingson, E. (eds) (1998/99) 'Keeping the promise: intergenerational strategies for strengthening the social compact (special issue)', *Generations*, vol 22, no 4.

Kalish, R.A. (1969) 'The old and the new as generation gap allies', *The Gerontologist*, vol 9, no 2, pp 83-9.

Kaplan, M. and Lawrence-Jacobson A. (2006) 'Intergenerational programs and practices', in L. Sternod, C.A. Flanagan and R. Kassimir (eds) *Youth activism:An international encyclopaedia* (pp 357-61),Westport, CT: Greenwood.

Kaplan, M. and Liu, S.-T. (2004) *Generations united for environmental awareness and action*,Washington, DC: Generations United.

Kingson, E., Cornman, J. and Leavitt, J.K. (1997) *Strengthening the social compact: An intergenerational strategy*, Washington, DC: Generations United.

Kuehne,V.S. (1998/9) 'Building intergenerational communities through research and evaluation', *Generations*, vol 22, no 4, pp 82-7.

Letki, N. (2008) 'Does diversity erode social cohesion? Social capital and race in British neighbourhoods', *Political Studies*, vol 56, no 1, pp 99-126.

MacCullum, J, Palmer, D,Wright, P, Cummings-Patvin,W, Northcote, J, Brooker, M and Tero, C. (2006) *Community building through intergenerational exchange programmes*, Report to the National Youth Affairs Research Scheme, Department of Families, Community Services and Youth Affairs, Canberra: ACT, Australia.

Mercken, C. (2003) *Generations in action*, Utrecht, the Netherlands: NIZW.

NIO (Northern Ireland Office) (2009) *Safer ageing:A strategy and action plan for ensuring the safety of older people*, Belfast: NIO.

ODPM (Office of the Deputy Prime Minister) (2005) *Sustainable communities: People, places, prosperity*, Cm 6425, London:The Stationery Office.

Pain, R. (2005) *Intergenerational relations and practice in the development of sustainable communities*, London: OPDM.

Portney, K.E. and Berry, J.M. (2001) 'Mobilising minority communities: social capital and participation in urban neighbourhoods', in B. Edward, M.W. Foley and M. Diani (eds) *Beyond Tocqueville: Civil society and social capital in comparative perspective*, Hanover, Germany: Tufts University.

Putnam, R.D. (2000) *Bowling alone: The collapse and revival of American community*, New York, NY: Simon & Schuster.

Rein, M. (1994) *Solidarity between generations: A five country study of the social process of aging,* Vienna: Institut fur Hohere Studien Reihe Politikwessenschaft.

Sanchez, M. (ed) (2008) *Programas intergeneracionales, solidaridad intergeneracional y cohesión social, Hacia una sociedad para todas las edades: La vía de los programas intergeneracionales,* Barcelona: Fundación La Caixa.

Spicker, P. (2003) *Solidarity between generations: A conceptual account*: Antwerp, Belgium: International Research Conference on Social Security.

Springate, I., Atkinson, M. and Martin, K. (2008) *Intergenerational Practice: a Review of the Literature,* LGA Research Report F/SR262, Slough: NFER.

Stearns, P.N. (1989) 'Historical trends in intergenerational contacts', in S. Newman and S.W. Brummel (eds) *Intergenerational programs: Imperatives, strategies, impacts, trends* (pp 21-32), Binghamton, NY: Haworth Press.

UN (2003) *Young people in a global world,* New York, NY: United Nations Publications.

Walker, A. (2001) *Seminar transcript ageing and intergenerational relationships,* London: Daiwa Anglo-Japanese Foundation.

Welsh Assembly Government (WAG) (2008) *Strategy for older people in Wales: A strategy for intergenerational practice in Wales,* Cardiff: WAG.

Part Four

Conclusion

Conclusion: towards a theory of change for social cohesion

Ines Newman and Peter Ratcliffe

In this conclusion we aim to do three things. First, we want pull together the chapters of this book into a theory of change (ToC) that can provide a new basis for the evaluation of social cohesion. Second, we want to highlight the problems with implementing this new approach as a result of the financial crisis and change of government. Finally, we want to end on an optimistic note and identify the levers that might help sustain a broader approach despite the difficulties.

We started writing this book under a Labour government that had fetishised community cohesion and we were very critical of its implicit ToC, which we viewed as dominated by a culturalist approach to policy. We argued that its theory saw those deemed to be 'socially excluded' as 'the problem' (Gough et al, 2006). It was *they* who had to integrate with British society, learn English, gain qualifications, raise their aspirations, shun 'extremism', vote, become active citizens and get a job. The problem of modern society, and especially poor urban communities, was seen to stem from people becoming isolated from the sources of help and support that would help them to help themselves. The solution therefore lay in a set of policies addressing the 'problems' of the socially excluded individual rather than policies that tried to make the wider society more inclusive and equitable. Such policies included: reconnecting people to their local jobcentre and motivating them to look for work; raising aspirations at school; pursuing the 'Prevent' agenda and new citizenship tests; bringing together the old and the young and the migrants and established populations through cultural activities; dispersing Black and minority ethnic and migrant communities; and encouraging volunteering and processes that enabled disadvantaged 'communities' to take greater control and responsibility for their futures.

In Chapter Three, Fuller argued that performance management regimes reinforce these social constructions, as what is measured is what is valued. While in reality people have multiple identities and networks that stretch far beyond their neighbourhood, performance management regimes have sought to identify communities where social relationships are affected by their policy solutions. They have focused on people's perceptions of their local area and the local services they receive, on how much influence they feel they have on local decision making, on how 'different' people 'get along' together, on how much they volunteer, on whether they feel they 'belong' to the neighbourhood and whether different ethnic groups are respected.

While we have argued that a society will never be completely devoid of internal conflicts and some tensions are additional to those derived from material inequality, the government's conceptualisation marginalises the principal underlying causes of the lack of cohesion: poverty, differential access to basic services and life opportunities and discrimination and xenophobia. These issues have been acknowledged in the definitions of community cohesion, as outlined in Chapter One, but have not been seen as fundamental causal agents within governments' ToCs. Yet, research has consistently shown that deprivation, low socioeconomic status, and poverty are the principal correlates of 'cohesion' (Laurence and Heath, 2007). The Labour governments were concerned with inequality and did seek to reduce child poverty by increasing employment levels, minimum income and child benefits. They also sought to enhance life opportunities by improving access to basic public services and programmes like Sure Start. But, while government policy has prioritised community cohesion, it has primarily relied on economic growth and the market to deliver enhanced life opportunities for disadvantaged groups despite historic evidence during the 1980s that increased wealth in the United Kingdom (UK) failed to 'trickle down' and indeed was associated with increasing inequality in England and Wales with widening gaps between individuals, neighbourhoods and regions. Cohesion funds have been focused on projects and the promotion of best practice to improve good relationships. These projects may well have marginally helped to keep the lid on overt conflict, but at no time did New Labour governments seriously challenge the growth of inequality, the rising wealth of the top 1-5%,[1] the lack of social housing and the reduction in social mobility, despite the fact that:

> Time and time again articles were written explaining that: 'Extreme social inequality is associated with higher levels of mental ill health, drugs use, crime and family breakdown. Even high levels of public service investment, alone, cannot cope with the strain that places on our social fabric.' (O'Grady, 2007, pp 62-3, quoted in Dorling, 2010, p 318)

Dorling (2010) argues that the failure to deal with social inequality rests on the powerful in the economically affluent and unequal countries, not just the UK, propagating five new sets of beliefs that are presented as natural and longstanding but in fact are relatively new constructs. These sets of beliefs are based on elitism, exclusion, prejudice, greed and despair and are interlinked:

> Elitism suggests that educational divisions are natural.... Elitism is the incubation chamber within which prejudice is fostered. Elitism provides a defence for greed.... It perpetuates an enforced and inefficient hierarchy in our society.... The exclusion which rises with elitism makes the poor appear different, exacerbates inequalities between ethnic groups and, literally, causes racial difference.... The prejudice that rises with exclusion allows the greedy to try and justify their greed and makes others think they deserve a little more than most. The ostracism that such prejudice engenders further raises depression and anxiety in those made to look different.... In turn despair prevents us from effectively tackling injustice. (Dorling, 2010, pp 309-10)

Dorling's view of the modern-day evils complements our call for social cohesion in which a more just and equal society enables wider tensions and divisions to be more successfully addressed.

Towards a theory of change for social cohesion

How would one evaluate progress towards achieving social cohesion? This question has been at the core of this book. Here we start to put forward some tentative steps for moving towards a wider evaluation, drawing particularly on Chapter Two by Sullivan and also on the different issues highlighted by the authors in this book.

The first task is to specify the desired outcome and then elucidate our theory of causality. We have made the case for the desired outcome to be social cohesion. This, we have argued, cannot be achieved unless internal divisions based on material inequalities and multiple and complex identities have been addressed successfully. 'Success', we have suggested, is judged by sustainable, lasting stability based on the firm foundation of achieved equality targets and also on a serious push to ensure harmonious relations within a clearly prioritised policy strategy.

In terms of causality, our ToC suggests that pursuing social cohesion will narrow the gaps in outcomes and life opportunities and that this is a prerequisite for reducing community tensions and facilitating better relationships. While we have sought to show that equality is necessary for cohesion, we have still argued that policies around reducing tension (tackling discrimination; tackling media myths and fear of the Other; seeing the positives in multi-ethnic societies and so on) can have a significant effect. By seeing such 'cohesion' policies in the context of a social cohesion framework, different types of intervention will be privileged. Current culturalist approaches see the individual as the source of 'the problem' and look at policies to modify their behaviour. Or they build from a communitarian, social capital framework and argue for policies that are assumed to build bonding capital based on the creation of an enhanced social housing 'mix'.

In contrast, a social cohesion approach would look at the barriers that are created by a society that is unequal and seek to address these issues. It would explicitly recognise the internal divisions in society (stemming from racism, sexism, homophobia and religious intolerance) that obscure inequality and are embedded in an unjust world. It would also have a more nuanced idea of both the target population and the spatial implications of policies.

So an equalities approach to cohesion would look first to address inequality and in this book we have highlighted the need for more social housing, better outcomes for disadvantaged groups at school and the creation, or in the current climate the retention, of good-quality jobs that offer career potential. On the cohesion side, we stressed the importance of bringing together groups where tensions exist and seeking to build programmes based on common interests (as in the planning examples in Northern Ireland in Chapter Eight; and in building links between those in work in trades unions and the workless in Chapter Ten; and in bringing together the young and old in Chapter Twelve). This approach would also recognise that real integration requires change in existing populations as well as migrants. Tensions will continue if migrants are made to feel that racism, Islamophobia, xenophobia and extreme intolerance are their fault and if established residents' fears are not addressed. The work of Praxis (the non-governmental organisation featured in Chapter Eleven, which seeks to help new migrants to settle) in going beyond help to individual migrants and adopting a community development approach to empower both established communities and migrant communities is an attempt to ensure that everyone's voice is heard. It is assumed this will lead to better integration, since not only is understanding of the Other improved but power inequalities over decision making on policies that affect everyday lives are addressed.

The ToC emphasises the need to seek the views of stakeholders in defining the ToC itself and in monitoring and evaluating the outcomes of the changes that follow from adopting relevant interventions: responsive/interactive evaluation. In Chapter Two, Sullivan argues that there is a need to be sensitive to unequal power among stakeholders when seeking their views, particularly in the UK. This element of the ToCs is particularly explored in Chapter Eleven by Mayo and her colleagues on the work of Praxis, where there is an attempt to involve the broadest possible range of voluntary and community organisations in the research process (itself a way of empowering both established and migrant communities). But it is also reflected in other chapters, for example: in Newman's call to give the unemployed a voice in the policies that address their worklessness (Chapter Ten); in Grimshaw and Smart's conclusion that it is vital to assess communications' impacts among representative segments of local communities to understand how the connectedness of groups is mediated and rendered meaningful by communications (Chapter Six); and in Osler's insistence that the learner needs to be recognised as a holder of human rights and given opportunities to explore and reflect on various identities and cultural attributes, create personal narratives and develop collective narratives and cognitive models that enable learners as a group to make sense of the world (Chapter Nine). As the contribution from Grimshaw and Smart indicates, communications in a new information age have a material impact on the quality of social understanding; audiences interpret dominant communications in the press using the information resources at their disposal (which vary substantially). Access to multiple sources of information that promote better understanding among communities is partly a function of social competences that are enhanced by effective education. Equality in education is therefore an integral part of a socially cohesive policy and fundamental to evaluation goals.

The new evaluation criteria that would facilitate the monitoring and evaluation of the ToC for social cohesion are not necessarily very complex to develop or evidence and the authors have provided practical information. We have emphasised the need to be clear about the target population and Chapter Four by Simpson puts together some useful guidance. In Chapter Three, Fuller emphasises the need to understand how communities live through multi-spatial networks, in which they do not necessarily relate to a fixed notion of place such as a 'neighbourhood'. Indicators need to relate to the problems that are causing tension and elucidate issues of faith, gender, sexuality, age and socioeconomic class as well as 'race'/ethnicity. The equalities framework developed by IDeA/Local Government Improvement and

Development already provides a starting point and also shows how implicit knowledge and local authorities' qualitative knowledge of their communities should complement quantitative data. In Chapter Five, Eversley and Mayhew show how administrative data can be used in Equality Impact Assessment work and how it can provide useful evaluation data.

The book has also emphasised that, if stakeholders are to be involved in evaluation, mixed techniques need to be used, including some data monitoring; interviews with stakeholders and key decision makers; focus groups; action learning sets; deliberative debate; direct observations/ ethnographic research; long-term case studies, critical literature and document analysis; and the many other forms of participative research. As Praxis found, it is necessary to build up a picture of the contributions of the initiative towards improving social cohesion at different levels, that is, individuals, families, specific migrant communities and the whole community/neighbourhood. As a theory of evaluation is specified in more detail, more thought would need to be given to the role of different local actors at various levels.

Stakeholders who are the subjects of evaluation have to be able to hold those with power to account. Sullivan, in setting out the ToC, emphasised the need for thresholds of, and a timeline for, change. New Labour had a number of key outcome targets, such as the elimination of child poverty by 2020 and its halving by 2010. However, the necessary political leadership was not forthcoming when it became clear in 2006/07 that new policies were required to achieve the milestones. In this case, attention switched to privileging community cohesion above equality. The target of eradicating child poverty by 2020 remains, backed by new legislation (passed in March 2010). This provides a clear definitional framework, setting four challenging UK-wide targets based on the proportion of children living in: relative low income, combined income and material deprivation, absolute low income and persistent poverty. It also requires that these targets continue to be met after 2020 and places a duty on local authorities and their partners to cooperate in tackling child poverty. However, the new coalition government and Frank Field MP, the chair of the Review on Poverty and Life Chances, are already disputing the definitions of child poverty.[2] So this brings us to Sullivan's last point. Is the evaluation of social cohesion that we are proposing politically acceptable: is it *realistic evaluation*?

New government, new challenges

For at least two major reasons, the omens for the endorsement of our approach to social cohesion do not look good. First, the outgoing government's 'community cohesion' agenda, as it stood in 2010, appeared to be dominated by one major issue – radical Islamism – with concerns about the implications of immigration at times running at a close second. The second major area of concern stems from the outcome of the General Election in 2010.

We have argued that New Labour continued the Thatcherite process of forcing the disadvantaged to take responsibility for their 'own problems'. This has led to the assumption that the 'failure' to have a job, or to fully integrate, or to succeed in school, or to access home ownership or to avoid drugs, alcohol and crime is primarily an individual failure and not a failure of the state or of broader society. This assumption is becoming increasing embedded in policy thinking.

The new coalition government is set to take this agenda one step further. In the run-up to the General Election in May 2010, David Cameron highlighted the idea of the 'Big Society' and outlined proposals to devolve power to a new 'neighbourhood army' of 5,000 professional community organisers[3] who would give communities the help they need to work together and take over the running of certain public services. 'Collective strength will overpower our problems', he wrote in the foreword to the Conservative Manifesto. At the launch of this Conservative Manifesto on 13 April 2010, Cameron focused on a New Citizen Service for 16-year-olds, funded through reallocating the 'Prevent' programme (Conservatives, 2010).

> It's going to mix young people from different backgrounds, different ethnicities and religions, in a way that doesn't happen right now. It's going to teach them what it means to be socially responsible by asking them to serve their communities.[4]

Simon Jenkins was to argue by 14 May 2010: 'Because [the Big Society] lacked the slightest substance – yielding a truly awful Michael Gove *Today* programme interview[5] – it did not "play well on the doorstep", and was dropped' (Jenkins, 2010). Further research in the *Financial Times* showed that most people who were interested in getting involved were already volunteering.[6] The evaluation of the pilots for the National Citizen Service (NCS) was claimed in the launch document to be positive but in fact had revealed that the pilots had a less positive impact on children from deprived areas than for those from affluent backgrounds.[7]

However, the Big Society was not dropped and has re-emerged as an ideological underpinning to current policy. Nick Hurd was appointed as the Minister for Civil Society and given a small budget to get the NCS off the ground. In July, the Big Society was relaunched with four pilots (including a local buy-out of a rural pub, efforts to recruit volunteers to keep museums open, support to speed up broadband supply, and devolving a half a million pound capital budget for local parks and libraries to local communities) and the promise to use funds from dormant bank accounts to establish a Big Society Bank, by the Prime Minister David Cameron, who said: '[w]hile reducing the budget deficit was his "duty", giving individuals and communities more control over their destinies was what excited him and was something that had underpinned his philosophy since he became Conservative leader in 2005' (BBC, 19 July 2010, www.bbc.co.uk/news/uk-10680062).

More significantly, Iain Duncan-Smith's vision of 'broken Britain' was to underpin welfare reform as he took the lead at the Department for Work and Pensions. Central to his agenda is the concept of protecting the 'vulnerable' but making others who are in poverty take responsibility for their own difficulties: a policy reinforced by increasing the stigma and penalties for those who do not conform to the (assumed) norms of society.

> Breakthrough Britain identifies five pathways to poverty: family breakdown, economic dependency and worklessness, educational failure, addiction and serious personal debt. It also provides policies for the role of the voluntary sector in reversing breakdown. Our approach is based on the belief that people must take responsibility for their own choices but that government has a responsibility to help people make the right choices. Government must therefore value and support positive life choices. At the heart of this approach is support for the role of marriage and initiatives to help people to live free of debt and addiction. (Policy Page Centre for Social Justice; www.centreforsocialjustice. org.uk/default.asp?pageRef=226)

The five pathways to poverty are defined in terms of personal failure rather than societal, economic or state failure. The 'vulnerable' are narrowly defined – a definition that most of society colludes in because they themselves do not wish to be seen as vulnerable, given the stigma this carries. Solutions are individualised and moralised: marriage or living within one's means and free of debt. The approach draws the third sector into provision of programmes to 'make people make the right choices' and away from advocacy. It withdraws responsibility from the state and helps to justify a programme of public expenditure cuts. It allows those who are 'deserving' and rich to keep their wealth. And ultimately it seeks to embed its assumptions so that there is no debate, for example, on reintroducing a wealth tax as part of the deficit reduction plans: while cutting Child Benefit and hitting the very poor through a £7 billion welfare reduction package in the Spending Review (SR) is 'necessary', the idea of a wealth tax is 'utopian' or 'socialist' (both seen as derogatory terms) and totally unrealistic.

This agenda of 'responsibilisation' is likely to increase inequalities, which in turn will make 'good relations' between different groups in society harder to achieve. The coalition government has also initiated a more direct attack on equality. Thus, public expenditure cuts of 25% in the SR (or more – local authority funding was cut by 27% in real terms over the SR period) on services other than health and international development will significantly increase inequality not only because they remove essential services from those in need and reduce benefit income but also because they stigmatise the remaining services as only suitable for the poor and vulnerable.

The residualisation of local authority housing and the failure to compensate for this by an equivalent expansion of the remainder of the social housing sector has led to a rapid reduction in provision and an increase in 'problem' estates and dwindling defence for social housing. The June 2010 Budget and the SR saw the social housing capital budget cut from £8.4 billion in the last spending round to £4.5 billion in this one, rents for new tenants rising to 80% of market rents and Housing Benefit capped generally and reduced by 10% for those who have been on Jobseeker's Allowance for more than 12 months. It has been estimated that this package could drive some 80,000 poorer tenants out of Central London, increasing the competition for cheaper housing in poorer Outer London areas, turning neighbour against neighbour (Cecil, 2010). We can expect this pattern of outcome for other services that are only deemed necessary for the poor.

Furthermore, the public sector cuts reduce the number of reasonable quality jobs with pensions (which are also under attack) in a sector where equal opportunities has been prioritised and where many disadvantaged groups who have faced discrimination in the private sector have found employment. The cuts will therefore impact differentially on both individuals and place and particularly affect disadvantaged groups throughout their lifetime.

There has been an early attack too on the bodies charged with promoting equalities. The Equality and Human Rights Commission was ordered to cut 15% from its budget as part of the coalition government's initial £6 million austerity measures. The cuts amount to £7 million from its £60 million budget for 2010/11. The Comprehensive Area Assessment run by the Audit Commission, which sought to monitor whether local authorities and their partners were meeting their statutory equalities duties by looking at the outcomes they were delivering, has also been scrapped. At central government level the equalities agenda has been further marginalised by giving it to one of the few women in the Cabinet, Theresa May, and by making it appear as a minor add-on to her main responsibilities (as Home Secretary).

Meanwhile, immigration is still seen in a negative way and is to be capped (for non-European Union [EU] citizens), despite the fact that levels have been dropping rapidly.[8] The coalition government is still talking about a review of 'existing measures and obligations' in the Human Rights Act following the decision on 18 May 2010 by the Special Immigration Appeals Commission (SIAC) that two men allegedly involved in a terror plot could not be deported to Pakistan.[9] More immediately, the national curriculum is to be rewritten. Michael Gove told *The Times* on 6 March 2010: 'Lessons should celebrate rather than denigrate Britain's role through the ages, including the Empire. Guilt about Britain's past is misplaced.'[10] We are likely to continue to see the citizenship curriculum and history education used to promote a sense of national cohesion or national loyalty, and integration will continue as a one-way process, focused on both newcomers and established visible minority groups, as Osler identified in Chapter Nine.

So, is our approach to evaluating social cohesion utopian and unrealistic? In the final section we shall argue that it is important to continue to pursue the framework outlined in this book and suggest that all is not doom and gloom.

Levers for a broader approach

The Equality Act 2010 was a key achievement of the last government. We have emphasised in this book that legislation is only a first step as it needs to be rigorously implemented and enforced. However, legislation does provide a new context. From the enactment of early 'race relations' legislation of the 1960s to the major legislation of the 1970s and more recent amendment legislation, we have gradually witnessed the generation of a new discursive climate. The overt racism of the 1950s and 1960s is unacceptable to the majority, and particularly the young. There is consequently a real hope that gradually the understanding that inequality is unjust (Dorling, 2010) will become more widely accepted and the coalition government's attempt to portray its SR as 'fair' is part of this shift in understanding. This is not to suggest that neoliberalism will be defeated and that a more equal world will be created in the near future. It is merely to point out that the current attack on furthering equality will increasingly face opposition and that the Equality Act provides an important lever in this process. Other legislation, such as the Duty to Involve 2009[11] and the Child Poverty Act 2010, also provide useful levers. There has been a general welcome by the voluntary and community sector for the new integrated public sector Equality Duty, the Socio-Economic Duty[12] and dual discrimination protection (Russell et al, 2010). Initial evaluations of the Comprehensive Area Assessment (CAA) by the Audit Commission showed that equalities approaches not only improved service delivery but were also cost efficient. As Chapter Seven by Doran and Keating suggests, linking equalities with the human rights agenda provides a strong and necessary basis for arguing for the importance of services that may be considered expensive or even unpopular in purely cost terms. The challenge from the Fawcett Society (www.fawcettsociety. org.uk/index.asp?PageID=1165) seeking a Judicial Review through the High Court of the government's June 2010 emergency budget (on the grounds that under equality laws the government should have assessed whether its budget proposals would increase or reduce inequality between women and men), shows the potential of using the new legislative framework.[13] Evaluation based on the wider concept of social cohesion and based on a strong foundation in equalities and human rights will be an important driver for local government decision making.

Linked to this will be increasing opposition at local level. There is a general pattern, in England and Wales, for local elections to produce local government controlled by political parties who are opposed to those who hold sway over central government at Westminster. This trend is likely to continue. It is worth noting that a major drive on equalities at the local level, particularly in local authority workforces, came under the Thatcher governments in the early 1980s. This notwithstanding, as Chapter One has argued, the Thatcher era was ideologically opposed to much of the equalities agenda and devolution. The Greater London Council was abolished, equality work starved of funds and the Local Government Act 1988 sought to destroy local authority trades union power and move jobs to the less equalities conscious private sector. Yet, as Atkinson and Wilks-Heeg (2000, p 2) have argued, 'while local authorities [under the Conservatives] have been forced to concede important sources of autonomy, they have also found a variety of ways of protecting and expanding their independent policy-making capacity in other areas' and they achieved this in the organisational change (including equalities) policy area.

So progress can be made on the new equalities duties at the local level. There are numerous examples in this book of the success of local initiatives in enhancing social cohesion. In many areas local authorities have also been working to empower their communities[14] and to counter increases in tension. Local authorities can find ways of using much of the methodology laid out in the chapters of this book. For example, London equality officers network help each other to look at different aspects of policy and their implications for different groups. In this way they can reduce the costs of ensuring they are fulfilling their equality duties and carrying out full Equality Impact Assessments. Developing partnerships and policy networks will be central to generating some creative autonomy.

But progress will depend on local leadership and local champions. The Joseph Rowntree Foundation has been running a programme on public interest in poverty issues, arguing that '[p]ublic support is needed to ensure that the Government and other organisations take action to tackle poverty in the UK [but t]he perception of poverty is often misguided, with people believing that it is a result of laziness, or an inevitable part of modern life' (Delvaux and Rinne, 2009, Summary, p 1). The research shows that while poverty campaigns have had some success in changing perceptions and behaviour, it is very difficult to change attitudes. One of the report's conclusions is that it is vital to use a champion: 'someone who is passionate about and committed to tackling poverty and is willing and able to convince people to engage with the UK poverty agenda' (2009, p 49).

The media play a similar role in 'shaping, amplifying and responding to public attitudes towards poverty' as they do in shaping attitudes to migrants (McKendrick et al, 2008). But in Chapter Six of this volume, Grimshaw and Smart have shown that such attitudes can be challenged through using a theoretically cogent strategy for effective communication involving more face-to-face contact within neighbourhoods and a variety of ways of confronting the power of the national press. As Dorling argues (2010, pp 315-6): 'Greater equality is easily possible; we have had it so recently before.... People can choose between falling into line, becoming both creatures and victims of markets, or they can resist and look for other ways, other arguments, different thinking.

In the immediate future there is likely to be growing discontent as inequality increases, public services are threatened and the contradictions emanating from government policy multiply. In this context it will be important for those committed to social cohesion to carry out thorough evaluations based on a clear ToC that will ultimately allow disadvantaged groups, as Sullivan has argued in Chapter Two, to be able to access evidence in relation to the *need* for interventions, the *pertinence* of interventions they would choose to address their needs as opposed to interventions that the government has chosen on their behalf and the intended *consequences* or outcomes of such interventions. To do otherwise would allow injustice to continue without challenge.

Notes

[1] Dorling (2010, p 191) presents a graph showing the share of all income received by the richest 1% in Britain from 1918 to 2005. Since 1980, the post-tax share has not affected the pre-tax share, which has now reached the level last experienced in the 1920s.

[2] See Frank Field interview, *Times Online*, 11 June 2010.

[3] Conservatives, 31 March 2010, 'Cameron unveils "Big Society" plan', www.conservatives.com/news/news_stories/2010/03/plans_announced_to_help_build_a_big_society.aspx

[4] Conservatives, 8 April 2010, www.conservatives.com/News/News_stories/2010/04/Conservatives_launch_plans_for_a_National_Citizen_Service.aspx

[5] BBC 'Today' interview with Michael Gove, 3 May 2010, http://news.bbc.co.uk/today/hi/today/newsid_8657000/8657744.stm

[6] *Financial Times*, 21 April 2010, 'Public appetite for Tory "big society" limited'.

[7] *Regeneration and Renewal*, 4 May 2010, p 4, 'Doubts cast on Tory scheme'.

[8] *The Guardian*, 28 May 2010, stated: 'Net migration to Britain is set to drop below 100,000 a year ... official immigration figures show that more eastern European migrants are leaving Britain than arriving'.

[9] www.ekklesia.co.uk/node/12183

[10] www.timesonline.co.uk/tol/news/politics/article7052010.ece

[11] The Duty to Involve came into force on 1 April 2009 and came out of the Local Government and Public Involvement in Health Act 2007. Local authorities must now ensure that people have greater opportunities to have their say on local matters. The Duty to Involve goes further than consultation, setting out three ways of securing the involvement of representatives of local people, informing them, consulting them or involving them in other ways. Authorities will need to provide support for the process that is adopted.

[12] The government has subsequently dismissed the socio-economic duty as "ridiculous" and said it would not be enacted, www.guardian.co.uk/society/2010/nov/17/theresa-may-scraps-legal-requirement-inequality

[13] The point still stands although the Society was refused permission by the High Court to challenge the legality of the government's emergency budget. The judge, Mr Justice Ouseley, ruled the Fawcett Society's judicial review application 'unarguable – or academic' and dismissed it, www.bbc.co.uk/news/uk-politics-11922551

[14] See the work of the National Network of Empowering Authorities at www.idea.gov.uk/idk/core/page.do?pageId=16639499

References

Atkinson, H. and Wilks-Heeg, S. (2000) *Local government from Thatcher to Blair. The politics of creative autonomy*, Cambridge: Polity Press.

Cecil, N. (2010) 'Housing reform will turn London into a middle class ghetto, says MP', *Evening Standard*, 25 October 2010, www.thisislondon.co.uk/standard/article-23891162-housing-reform-will-turn-london-into-middle-class-ghetto-says-mp.do

Conservatives (2010) National Citizens Service, www.conservatives.com/News/News_stories/2010/04/~/media/Files/Downloadable%20Files/NCSpolicypaper.ashx

Delvaux, J. and Rinne, S. (2009) *Building public support for eradicating poverty in the UK*, York: Joseph Rowntree Foundation.

Dorling, D. (2010) *Injustice: Why social inequality persists*, Bristol: The Policy Press.

Gough, J., Eisenschitz, A. and McCulloch, A. (2006) *Spaces of social exclusion*, London: Routledge.

Jenkins, S. (2010) 'What happened to the Big Society? It was killed by proximity to power', *The Guardian*, 14 May, p 33.

Laurence, J. and Heath, A. (2007) *Predictors of community cohesion: Multi-level modelling of the 2005 Citizenship Survey*, London: DCLG.

McKendrick, J.H., Sinclair, S., Irwin, A., O'Donnell, H., Scott, G. and Dobbie, L. (2008) *The media, poverty and public opinion in the UK*, York: Joseph Rowntree Foundation.

O'Grady, F. (2007) 'Economic citizenship and the new capitalism', *Renewal: A Journal of Social Democracy*, vol 15, no 2/3, pp 58–66.

Russell, H.E. in conjunction with Lepine, E., Newman, I., Dickinson, S., Meegan, R., Lawrence, R., Luanaigh, A.N., Swift, J., Grimshaw, L. and Chapman, R. (2010: forthcoming) *EHRC Local Partnerships Project: The role of Local Strategic Partnerships and Local Area Agreements in promoting equalities*, Research Report 63, London: Equality and Human Rights Commission.

Index

The letter 'f' following a page number represents a figure, 'n' an endnote and 't' a table.